THE SOUTH CORNER OF TIME

Originally published as

SUN TRACKS

An American Indian

Literary Series

edited by Larry Evers
with
Anya Dozier
Danny Lopez
Felipe Molina
Ellavina Tsosie Perkins
Emory Sekaquaptewa
Ofelia Zepeda

THE SOUTH CORNER OF TIME

hopi navajo papago yaqui tribal literature

Sun Tracks could not exist outside the supportive atmosphere of the University of Arizona. We appreciate the help of the American Indian student organization, the Amerind Club, and the encouragement we get from the American Indian Studies Program and the Department of English. We are especially grateful to Vine Deloria, Jr. and Dean Paul Rosenblatt for helping us to continue.

We would like to thank a few of the many individuals who contributed time and energy to get this issue together: Robert Hale for drawing the maps, Elly Evers for advice on the manuscripts, Leslie Silko for encouragement and the title, Dennis Carr for designing the issue and helping with decisions all along the way, and Barbara Grygutis for constant support.

Sun Tracks is an American Indian literary series sponsored by the American Indian Studies Program and the Department of English, University of Arizona, Tucson, Arizona. All correspondence should be sent to: *Sun Tracks*, Department of English, Modern Languages Building #67, University of Arizona, Tucson, Arizona 85721.

The original edition of this special issue was made possible by grants from the Coordinating Council of Literary Magazines and the National Endowment for the Arts.

This book was set in 12/14 Paladium on a Compugraphic UTS system.

Second printing 1981

The University of Arizona Press

Manufactured in U.S.A.

Library of Congress Catalog Card Number 76-617570
ISBN 0-8165-0732-5
ISBN 0-8165-0731-7 pbk.

HOPI

Michael Kabotie. "I Have Come" from **Sun Tracks Five** (1979). Copyright ©1979 by Michael Kabotie. Reprinted by permission of the author.

Edmund Nequatewa. "Dr. Fewkes and Masauwu" from **Truth of a Hopi** (1936; rpt. Flagstaff: Northland Press, 1967). Copyright ©1967 by Northern Arizona Society of Science and Art, Inc. Reprinted by permission of Museum of Northern Arizona Press.

Wendy Rose. "To Some Few Hopi Ancestors" from **Academic Squaw** (Blue Cloud Press, 1977). Copyright ©1977 by Wendy Rose. "Vanishing Point: Urban Indian" from **Long Division: a Tribal History** (Strawberry Press, 1976). Copyright ©1977 by Wendy Rose. Poems reprinted by permission of the author.

Emory Sekaquaptewa. "A Clown Story" from **Sun Tracks Five** (1979). Copyright ©1979 by Emory Sekaquaptewa. "One More Smile for a Hopi Clown" from **Parabola,** vol. 4, no. 1 (1979). Copyright ©1979 by Society for the Study of Myth and Tradition. Both essays reprinted by permission of the author.

Herschel Talashoma. "How Maasaw and the People of Oraibi Got Scared to Death Once" from **Hopitutuwusi: Hopi Tales** (Museum of Northern Arizona, 1978) by Ekkehart Malotki. Copyright ©1978 by Ekkehart Malotki. Reprinted by permission of the author and Museum of Northern Arizona Press.

Albert Yava. "In the Beginning" from **Big Falling Snow: a Tewa-Hopi Indian's Life and Times and the History and Traditions of His People** (Crown Publishers, 1978), edited by Harold Courlander. Copyright ©1978 by Harold Courlander. Reprinted by permission of Harold Courlander.

NAVAJO

nia francisco. "navaho inn" and "morning and myself" from **Sun Tracks,** vol. 2, no. 1 (fall 1975). Copyright ©1975 by nia francisco. Reprinted by permission of the author.

Betty John. "Hasda'jii'eezh" printed by permission of the author. Copyright ©1980 by Betty John.

Irene Nakai. "Sandpainting," "Story of a Cricket: Spring 1978," "Bridge Perspective," and "Sunrise Flight into Acid Rain/Cancelled" printed by permission of the author. Copyright ©1980 by Irene Nakai.

Andrew Natonabah. "Song of a Mountain" by permission of the singer.

Tom Ration. "A Navajo Life Story" from **Stories of Traditional Navajo Life and Culture** (Tsaile, Arizona: Navajo Community College Press, 1977), edited by Broderick H. Johnson. Copyright ©1977 by Navajo Community College Press. Reprinted by permission of Broderick H. Johnson.

Sandoval, Hastin Tlo'tsihee. "The Beginning" from **The Diné: Origin Myths of the Navajo Indians** (Washington: D.C.: Government Printing Office, 1956), edited by Aileen O'Bryan.

Agnes Tso. "male rain," "female rain," and "awakening" from **Sun Tracks,** vol. 2, no. 1 (fall 1975). Copyright ©1975 by Agnes Tso. Reprinted by permission of the author.

Gary Witherspoon. "Beautifying the World through Art" from **Language and Art in the Navajo Universe** (Ann Arbor: University of Michigan Press, 1977). Copyright ©1977 by the University of Michigan. Reprinted by permission of the University of Michigan Press and the author.

Nancy Woodman. "The Story of an Orphan" from **Navajo Historial Selections** (Phoenix: Phoenix Indian School Print Shop, 1954), edited by Robert W. Young and William Morgan. Reprinted by permission of Gloria Emerson, Director, Native American Materials Development Center.

PAPAGO

Susie Ignacio Enos. "Papago Legend of the Sahuaro" from **The Arizona Quarterly,** vol. 1, no. 1 (spring 1945). Copyright ©1945 by the Arizona Board of Regents. Reprinted by permission of Albert Frank Gegenheimer, Editor, **The Arizona Quarterly.**

Geri Felix. "From This World" from **Sun Tracks Five** (1979). Copyright ©1979 by Geri Felix. Reprinted by permission of the author.

Ventura Jose. "Ho'ok'oks" printed by permission of Daniel Matson.

Alice Listo. "Kiho Do'ak" printed by permission of Alice Listo. Copyright ©1980 by Alice Listo.

Danny Lopez. "O'odham Ha-ñeñei: Songs of the Papago People" printed by permission of the author. Copyright ©1980 by Daniel Lopez.

Frank Lopez. "The Boy Who Gets Revenge" printed by permission of Bernard L. Fontana. Copyright ©1980 by Frank Lopez.

Ted Rios. "The Egg" printed by permission of Kathleen Sands. Copyright ©1980 by Kathleen Sands.

Ruth Murray Underhill. "Ocean Power" from **Singing for Power** (Berkeley: University of California, 1938). Copyright ©1938 by the Regents of the University of California. Reprinted by permission of the author and the University of California Press.

Ofelia Zepeda. "Thoughts by My Mother's Grave" printed by permission of the author. Copyright ©1980 by Ofelia Zepeda.

YAQUI

Ruth Warner Giddings. "Tesak Pascola's Watermelons" and "The Snake People" from **Yaqui Myths and Legends** (Tucson: University of Arizona Press, 1959). Reprinted by permission of the University of Arizona Press.

Mini Valenzuela Kaczkurkin. "The Evil Eye" and "Let's Make Thunder" from **Sun Tracks,** vol. 2, no. 2 (spring 1976). Copyright ©1976 by Mini Valenzuela Kaczkurkin. Reprinted by permission of the author. "Surems and the Talking Tree," "Christianity," "Enchanted Pascola," "The Yaqui Curandero," and **"Ku Wikit"** from **Yoeme: Lore of the Arizona Yaqui People** (Tucson: Sun Tracks, 1977). Copyright ©1977 by Mini Valenzuela Kaczkurkin. Reprinted by permission of the author.

Felipe Molina. "Maso Buikam: Yaqui Deer Songs" and "How the Mountains were Created" printed by permission of the author. Copyright ©1980 by Felipe Molina.

Refugio Savala. "Growth: Merging of Labor and Love" from **The Autobiography of a Yaqui Poet** (Tucson: University of Arizona Press, 1980), edited by Kathleen Sands. Copyright ©1980 by the Arizona Board of Regents. Reprinted by permission of the University of Arizona Press. "The Legend of Skeleton Mountain" and "The Singing Tree" from **The Arizona Quarterly,** vol. 1, no. 1 (spring 1945). Copyright ©1945 by the Arizona Board of Regents. Reprinted by permission of Albert Frank Gegenheimer, Editor, **The Arizona Quarterly.**

Jim Darnton

THE SOUTH CORNER OF TIME

CONTENTS

Introduction

the track of the sun
across the sky
leaves its shining message
illuminating,
strengthening,
warming,
us who are here,
showing us we are not alone.
we are yet alive!
and this fire . . .
our fire . . .
shall not die.
Atoni (1971)

The South Corner of Time first appeared as a volume of *Sun Tracks*, an American Indian literary series published by Indian students and faculty at the University of Arizona. Our purpose in this cooperative project is to help all people recognize and appreciate this country's native literary heritage.

We also want to promote literary expression and appreciation among all Indian people. Our efforts focus on literature at a time when we are everywhere reminded that American Indians are at the bottom of most statistical measures of well being. We believe that no litany of cold statistics can adequately portray the rich, full range of human experience that is contemporary Indian life. On these pages Indian people speak for themselves, and with this special issue we renew the promise Atoni set for us in our first issue nearly ten years ago. We are alive. Our fire shall not die.

Over the last nine years we have published ten issues. Our focus in these issues has been on expressions of the American Indian heritage written in English. We have published poems, stories, interviews, and essays from more than a hundred tribal writers throughout the country. In this issue we narrow our focus to the literature of four tribal peoples. At the same time we broaden our scope to include *historic* as well as contemporary literature, *oral* as well as written literature, and literature written in *native languages* as well as literature written in English. In this collection we offer representative and accurate selections from the whole continuum of imaginative expression that forms the literature of Hopi, Navajo, Papago, and Yaqui communities.

We have organized this collection in four sections, one for each of the tribes. In so doing we wish to emphasize that American Indian literature really consists of many literatures supported by many distinct tribal traditions.

Literature and community

Language as much as anything else defines tribal communities, and the people who contributed most significantly to shaping this collection are linguists. Emory Sekaquaptewa, Ellavina Perkins, Danny Lopez, Ofelia Zepeda, and Felipe Molina are all committed to the description and maintenance of their native languages, and each is actively involved in teaching his language. With their guidance and help we offer you bi-lingual material in four native American languages here. We hope these selections will give those of you who speak one or more of the languages presented here an opportunity to exercise your reading abilities. Those of us who don't speak any of the four should be reminded by these selections that the languages are alive and well and *spoken* by thousands who call themselves *Hopiitu, Diné, O'odham,* and *Yoeme.*

Speaking the same language means more than being able to recognize and produce the same sound patterns. The oral tradition is a distillation of the shared experience that gives language meaning. Stories, songs, the whole oral tradition of a community, expresses its ideals, wisdom, and humor. In a significant way it is the singers and storytellers who hold tribal communities together, for in their telling and singing they preserve and re-create their community's idea of itself. In this way tribal communities shape, and are shaped by, literature.

Oral literature

We understand literature to consist of oral as well as written forms, and in each of the four tribal sections of this collection you will find both. In fact, oral literature forms the core of the whole collection. In each of the sections you will find songs, tales, autobiographical narratives, and historical narratives. These songs and stories may be very different from other literature you have encountered, and in many cases it will require some extra effort and imagination on your part to appreciate them.

Audience. One thing to keep in mind as you read the songs and stories translated here from oral traditions is their intended audience. The singers and tellers perform for audiences in their own communities. Those audiences are able to understand many references and supply many associations that those of us who live outside their communities cannot. This is probably what Papago singer Maria Chona had in mind when she told Ruth Underhill, "The song is very short because we understand so much." In each section we have included at least one essay addressed especially to those of us who are outsiders. The essays of Emory Sekaquaptewa, Gary Witherspoon, Ruth Underhill, and Felipe Molina should help you understand the long story behind short songs. Careful readers will also note that often the selections in each section build on each other to provide references and supply associations. For example, those who read the whole Navajo section in sequence should have a greater appreciation of Andrew Natonabah's "Song of a Mountain" than those who choose to read the song in isolation. An annotated list of "Other Sources" at the end of each section provides suggestions for those who seek greater understanding through further reading.

Performance. A second factor to remember in reading this collection is that stories and songs are performed by living, breathing, gesturing people, not by faceless typesetting machines. Simon Ortiz reminds us of this when he writes of how his father taught him a song as he was growing up at Acoma Pueblo:

> He was singing this song, and I didn't catch the words off hand. I asked him, and he explained, "This song, I really like it for this old man." And he said, "This old man used to like to sing, and he danced like this," motioning like the old man's hands, arms, shoulders, and he repeated, "This song, I really like it for this old man."

The way a song or story is performed contributes as much to its meaning as its words. The pieces we print here from oral traditions are but written approximations of oral performances. As we read these stories and songs each of us needs to try to hear the voices and see the motion behind the print on the page.

Translation. Many different kinds of translations are included in this collection. Some are the efforts of linguists who strive to represent literally every word of the original. Other translators are less interested in the translation of each and every word than they are in presenting what they judge to be the true spirit of the original. Whether they emphasize letter or spirit it is important to remember that every translation is itself a creation, one based on a creation in another language. While it is true that in every translation something of the original is lost, it is equally true that in the best translations so too is something new gained.

Written literature

Among each of the tribal communities represented here there are now many individuals committed to developing ways of expressing themselves by writing in their native languages. These efforts may find some of their deepest and most nourishing roots in the pictographic writing systems of native America, as Victor Masayesva's photo-narrative "Tsinijinnie's Hardrock Romance" playfully suggests. In historic times, the Cherokee syllabary, developed by Sequoyah in 1821, is a well known antecedent. But writing in native languages is more narrowly a tradition grown out of the work done by linguistic anthropologists and their native American "informants" around the turn of this century. Especially during the last ten years, as Professor Kenneth Hale and other linguists have begun to take native American linguists into their work as full partners, writing in many native languages has begun to appear. The work of Ofelia Zepeda, Felipe Molina, and others included here may be a harbinger of a new kind of native American literature, one written in native American languages.

Indian people have been writing imaginatively in

English for well over a century, but it has only been during the last ten years that American readers have paid much attention. As our colleague Vine Deloria, Jr. points out, though, American interest in Indian matters is trendy, surfacing for a year or two once each generation and then ebbing. The problem, of course, goes beyond the interests of the American reading public to the policies of the major commercial presses and their parent media conglomerates. Although the major publishing houses have allowed a few American Indian writers a place on their lists, aggressive promotion of books on Indian topics seems always reserved for those written by non-Indian authors.

That Indian people continue to write at all in the face of this pattern of neglect indicates not only a remarkable patience and perseverance in attempting to reach non-Indian readers with their work, but also a real commitment to writing for their own communities. And it is the tribal relations of the work of Irene Nakai, Agnes Tso, Refugio Savala, and others that we wish to emphasize by presenting their work in this collection. We wish to suggest that an important and sustaining relationship exists between their written work in English and the oral traditions of their native communities.

Place, time, and literature

Finally, a word about out title. Place, time, and literature came together in very particular ways in native American communities. Late in N. Scott Momaday's novel *House Made of Dawn* a Pueblo grandfather remembers instructing his grandsons:

> He made them stand just there above the point of the low white rock, facing east. They could see the black mesa looming on the first light, and he told them there was the house of the sun. They must learn the whole contour of the black mesa. They must know it as they knew the shape of their hands, always and by heart. . . . They must know the long journey of the sun on the black mesa, how it rode in the seasons and the years, and they must live according to the sun appearing, for only then could they reckon where they were, where all things were in time.

The track of the sun marks place, time, identity in the four literatures we gather here too. So it is that we choose to locate this collection by the sun's rising, at the time when the winter solstice marks a special storytelling time for native American communities. During that special literary season, they say, the sun is in the south corner of time. We hope this collection will help you experience some of the pleasure of that literary season all through the year.

Larry Evers

HOPI LITERATURE

Emory Sekaquaptewa
editorial consultant

Hopi Alphabet

Ekkehart Malotki

A total of twenty-one symbols is sufficient to render all of the functional sounds which occur in the dialect of the Third Mesa villages. Nineteen of these are drawn from the English alphabet (a e g h i k l m n o p q r s t u v w y), one is borrowed from German orthography (the umlauted ö). The apostrophe is used to represent the glottal stop, one of the Hopi consonants. Stress and falling tone — the latter occurring in conjunction with long vowels, diphthongs, and certain vowel-nasal sequences — are not marked in the text. The following inventory lists all the functional sound units, with the exception of those characterized by falling tone, which exist in the Third Mesa dialect area and illustrates their use in sample words.

1. Vowel sounds:

(a) short vowels

a	pas	'very'
e	pep	'there'
i	sihu	'flower'
o	momi	'forward'
ö	qötö	'head'
u	tuwa	'he found it, saw it'

(b) long vowels

aa	paas	'carefully; completely'
ee	peep	'almost'
ii	siihu	'intestines'
oo	moomi	'he is pigeon-toed'
öö	qöötö	'suds'
uu	tuuwa	'sand'

2. Diphthongs:

(a) with y-glide

ay	tsay	'small, young'
ey	eykita	'he groans'
iy	hangwniy	'his ditch' (objective case)
oy	ahoy	'back to'
öy	öyna	'he gave him enough to eat'
uy	uyma	'he has been planting'

(b) with w-glide

aw	awta	'bow'
ew	pew	'here (to me)'
iw	piw	'again'
ow		nonexisting
öw	ngölöwta	'it is crooked'
uw	puwmoki	'he got sleepy'

3. Consonantal sounds:

(a) stops

p	paahu	'water, spring'
t	tupko	'younger brother'
ky	kyaaro	'parrot'
k	koho	'wood, stick'
kw	kwala	'it boiled'
q	qööha	'he built a fire'
qw	angqw	'from him; from there'
'	pu'	'now, today'

(b) nasals

m	malatsi	'finger'
n	naama	'both'
ngy	yungyapu	'wicker plaque'
ng	ngöla	'wheel'
ngw	kookyangw	'spider'

(c) affricate

ts	tsuku	'clown'

(d) fricatives

v	ivasa	'my field'
r	roya	'it turned'
s	sakuna	'squirrel'
h	ho'apu	'carrying basket'

(e) lateral

l	laho	'bucket'

4. Glides:

(a) preceding a vowel

w	waynuma	'he is walking about'
y	yas	'last year'

(b) following a vowel
see diphthongs

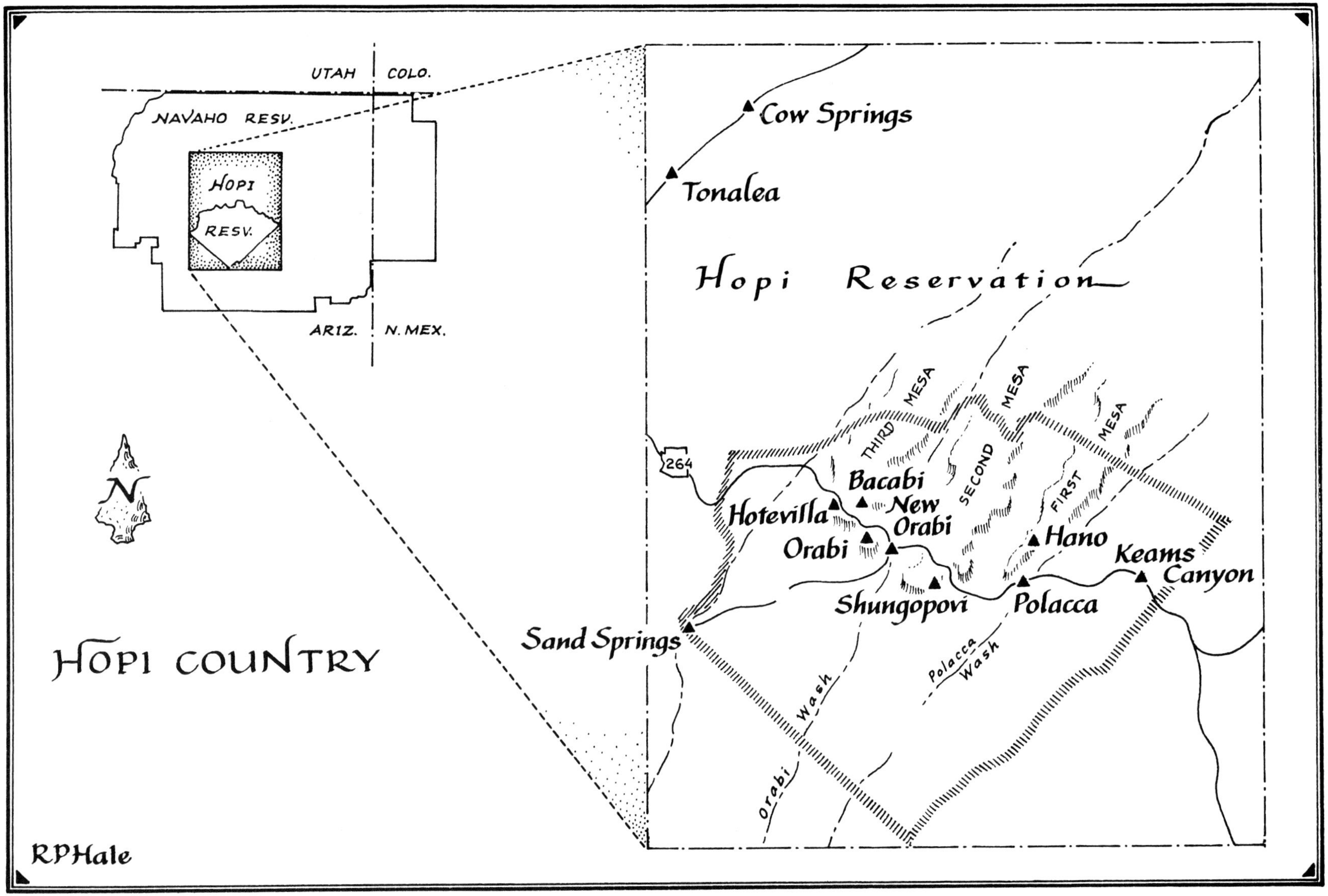
UTAH
COLO.
NAVAHO RESV.
HOPI
RESV.
ARIZ.
N. MEX.
N
HOPI COUNTRY
RPHale
Cow Springs
Tonalea
Hopi Reservation
THIRD MESA
SECOND MESA
FIRST MESA
264
Bacabi
New Orabi
Hotevilla
Orabi
Hano
Keams Canyon
Shungopovi
Polacca
Sand Springs
Polacca Wash
Orabi Wash

Way Back in the Distant Past

Albert Yava

A descendant of the Tewa Pueblo people who emigrated to Hopi country several centuries ago, Albert Yava was educated in two native American cultures: the Hopi and the Tewa. The following segment from his autobiography **Big Falling Snow** *(New York: Crown Publishers, 1979) tells how Hopi people came into this world.*

I am going to recall some of the things I know, the way I saw them or heard them, or the way they were taught to me. Maybe our young people will get an inkling of what life was like on this mesa when I was a boy, or how it was in the time of our fathers and grandfathers. If I seem to say a lot about myself, it is really my times that I am thinking about. I am merely the person who happened to be there at a particular time. It is hard to put down something with myself as a center of interest — that is, to say I did this or that. It makes me out as important, which isn't the way I see it. We Tewas and Hopis don't think of ourselves that way. In our histories and traditions we don't have individual heroes with names to remember. It is the village, the group, the clan that did this or that, not a man or woman. If an individual happens to stand out, we probably don't remember his real name, and if a name is required we probably have to make it up. Anyway, I am going to tell about some of the things that I know or remember, and you will understand that I am really talking about my people, the Tewas and the Hopis, and their experiences and recollections.

Way back in the distant past, the ancestors of humans were living down below in a world under the earth. They weren't humans yet, merely creatures of some kind. They lived in darkness, behaving like bugs. Now, there was a Great Spirit watching over everything, and some people say he was Tawa, the sun. He saw how things were down under the earth. He didn't care for the way the creatures were living. He sent his messenger, you might say his representative, Gogyeng Sowuhti — that is, Spider Old Woman — to talk to them. She said, "You creatures, the Sun Spirit who is above doesn't want you living like this. He is going to transform you into something better, and I will lead you to another world."

So Tawa made them into a better form of creatures, and Gogyeng Sowuhti led them to another world above the place where they were living. This was the Second World, still below the ground. The creatures lived here for some time, but they were still animals in form, not humans. There were some with tails, some without. The ones that were eventually to become human did not have tails.

But life in the Second World wasn't good. The creatures didn't behave well. They didn't get along. They ate one another. There was chaos and dissension. So the Great Spirit sent Gogyeng Sowuhti down again after he transformed those beings without tails into a humanlike form. But they weren't yet true humans, because they were undisciplined — wild and uncivilized. Gogyeng Sowuhti led them to another world up above, the Third World. Things were better at first, but after a while there was more chaos and dissension. Evil individuals caused all kinds of difficulties. There were sorcerers who made people fall sick or quarrel with one another. The evil ones made life hard for everyone.

When at last things became too difficult to bear, the ones who wanted to live orderly and good lives said, "This must come to an end. When the Great Spirit brought us up here he wanted us to be better than we were before. How can we get away and leave the evil ones behind?"

Gogyeng Sowuhti told them, "Above us is a Fourth World. Up there life will be better for you. But to get there we have to go through the sky of the Third World. And there are other problems. The Fourth World is owned by Masauwu, the Spirit of Death. You will have to have his permission to go there."

The way this story is told by our old ones, there were four layers of worlds. You might say that this idea describes a way of existing, the transformations that had to be gone through for the people to become truly human. In the Fourth World they were supposed to acquire good values and become civilized.

The people who wanted to escape from the Third World decided to send a scout up to see what it was like up there and make contact with Masauwu. They chose a swift bird, the swallow. The swallow was swift, all right, but he tired before he reached the sky and had to come back. After that they sent a dove, then a hawk. The hawk found a small opening and went through, but he came back without seeing Masauwu. Finally they sent a catbird. He was the one that found Masauwu.

Masauwu asked him, "Why are you here?"

The catbird said, "The world down below is infested with evil. The people want to come up here to live. They want to build their houses here, and plant their corn."

Masauwu said, "Well, you see how it is in this world. There isn't any light, just greyness. I have to use fire to warm my crops and make them grow. However, I have relatives down in the Third World. I gave them the secret of fire. Let them lead the people up here, and I will give them land and a place to settle. Let them come."

After the catbird returned to the Third World and reported that Masauwu would receive them, the people asked, "Now, how will we ever get up there?" So Spider Old Woman called on the chipmunk to plant a sunflower seed. It began to grow. It went up and almost reached the sky, but the weight of the blossom made the stem bend over. Spider Old Woman then asked the chipmunk to plant a spruce tree, but when the spruce finished growing it wasn't tall enough. The chipmunk planted a pine, but the pine also was too short. The fourth thing the chipmunk planted was a bamboo. It grew up and up. It pierced the sky. Spider Old Woman said, "My children, now we have a road to the upper world. When we reach there your lives will be different. Up there you will be able to distinguish evil from good. Anything that is bad must be left behind down here. All evil medicine must be thrown away before you go up. Sorcerers cannot come with us, or they will contaminate the Fourth World. So be careful. If you see an evil person going up, turn him back."

The people began climbing up inside the bamboo stalk. How they got through the bamboo joints I don't know, because the story doesn't explain about that. The mockingbird guarded them on the way up. He was like a scout. He went ahead, calling, "Pashumayani! Pashumayani! Pash! Pash! Pash! — Be careful! Be careful!" The people came up in groups, until everyone reached the top. The opening in the place where they came out was called the sipapuni. The people camped near where they emerged. The light was grey and they didn't know where they would be going.

Spider Old Woman — that is, Gogyeng Sowuhti — said, "Well, we are all here. Did you leave the evil ones down below?"

They said, "Yes, we didn't see any evil ones coming up."

Spider Old Woman said, "Good. Now plug the bamboo up with this cotton."

All this time, the mockingbird was telling the people how to arrange themselves, some over here, some over there, group by group, and he gave each group the name of a tribe. So there were Utes, Hopis, Navajos and so on, and one of the groups was called Bahanas, or white people.

After the bamboo was plugged with cotton, it turned out that an evil one had come up without being detected. When they discovered him he laughed.

They said, "We don't want you here. It was because of people like you that we left the Third World."

He said, "You couldn't get along without an evil one. I have a part to play in this world."

So according to this version of the story, the evil one taught them how to make the sun, moon and stars and to loft them into the sky to make the world light.

There are other explanations of who put the sun, moon and stars in the sky. Some say that Spider Old Woman told the people how to do it. There is also a story that Coyote scattered the stars in the sky. Over in Oraibi some of the traditions say that the spirit Huruing Wuhti, Hard Substances Old Woman, put the sun up there. But the way it was told to me, it was the evil one who came through the sipapuni with the people who showed them how to get the sky work done. Sometimes you hear that the evil one was a powaka, a witch or sorcerer. Because he came into the upper world instead of staying below, sorcery and evil have plagued the people ever since. In my version of the story, sorcery and knowledge were sort of linked together. A sorcerer was supposed to know how to do things that ordinary people couldn't do. I suppose that in the old days they would have said that he was a man with powerful medicine. That's how the evil one knew what to do about making the sun and moon.

When the Hopis left the sipapuni to begin their migrations, they told the sorcerer that he couldn't come with them, because the whole purpose of the emergence was to get away from evil. So he went with the Bahanas, or white people, instead, and the Hopi leaders said that everyone must be wary of Bahanas if they met them anywhere, because their possession of the sorcerer would give them more knowledge than the Hopis could cope with. But time and again in later days other sorcerers found the Hopis and caused dissension and corruption in the villages.

You can see that the theme of dissension and evil, and of the search for a place of harmony, starts with the emergence story. I've told only a little of that story, because it's very long. Different villages and clans have their own special details, and different explanations. A clan in Shongopovi or Oraibi has different explanations than the same clan in Walpi has. The reason is that clan groups kept branching off during the migrations. The Bear Clan was going in a certain direction, then part of the clan left the group and went another way. They all expected to meet again somewhere, maybe at the place foretold in their prophecy. When the Water Clan was coming north from Palatkwa, it was the same thing with them. So you had different branches of clans scattered all across the country, and then they started coming together again at the Hopi mesas. By that time the fragments of the clan had accumulated different experiences. Up to the point when they'd separated, they all had the same traditions, but after that each branch acquired experiences of its own. When they came together again they couldn't tell the same story any more.

Nevertheless, the tradition that the people emerged from the underworld with the guidance of Gogyeng Sowuhti is accepted by most Hopis. The emergence through the sipapuni is commemorated in a great many ceremonies. Sometimes it is discussed and debated in the kiva. Like one night we were talking about it and someone said, "Now how in the world could all those people come through a bamboo? How could they get in? How could it hold their weight? How could they get through the joints?"

Those clowns that come out when a big dance is going on, they are there to entertain the people, of course, but they have a special meaning in some of the things they do. For older people like myself, they're a part of the serious ritual, though most spectators aren't aware of it. There used to be a Clown Fraternity in the old days. If you were initiated into that group you were a clown as long as you lived. That Clown Fraternity doesn't exist here any more. Nowadays when they need clowns they invite certain members of the community to be performers. I can't say for sure about the Hopi clowns, but our Tewa clowns have to go through preparations just as the dancers do. They abstain from various things to purify themselves and make themselves ready. They stay away from their women, don't have any intercourse with them. Sometimes they sleep in the kiva. They deny themselves salt or meat. It is a tribute to you if you are asked to be a clown. If you accept the invitation, your aunts on your father's side will furnish you with food.

I was telling you about the emergence from the underworld. Now, that tradition is involved in the clown rituals. Before they go to perform, the clowns have their own ceremony in the kiva. Just as in other ceremonies, the central themes of their ritual is rain. They sit in a circle, go through prescribed routines and sing. When they are finished wth the song they all holler, "Yah hay!" Then they reenact the coming from the underworld. The leader climbs the ladder to the top. He sticks his head out, says, "Yah hay!" and ducks his head down again. He does that four times. Says, "Ne talat aou yama, I came out into the light!" After that, the next fellow does the same thing. It's a reenactment of the emergence into the upper world.

When they are all outside the kiva, they go to different places in the village. First they go to the home of the eldest woman of the Corn Clan or of the Tobacco Clan. This woman offers them piki, and they take small pieces four times. They thank her. They have in mind that corn is life, that it is the substance of our bodies. They have in mind that all things come from the Great Spirit. The piki that they receive from the woman is symbolic. It gives them the strength to perform. These things take place the day before the dance. They go to where the dancers and kiva leaders are having their rehearsal, and they rehearse with them, planning what they are going to do to entertain the spectators. They stay there all night, and early in the morning they return to their own kiva for a while before they make their appearance at the ceremony.

Many of the things they do in their performance are mischievous or, you might say, naughty. This behavior is really telling people how *not* to behave. Sometimes the things they do refer to certain individuals in the community. If someone has been acting in an improper manner, the clowns' actions or dialogue allude to this. They can be criticizing even an important person. While it may seem funny to many of the spectators, some of them understand that it is serious criticism. Those clowns are freed from the usual restraints, and it gives them an opportunity to say things that ordinarily wouldn't be said. But a lot of things they do are just nonsense, as if they didn't understand any proprieties. You see, they sort of represent people as they were when they came from the underworld. They are funny looking and they don't understand good manners. They are, you could say, uncivilized, as people were when they first emerged. By their actions they remind everyone how important it is to be decent and respectful and harmonious in their way of living.

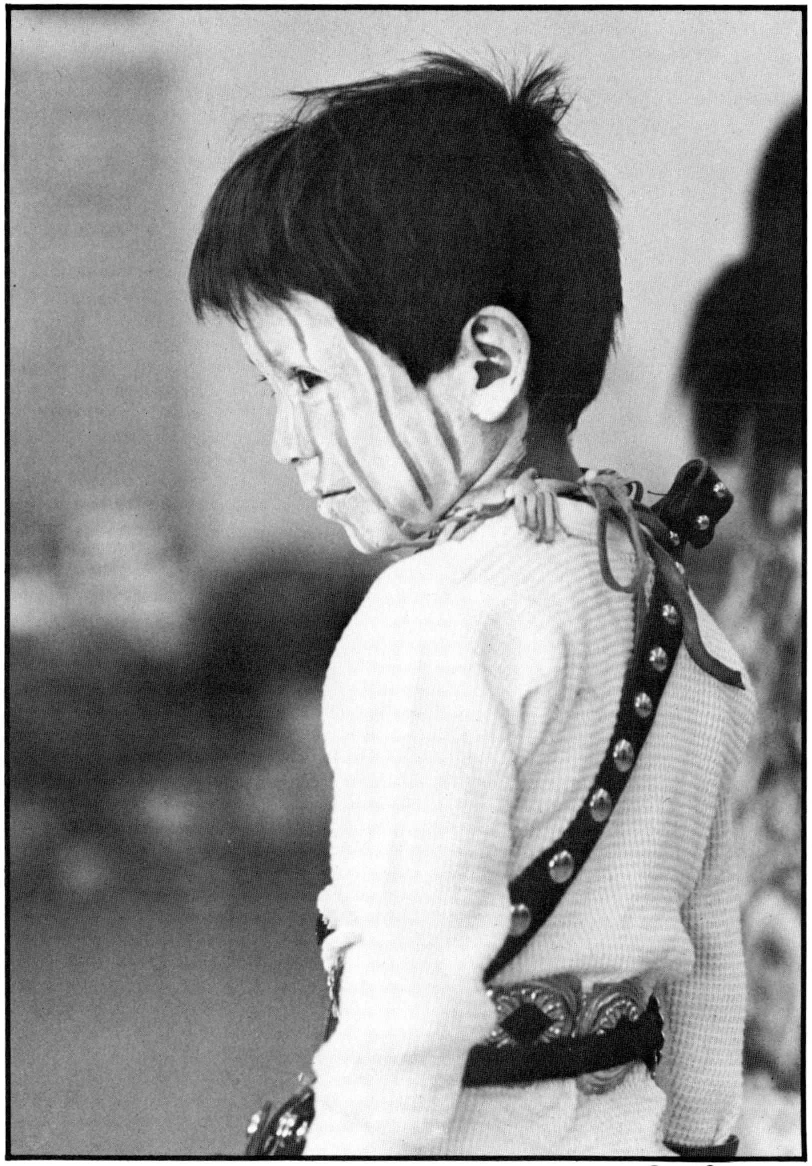

Owen Seumptewa

One More Smile for a Hopi Clown

Emory Sekaquaptewa

The heart of the Hopi concept of clowning is that we are all clowns. This was established at the very beginning when people first emerged from the lower world. In spite of the belief that this was a new world in which no corruption and immorality would be present, the people nevertheless took as their own all things that they saw in the new world. Seeing that the people still carried with them many of the ways of the corrupted underworld, the Spirit Being divided them into groups and laid out a life-pattern for each of them, so that each would follow its own life-way.

Before the Hopi people left from the emergence place, one man chosen by them as their leader went up on a hill. I can just imagine the throng of his people around him who were excited and eager in getting ready to be led out to the adventures of a new world. The leader gets up on this hill and calls out, "yaahahay!" four times. Thus gaining their attention he said, "Now you heard me cry out to you in this way. You will hear me cry in this way when we have reached the end of our life-way. It will be a sign that we have reached the end of the world. We will know then whether we have fulfilled our destiny. If we have not we will see how it is to be done." The leader who was a visionary man chose this way of reminding his people that they have only their worldly ambition and aspirations by which to gain a spiritual world of eternity. He was showing them that we cannot be perfect in this world after all and if we are reminded that we are clowns, maybe we can have, from time to time, introspection as a guide to lead us right. From this beginning when we have been resembled to clowns we know that this is to be a trying life and that we will try to fulfill our destiny by mimicry, by mockery, by copying, by whatever.

This whole idea of clowning is re-enacted at the time of the *katsina* dances. When they are dancing in the plaza the *katsinas* represent the spiritual life toward which Hopi destiny is bent. The *katsinas* dance in the plaza at intervals throughout the day and sometimes for two days. When the clowns come they represent man today who is trying to reach this place of paradise. That is why the clowns always arrive at the plaza from the rooftops of the houses facing the plaza where the *katsinas* are dancing. The rooftops signify that even though we have reached the end, we are not necessarily ready to walk easily into the spiritual world. The difficulties by which clowns gain the place of the *katsinas* make for fun and laughter, but also show that we may not all be able to make it from the rooftop because it is too difficult. We are going to clown our way through life making believe that we know everything and when the time comes, possibly no one will be prepared after all to enter the next world. We will still find the way difficult with obstacles in front of us. Maybe some of us won't make it.

The clowns come to the edge of the housetops around noon and they announce themselves with the cry "yaahahay!" four times. This announces as foretold at emergence the arrival at the end of the life-way journey. And then they make their way into the plaza with all sorts of antics and buffoonery representing the Hopi life quest. In their actions they reveal that we haven't yet fulfilled our destiny after all. By arriving at the late hour, noon, they show that we are lagging behind because we think we have many things to do.

Once in the plaza they act just as people did when they emerged in this world. They presume that they are in a new world, clean and pure. They are where they can finally have eternal life like the *katsinas*; indeed, this is the day all Hopi look forward to. But as they are remarking on the beauty of this place filled with plants and good things they hear the *katsina* songs. They grope around the plaza looking for someone. They pretend they cannot see them because they are spirits. Finally, one of the clowns touches a *katsina* and upon his discovery of these beautiful beings, the clowns immediately try to take possession of them. "This is mine!" "This is mine!" They even fight each other over the possession of the *katsinas* and over the food and things they find.

The remainder of the afternoon is filled with all sorts of clown performances, many of which are planned in advance. Others just happen. These are satires focused on almost anything whether it be in the Hopi world or in the non-Hopi world. Clowns make fun of life and thereby cause people to look at themselves.

Imagination is important to the clown. There are good clowns and not so good clowns when it comes to being funny and witty. But all clowns perform for the smiles and laughter they hope to inspire in the people. When the clowns leave the kiva on their way to the plaza the last request by each is a prayer something to the effect, "If it be so, may I gain at least one smile."

The clown skits and satiric performances done throughout the afternoon are reminiscent of the corruption that we experienced in the underworld, where we presumably had Conscience as a guide. We chose not to follow the Conscience and it comes into play during the clown performances in the form of *katsinas* that visit the plaza. The Owl *katsina* on his first visit comes with a handful of pebbles, carrying a switch. He appears at each corner of the plaza presumably unseen by the clowns and throws little pebbles at the clowns, occasionally hitting them. These pangs of Conscience are felt but not heeded by the clowns. Owl *katsina* returns to the plaza later accompanied by several threatening *katsinas* carrying whips. And this time, instead of pebbles, he may brush up against one of the clowns. He may even knock him down. Conscience keeps getting stronger and more demanding and insistent. On Owl's third visit, the clowns begin to realize that they may suffer consequences if they don't change their ways. Still, they try to buy their safety by offering Owl a bribe. On the sly, the head clown approaches Owl, presumably unseen by anyone, but, of course, they are in the middle of the plaza and are witnessed by all the spectators. Those two kneel together in an archaic conversation modeled upon an ancient meeting.

Owl finally accepts the bribe of a string of beads and thus leads the clown to believe that he has bought his safety. The head clown asks Owl to discipline the other clowns so as to get them back on the right road, but he thinks he will be safe.

With each of Owl's visits more and more *katsinas* accompany him. They do not come as one big group, but in groups of two or three. Throughout the afternoon the tension builds with the threatening presence of the whip-carrying *katsinas.* All of the spectators begin to identify with the plight of the clowns. You feel like you are the one who is now being judged for all these things.

Owl's fourth visit may not come until the next day. On this visit he brings with him a whole lot of warrior *katsinas.* The atmosphere is one of impending catastrophe. They move closer and closer, finally attacking the clowns, who are stripped and whipped for all they have done. In this way they force the clowns to take responsibility for their actions. After they are whipped, water is poured on them and sprinkled about the audience to signify purification.

When it is all over the threatening *katsinas* come back to the plaza again, but this time they are friendly. They shake hands with the clowns signifying that they have been purified. Then they take each clown the length of the plaza and form a semi-circle around him. At this time the clowns make confessions, but even here they are clowns for their confessions are all made in jest. Having worked up satires for the occasion they jump and sing before the *katsinas.* Their confessions usually are focused on their clan, who, by way of being satirized, are actually honored.

I'll tell you one I heard not long ago. When it was time for this young clown man to make his confession he jumps up and down in front of the *katsina* and says, "Ah ii geology, geology, ah ii." Then he made a beautiful little breakdown of this word so that it has Hopi meaning. "You probably think I am talking about this geology which is a white man's study about something or other. Well, that's not it," he says. "What it really is is that I have a grandmother, and you know she being poor and ugly, nobody would have anything to do with her. She is running around all summer long out in the fields doing a man's job. It breaks her down. She would go out there every day with no shoes and so her feet were not very dainty and not very feminine. If you pick up her foot and look at her sole, it is all cracked and that's what I am talking about when I say geology." Every Hopi can put that together. *Tsiya* means "to crack" and *leetsi* means things placed "in a row," so these cracks are in a row on the bottom of the feet, geology. Things like that are what the confessions are like.

There is a story about the last wish of a Hopi man who died many years ago that shows the character of clowning.

In those days the clown society was very much formalized. It was a practice for men who had great devotion for their ritual society to be buried in the full costume of their office. Of course, this was not seen by the general public since Hopi funerals are rather private affairs.

This story is about a man who had gained great respect for his resourcefulness and performance as a clown. Clowning had become a major part of his life and he was constantly attending to his work as a clown by thinking up new skits and perfecting his performance. As he reached old age he decided that clowning had made his place in this world and he wanted to be remembered as a clown. So he made a special request for what was to be done with him at his death as he realized his time was short. He made his request to his family very firmly.

When he died his nephews and sons began to carry out his request. In preparation for burial the body was dressed in his clown costume. Then the body was carried around to the west side of the plaza and taken up on a roof. While this was being done the town crier's voice rang out through the village calling all the people to the plaza. Everybody was prompt in gathering there. I can just see the women, as with any such occasion, grabbing their best shawl on their way to the plaza. It didn't matter whether they were dressed well underneath the shawl.

When the people arrived they saw this unusual sight on the roof of the house on the west side of the plaza, men standing around a person lying down. When all of the people had gathered, the attendants — pallbearers I guess you could call them — simply, quietly, picked up the body and took it to the edge of the house near the plaza. They picked it up by the hands and legs and swung it out over the plaza as if to throw it and they hollered, "Yaahahay!" And they'd swing it back. Then they'd swing it once more. "Yaahahay!" Four times! On the fourth time they let the body go and it fell down, plop, in the plaza. As they threw the body the pallbearers hollered and laughed as they were supposed to. It took the people by surprise. But then everybody laughed.

Owen Seumptewa

A Clown Story

Emory Sekaquaptewa

It was during the Bean Dance season, which occurs around February or the month called Powamuya. *This is the time when many ceremonies occur, all culminating in what is referred to as the Bean Dance. One of the ceremonies is the appearance of the so-called ogres. That's really a misnomer. This little story tries to bring out the Hopi conception of these Kachinas who come threatening to a child. An ogre in the English sense has no moral fiber in him. He's interested in consuming you regardless, but the Hopi Kachina known as* So'yoko *is a very moral spirit being and he threatens only those children that are bad, incorrigible and misbehaving. He threatens you with the alternative that you straighten out or he is going to eat you. So that's really not an ogre.*

These Kachinas referred to as ogres appear to Hopi children, actually to every child. But they are a little bit more vehemently threatening toward children who are considered as being pretty bad during the past year, and this particular extra threat is all prearranged so that their threats would put the "fear of God," so to speak, in the child's mind and that hopefully he would straighten out. But actually it's done in kind of a unique way, and this little story I'm about to tell shows it.

It seems that back in the older days of old Oraibi, before the division of Oraibi, there was a young man (and I think we'll keep him anonymous) who was considered a bad child by his parents. He was a pretty bad boy, so the ogres knew that when they came to him. They stood outside the door of his house, threatening him. There was the big uncle ogre. (He has to be the uncle figure because in Hopi the disciplinarians are your maternal uncles, not the father.) So there's this big uncle ogre with the mother ogre and the brother ogres and the whole throng of helpers ready with the ropes, burden baskets and so forth to carry off bad children. All this threatening outside is to build up the drama and anxiety in the child, really to get him to start thinking "My Gosh! Now I've had it! How am I ever going to get out of this thing?"

Well, he had been coached prior to this time but didn't remember it when he got scared. He'd been coached to do a little dance and it happened that it was to be a Clown dance. He consulted probably with his father or his grandfather who finally came up with the idea "Well, look. You know how to do this dance. Let's go out and show them we can do this and maybe if we can make them laugh or we can make them go along with the story we will have the advantage because if they laugh or if they go along in any way with the story, they've lost. They'll no longer have a right to take you away and eat you up." So the boy finally realized that this was the only chance he had for his own survival.

Quickly they dressed him up as a clown. And it so happened that Grandma had been cooking off to the side a sheep's head which is a kind of delicacy. The head with the skin on is buried in the hot coals overnight, and when it comes out it is really nicely roasted. Children love this stuff. So there was this young boy who was probably looking forward to having it himself, but now it is more important that he save his own skin first. He agreed to use this roasted head because it was necessary to this whole little skit that there be something which was important to himself and to the ogres that would make it look real.

So the child was led out under the protection of his father and his grandfather and they approached the ogres outside. The ogres were all making threats to grab the boy, so the grandfather said, "Hold it now. It's the custom that this boy be given a chance to make amends, to make an apology, to show you that there's something good in him." So the boy was given the signal and he — dressed up like a clown — went up in front of the whole line of ogres, and he sang this little song as he danced:

Tuma angwu noonova!
Tuma angwu noonova!
Oovi paatang kwivi,
siitang kwivi nöqvalkiwta.
Sikwitpeyu tuuva-a-a!
Aqw suunatuvay!

Then as he threw the head on the ground in

front of the ogres he took the pose as though to get ready to grab for it. Suddenly he feigned a grab for the head! Sure enough there were several ogres who moved to pounce on it. They were so taken by the child that they played along with his little story. So that's how he saved the day for himself.

The song is nothing more than "Let's eat; let's eat, because this thing here goes good with pumpkins; it goes good with . . ." you know, really putting up a dish of things which goes good together for a fine meal. And, "So I throw this meat down and now I G-R-A-B for it!" and all the others grab for it. And that was how he won his case before the ogres. The literal translation of the song is:

Let's go ahead eat!
Let's go ahead eat!
Because boiled squash,
boiled things crave meat.
His roasted meat he throws down!
Toward it he throws himself!

Owen Seumptewa A Portfolio

How Maasaw and the People of Oraibi Got Scared to Death Once

Herschel Talashoma

Tutuwutsi *is the Hopi term for stories about make believe things. According to Hopi tradition they should only be told during* Kyaamuya, *the winter month around the solstice. To tell one in the summer is to risk being bitten by a rattlesnake. The following* Tutuwutsi *was recorded by Ekkehart Malotki in his collection of Hopi stories* Hopitutuwutsi: Hopi Tales *(Flagstaff: Museum of Northern Arizona Press, 1978). Illustrations are by Anne-Marie Malotki.*

Aliksa'i. Yaw Orayve yeesiwa. Noq pu' yaw Orayviy aqlap, Mastupatsve, yaw Maasaw piw kiy'ta. Pay yaw pam panis soy'ta. Pam yaw sutsep mihikqw pep Orayve sinmuy tokvaqw, pu' Orayviy angqe pootangwu. Yan yaw pam pep Orayvituy tumalay'ta.

Noq yaw pam hisat piw pangqe Orayviy angqe pootiy'makyangw ahoy pitu. Yaw pam kiy aw pitut, yaw pam hiita navota. Pas yaw haqam suupan hiitu kwanonota. Pay yaw Orayve'ewakwhaqam. Pu' yaw pam angqw Oraymi hiisavo nakwsu. Nit pu' piw tuqayvasta. Noq pay yaw kur pas Orayve hakim hingqaqwa. Pay yaw pam panis yan navot, pu' yaw pay ahoy kiy aw'i. Pu' yaw pam pakiiqe pu' soy aa'awna, "Pas hapi Oraye-haqam hakim suupan haalayyay," yaw soy aw kita.

"Hep owi, pay nu' navotiy'ta. Puma pep mihikqw kivaape tootim, mamant, pu' taataqt, momoyam pep kivaape mihikqw sosotukwyangwu. Niiqe pas pu' nungwu pay qa iits tokwisngwu. Pay as mootiniqw suutokwisngwu, nit pay pu' pas qa iits tokwisngwu. Pay nu' oovi put navotiy'ta," yaw aw kita.

Paasat pu' yaw Maasaw lavayti, "Pas nu' as kur hisat nuutum awni. Hin pi hak sosotukwngwu."

Noq pu' yaw so'at aw pangqawu, "So'on pini, um qa panhaqam hintsakni. Puma hapi ung mamqasya, um oovi qa panhaqam hintsakni," kitaaqe pay yaw qa hin put nakwhana.

Pu' yaw pay aapiy i' Maasaw put wuuwankyangw mihikqw Orayviy angqe pootangwu. Pantsakkyangw pu' yaw pam hisat

Aliksa'i. People were living in Oraibi. Not far from the village, at Mastupatsa, was Maasaw's home, where he lived with his grandmother. Every night when the villagers went to bed, he inspected the area around Oraibi. In this way he guarded the Oraibians.

One day when he was returning from his inspection tour around the village, he heard something just as he reached his house. It sounded as if someone was having a good time, and the shouting and laughing seemed to be coming from Oraibi. So he went a little distance toward Oraibi and listened once more. Evidently some people were making a great deal of noise in Oraibi. As soon as he had realized this, he returned to his house. He entered and blurted out to his grandmother, "Some people in Oraibi really seem to be very happy."

"That's for sure, and I'm aware of it. Boys, girls, men, and women play *sosotukwpi* there in the kiva every night. It's getting so bad that they go to bed late. At first they used to go to bed right away, but now it's usually very late. So I'm well aware of what is going on."

Thereupon Maasaw replied, "I'd very much like to be there together with the others one of these days. I have no idea how to play *sosotukwpi*."

"That's out of the question," his grandmother replied. "You can't do that. They are afraid of you, so don't count on doing anything like that!" Her words made it clear that she would not give him permission to go under any circumstances.

From that day on Maasaw kept mulling this

piw pituuqe, pu' soy aw pangqawu, "Pay nu' pas sutsep Orayminiqay wuuwankyangw angqe pootangwu. Noq nu' oovi qaavo piw ahoy pite,' pu' nu' kur awni," yaw kita.

"Pay pi nu' as ura ung meewa, noq pay pi puye'em um son tuuqayni. Noq pay pii oovi um antsa awni. Pay ason um suus awni. Niikyangw um hapi awnen, um uupösaalay akw huur naakwapmani. Um hapi qa naw- lökintani, puma hapi ung mamqasya. Um hapi oovi paapu inumi tuuqayte' qa naahöltoynani," kita yaw awniiqe pay yaw put nakwhana.

Pu' yaw Maasaw qavomi mihikmi kwangwtoya. Pu' yaw oovi qavong-vaqw mihikqw pu' yaw pam piw Orayviy angqe poota. Panis yaw oovi pam ahoy pitut, pösaalay kwusut, pu' yaw pam pangqw Oraymi'. Piw naat yaw so'at meewa, "Um hapi qa ephaqam naahöltoynani. Pay um panis amumi yorikt, pay um ahoy angqw nimani."

Pu' yaw pam oovi Oraymi pitu. Noq yaw antsa sup kivaape yaw kur sosotukwyangwu. Noq yaw kivats'ove tootim, taataqt wuuhaqniiqamya. Noq pay yaw oovi pam qa pas kivats'omi wupt, pay yaw pam haaqw kiihut tuyqayat angqw wunuwkyangw tuuqayta. Pas pi yaw haalayya. Yaw kivaapehaq kwanok- manta.

Pay yaw oovi pam pangqw su'awsavo wunuwtaqw, pu' yaw kivats'o- veyaqam pay yaw himuwa kya pi öönate', pay nimangwu. Pantsakkyaa- kyangw pu' yaw pay hak pas suukya kivats'ove akwsingwa. Paasat pu' yaw pam pan wuuwa, "Nu' pi pas awnen pu' aqw

over as he made his nightly rounds at Oraibi. One day when he returned home, he said to his grandmother, "It's always on my mind to visit Oraibi when I'm inspecting the area there. So tomorrow, after I make the rounds, I will go there."

"Well, if you will recall, I forbade you to do that. On the other hand, I have a hunch that you don't intend to obey me. So why don't you go. But if you do go, be sure to cover yourself tightly with your blanket and don't let it slip off, for the people are very much afraid of you. For once, listen to me and don't reveal your face!"

Now at last he had her consent. Maasaw started looking forward to the following evening. And once more he made his inspection rounds. But as soon as he got home, he grabbed his blanket and headed towards Oraibi. Once again his grandmother had warned him, "You must not show your face under any circumstances! Take just a quick look at them and then come back."

He arrived in Oraibi and, sure enough, in one kiva they were playing *sosotukwpi.* Since there were a lot of boys and girls on the kiva roof, he did not climb up on the roof but stood at the corner of a house and watched. The people were in a happy mood. There was shouting and laughter in the kiva.

After he had stood there for a long time, the people watching from the roof one by one got tired and departed. Eventually only one person remained on the top of the kiva. Thereupon Maasaw thought, "I'll go up there and peek in.

kuyvani. Nen pu' nu' pas naap hin yorikni. Hintsatskyangwu piniiqe oovi pas haalayyangwu."

Kitaaqe pu' yaw pam angqw kivats'omi'. Pu' yaw pam put hakiy suukw akwsingwqat aqle' kivamiq tsooralti. Pay yaw pan oovi huur naakwap- kyangw, pay yaw pas poosiysa hihin kuytoyniy'ta. Pu' yaw pam pangqaqw pumuy tiimayi. Pas pi yaw kwangwa'ewlalwa.

Pu' yaw kur put amum oongaqwniiqa hisatniqw put aw yori. Noq pam yaw kur pas kawngwatimayqe, yaw kur pam pösaalay qa aw tunatyalti. Niiqe yaw kur pam qötöy hölökna, noq put yaw kur aqle' tsoorawtaqa tuwaaqe, pay yaw okiw sumoki. Pu' yaw pam pangqw nuutum hin unangway'ta. Pantsakkyangw pay yaw kur pam pösaalay posnat qa navota. Pantsakkyangw pu' yaw pay kur pam pas hin unangwtiqe, pay yaw pam kur pas kivamiq pakit qa navota.

Yaw oovi pam pas aw pakiqw, pu' yaw kur hak tuwa. Pu' yaw mimuywatuy aa'awna, "Himu pakiy," yaw kita. Noq pay yaw pas qa nanapta. Pu' yaw as pi'epningwu. Pas yaw hisatniqw pu' yaw kur nanapta. Paasat pu' yaw suuqe'toti. Pu' yaw kivaapeq kwiniwiq tupoq soosoyam yuutu.

Paasat pu' yaw Maasaw nuutum pansoq wari. Panis yaw oovi pam amumiq pituqw, pu' yaw piw taatöqwat yuutu. Pu' yaw pam piw nuutum aqw wari. Pu'yaw pay puma pepehaq naahoy pantsatskya. Pu'yaw kwiniwiq yuutukngwu. Pu' yaw pay piw pam nuutum aqw warikngwu. Puma hapi yaw kur as it angqw waytiwnumyaqw, pam nuutum waayangwu.

Then I can see for myself what the game is like. I have no idea why they are carrying on so happily."

Saying this, he climbed up to the kiva. He lay flat on top of the roof right alongside the one remaining person. He kept his head tightly covered and let only his eyes show a little bit. Then he started watching the players below. They were enjoying themselves tremendously.

After a while his neighbor took a look at him. Now, Maasaw had been having such a good time watching the players that he stopped paying much attention to his blanket. He had uncovered his head and when the person lying next to him saw his face, the poor soul passed out right away. Maasaw was by now just as excited as the others down in the kiva. He was completely unaware that he had dropped his blanket. In the end he got so worked up that he did not even notice that he had entered the kiva.

But someone had apparently heard him come in and announced to the others, "A stranger has come in!" However, the players paid no attention to him. Again and again the man tried to point it out to them. Finally they heard him. Their game stopped immediately and then all of them started running towards the northern wall base in the kiva.

Maasaw too ran there with them. He had hardly reached them when they started running back to the southern base. And again he ran with them. Thus they kept running back and forth. They headed for the northern part, but he ran there too. They tried to run away from him, but

Pas pi yaw putniqw is uti. Pay yaw pam piw tsawnaqe, oovi nuutum pepeq naahoy waytiwnuma. Hisatniqw pu' yaw soosoyam so'a. Pay yaw pam paasat naala epeq wunuwta. Aqle' yaw sinom aasaqawta.

Paasat pu' yaw pam pangqw suyma. Pu' yaw pösaalay sukwsut pu' yaw pam pangqw kiy aw waaya. Paysoq yaw pam kiy aqw poosi. Pavan yaw hin unangway'kyangw, "Hihiya, uti, is uti," yaw kita.

"Ya hinti?" yaw so'at kita.

"Nu' Orayve'e. Nu' pep nanavö'yaqamuy amumiq pakiqw, pay hintotiqe kivaapeq naanahoy yuyutyaqw, pas nu' kyaanavota. Is uti, pay nu' son paapu hisat awni. Pay pi taataqtuy qötöyamuy ooveq himu qöötsa puvuyaltimangwuqa, pay pam pas nuy tsaawina. Pay put nu' hiita pas mamqasi. Pas is uti," kita yawi'.

Paasat pu' yaw so'at lavayti, "Ya um piw pay pas kivamiq paki?"

"Owi, pas kwangwa'ewyaqw, oovi nu' amumiq paki. Noq pay naat nu' hiisavo epeqniqw, pay hintotiqe naanahoy yuyutya, noq paasat pu' nu' put hiita tuwaaqe put nu' angqw waytiwnuma."

"ya'e," yaw aw so'at kita, "puma hapi ung mamqasyaqe, oovi uungaqw puma waytiwnumyaqw, um pepehaq pumuy tsattsawina. Pay um oovi paapu qa hisat awni. Put hapi um mamqasqay pangqawqw, pam hapi pumuy kwavöönakwa'amu. Son pi pam ung hintsanni," kita yaw put so'at awniiqe yaw put qööqöya.

he kept running along beside them.

As he said later, it was awfully spooky. Because he, too, had become scared, he kept fleeing back and forth with the others. After a while all the players had fainted and he stood there all by himself. Next to him, people lay scattered on the floor.

He rushed out, snatched up his blanket and ran all the way home. He entered the house so fast that he more or less tumbled in. Excited and nearly out of his mind, he gasped, "How horrible, how dreadful!"

"What is it?" his grandmother asked.

"Well, I was in Oraibi, and I entered the kiva where they were playing and competing with each other. All of a sudden something happened and all the players started dashing back and forth in the kiva. It was dreadful for me! Let me tell you, I will never go back there. Something white hovered over the men's heads. It frightened me out of my wits. I really was scared stiff of that white thing, whatever it was. It was awful!"

Thereupon his grandmother spoke. "So you entered the kiva?"

"Yes, the people were having such a good time that I went in. And then, when I had been there only a few minutes, they all went crazy and started running back and forth. That's when I saw that white thing and started running from it, wherever it was."

"It was quite the contrary," his grandmother interjected. "They were afraid of you and so they took to their heels when you scared them. That's why you must never go there again. What you

Pu' yaw kivaapeq himuwa yaw hisatniqw yan unangwte', pu' pang- qaqw kiy aw waayangwu. Yan yaw puma Orayve tootim, taataqt, pu' momoyam, mamant Maasawuy pitsinayaqe pas yaw puma naatsawinaya. Paapiy pu' yaw pay qa hisat puma kivaapehaqam mihikqw nanavö'ya.

Paapiy pu' yaw Maasaw pay ahoy piw Orayvit tuuwalangwu. Naat kya oovi pu' piw haqam songqe angqe pootiy'numa. Pay yuk pölö.

said scared you were only the white eagle feathers they wear in their hair. They can't do you any harm." With these explanations his grandmother chided him.

In the kiva, meanwhile, as soon as somebody gained consciousness, he just got up and ran away home. Thus those boys and girls, and men and women who tempted Maasaw to Oraibi got frightened to death. Never again did they gamble in the kiva at night.

From that day on Maasaw guarded Oraibi again. I suppose he is still making his inspection tour there somewhere. And here the story ends.

Dr. Fewkes and Masauwu

Edmund Nequatewa

In the autumn of 1898, the late Dr. Fewkes, archaeologist of the Smithsonian Institution, was staying at Walpi, one of the Hopi Indian Pueblos. In the annual report of the director of the Bureau of Ethnology his visit is noted as follows:

"In November, Dr. J. Walter Fewkes repaired to Arizona for the purpose of continuing his researches concerning the winter ceremonies of the Hopi Indians, but soon after his arrival an epidemic of smallpox manifested itself in such severity as to completely demoralize the Indians and to prevent them from carrying out their ceremonial plans, and at the same time placed Dr. Fewkes in grave personal danger. It accordingly became necessary to abandon the work for the season."

The Hopis at Walpi have another story of the cause of Dr. Fewkes' departure.

Although Dr. Fewkes never reported this story to the outside world, the Hopis now tell that he related it to the priests in the kiva the next day after the strange occurrence.

One of the most important of the Hopi winter ceremonies is the Wuwuchim which comes in November. At a certain time during the ceremony the One Horned and the Two Horned Societies hold a secret rite in a certain part of the pueblo, and all the people who live on that plaza go away and close their houses. No one may witness this ceremony, for Masauwu, the Earth God, is there with the One Horned Priests who do his bidding in the Underworld and the Spirits of the dead are there and it is said that anyone who sees them will be frozen with fright or paralyzed or become like the dead.

Masauwu owns all the Hopi world, the surface of the earth and the Underworld beneath the earth. He is a mighty and terrible being for he wears upon his head a bald and bloody mask. He is like death and he clothes himself in the raw hides of animals and men cannot bear to look upon his face. The Hopi say he is really a very handsome great man of a dark color with fine long black hair and that he is indeed a great giant. When the Hopi came up from the Underworld and looked about them in fear, the first sign which they saw of any being of human form, was the great footprints of Masauwu. Now Masauwu only walks at night and he carries a flaming torch. Fire is his and he owns the fiery pits. Every night Masauwu takes his torch and he starts out on his rounds, for he walks clear around the edge of the world every night.

Dr. Fewkes had been in the kiva all day taking notes on what he saw going on there. Finally the men told him that he must go away and stay in his house for Masauwu was coming, and that part of the ceremony was very sacred and no outside person was ever allowed to see what was going on. They told him to go into his house and lock the door, and not to try to see anything no matter what happened, or he would be dragged out and he would "freeze" to death. So he went away into his house and he locked the door just as he had been told to do and he sat down and began to write up his notes.

Now suddenly he had a queer feeling, for he felt that there was someone in the room, and he looked up and saw a tall man standing before him, but he could not see his face for the light was not good. He felt very much surprised for he knew that he had locked the door.

He said, "What do you want and how did you get in here?" The man replied, "I have come to entertain you."

Dr. Fewkes said, "Go away, I am busy and I do not wish to be entertained."

And now as he was looking at the man, he suddenly was not there any more. Then a voice said, "Turn your head a moment," and when the Doctor looked again the figure stood before him once more, but this time its head was strange and dreadful to see.

And the Doctor said, "How did you get in?", and the man answered and said, "I go where I please, locked doors cannot keep me out! See, I will show you how I entered," and, as Dr. Fewkes watched, he shrank away and became like a single straw in a Hopi hair wisk and he vanished through the key hole.

Now Dr. Fewkes was very much frightened and as he was thinking what to do, there was the man back again. So he said once more to him, "What do you want?", and the figure answered as before and said, "I have come to entertain you." So the Doctor offered him a cigarette and then a match, but the man laughed and said, "Keep your match, I do not need it," and he held the cigarette before his horrible face and blew a stream of fire from his mouth upon it and lit his cigarette. Then Dr. Fewkes was very much afraid indeed, for now he knew who it was.

Then the being talked and talked to him, and finally the Doctor "gave up to him" and said he would become a Hopi and be like them and believe in Masauwu, and Masauwu cast his spell on him and they both became like little children and all night long they played around together and Masauwu gave the Doctor no rest.

And it was not long after that Dr. Fewkes went away but it was not on account of the smallpox as you now know.

To Some Few Hopi Ancestors

Wendy Rose

No longer the drifting
and falling of wind
your songs have changed,
they have become
thin willow whispers
that take us by the ankle
and tangle us up
with red mesa stone,
that keep us turned
to the round sky,
that follow us down
to Winslow, to Sherman,
to Oakland, to all the spokes
that have left earth's middle.
You have engraved yourself
with holy signs, encased yourself
in pumice, hammered on my bones
til you could no longer hear
the howl of the missions
slipping screams through your silence,
dropping dreams from your wings.
    Is this why
    you made me
    sing and weep
    for you?
Like butterflies made
to grow another way
this woman is chiseled
on the face of your world.
The badger-claw of her father
shows slightly in the stone
burrowed from her sight
facing west from home.

Vanishing Point: Urban Indian

Wendy Rose

It is I in the cities, in the bars, in the
dustless reaches of cold eyes who
vanishes, who leans

underbalanced into nothing; it is I
without learning, I without song, who
dies & cries the death time, who

blows from place to place hanging onto
dandelion dust, dying over & over. It is I
who had to search & turn the stones,

half-dead crawl through the bones, let
tears dissolve the dry caves where
woman-ghosts roll piki & insects move
to keep this world alive.

It is I who hold the generous bowl that
flows over with shell & stone,
that is buried in blood, that places its
shape within rock carvings.

It is I who die bearing cracked turquoise
& making noise
so as to protect your fragile immortality
O Medicine Ones.

I Have Come

Lomawywesa
(Michael Kabotie)

Ya Ha Hai!
          I have come

it was a long
hard death

scars of battle
struggling to die
crying, agony/fright

gasping for that
final breath
and finally
jerking in violent
spasms of death

But alas!

here I stand
crying and shouting
sounds of happiness
                    and joy

KUWAH WA DODA NGUI!

In death I am born.

Tsinnijinnie's Hardrock Romance

(A Sing at Coal Mine Canyon)

Victor Masayesva

Hopi Literature: Other Sources

Originally published by the Museum of Northern Arizona in 1936, Edmund Nequatewa's Truth of a Hopi *(Flagstaff: Northland Press, 1967) gives reliable "stories relating to the origin, myths and clan histories of the Hopi." Walter Collins O'Kane provides a readable overview of Hopi society in his* Sun in the Sky *(Norman: University of Oklahoma Press, 1950). Harry James'* Pages from Hopi History *(Tucson: University of Arizona Press, 1974) is a good source on Hopi documentary history.*

Ten Hopi stories as told by Herschel Talashoma, from the Third Mesa village of Bakavi, are printed in bi-lingual form in Ekkehart Malotki's Hopitutuwutsi: Hopi Tales *(Falgstaff: Museum of Northern Arizona Press, 1978). Malotki's introductory remarks and notes provide very clear and succinct information on Hopi literature and culture.*

Harold Courlander's People of the Short Blue Corn *(New York: Harcourt, 1970) is a good collection of Hopi stories for younger readers.*

A selection of Hopi kat'sina *songs in bi-lingual format is given in* Two Hopi Song Poets of Shungopavi: Milland Lomakema and Mark Lomayestewa *(Second Mesa, Arizona: privately printed, 1978). The book was edited by Michael Kabotie and is available from the Hopi Arts and Crafts Guild, Second Mesa, Arizona 86039. Four Hopi lullabies are well translated and discussed in "Four Hopi Lullabies: A Study in Method and Meaning" by Emory Sekaquaptewa and Kathleen Sands. The article appeared in the* American Indian Quarterly*, 4 (1978), pp. 195-210.*

There are a number of sound recordings of Hopi song presently available. Hopi Katchina Songs and six other songs by Hopi chanters *(FE 4394) is available from Folkways. It includes recordings made by Jesse Walter Fewkes in 1924. Canyon Records'* Hopi Social Dances, Vol. 2 *(C-6108) includes Butterfly, Water Maiden, Ribbon, Clown, and Elk dance songs from the Second Mesa village of Shungopavi.*

A number of excellent Hopi autobiographies are presently available. Albert Yava's Big Falling Snow: A Tewa-Hopi Indian's Life and Times and The History and Traditions of His People *(New York: Crown Publishers, 1978) was edited and annotated by Harold Courlander.* Sun Chief: the Autobiography of a Hopi Indian *(New Haven: Yale University Press, 1942) was edited by Leo W. Simmons from notebooks kept by Don Talayesva of Third Mesa.* No Turning Back *(Albuquerque: University of New Mexico Press, 1964) is an engaging account of the life of Hopi potter Polingayse Qoyawayma (Elizabeth Q. White).*

Hopi artist and writer Michael Kabotie (Lomawywesa) has printed selections of his poems in A Decade and Then Some *(Buffalo, N.Y.: Intrepid Press, 1976), edited by Allen DeLoach, and in* Sun Tracks Five *(1979). Wendy Rose's collections of poems include:* Hopi Roadrunner Dancing *(Greenfield Center, N.Y.: The Greenfield Press, 1973),* Long Division: A Tribal History *(New York: Strawberry Press, 1976),* Academic Squaw: Reports to the World from the Ivory Tower *(Marvin, S.D.: Blue Cloud Quarterly, 1977), and* Builder Kachina: a Home-going Cycle *(Marvin, S.D.: Blue Cloud Quarterly, 1979). A good selection of her poems appears in Duane Niatum's collection of contemporary American Indian poetry* Carriers of the Dream Wheel *(New York: Harper and Row, 1975).*

Qua-Toqti *is a weekly newspaper published on the Hopi reservation at New Oraibi, Arizona. It regularly contains writing in Hopi.*

For other written work on Hopi literature and culture see W. David Laird's annotated Hopi Bibliography *(Tucson: University of Arizona Press, 1977). It contains nearly three thousand entries.*

NAVAJO LITERATURE

Navajo Alphabet
Irvy Goossen

VOWELS

1. There are basically four vowels in the Navajo alphabet. The vowels are as follows, the first example being a Navajo word; the last, the closest aproximation in an English word.

a	gad — juniper	art
e	e'e'ahh — west	met
i	sis — belt	sit
o	hosh — cactus	note

2. Vowels may be either long or short in duration, the long vowels being indicated by a doubling of the letter. Actually, there are three regular vowel lengths, a short, a long and an extra long. The latter occurs regularly in syllables closed by a stop consonant, usually "d" or "'" (glottal stop). The length does not affect the quality of the vowel, except that "ii" is always pronounced as "i" in machine.

sis — belt	the vowel is short
siziiz — my belt	the second vowel is long

3. Vowels with hooks under them are nasalized. Some of the breath passes through the nose in their production.

tsinaabaas — wagon	naadą́ą́' — corn
bizees — his warts	háádéé' — from where
ashiih — salt	shilį́į́' — my horse
so' — star	dlǫ́ǫ́' — prairie dog

4. When there is a tone mark on a letter, raise your voice in pitch on that syllable. Say the first words of the examples given below, and then the one across from it, after hearing a Navajo say them.

ni — you	ní — he says
azee' — medicine	azéé' — mouth
nilí — he is	nílí — you are
doo — not	dóó — and

Notice the difference in the meanings of the words in the two columns. The tone alone indicates the difference.

5. The diphthongs are as follows: ai; aai; ao; aoo; ei; eii; oi; ooi.

ai	hai — winter	something like kite
ei	éí — that one	day
oi	deesdoi — it is warm	buoy

6. When only the first element of a vowel or a diphthong has a mark above it, the tone is falling. When the last element is marked, the tone is rising.

bilasáana — apple	deídíiltah — we will read it
dóola — bull	litsxooí — orange

CONSONANTS

7. (') This is the most common consonantal sound in Navajo. It is called a glottal stop and sounds like the break between the two elements of the English expression "oh, oh." The diference between "Johnny yearns" and "Johnny earns" is that the latter has a glottal closure between the two words.

e'e'ahh — west	a'ą́ą́n — a hole

8. Following are the rest of the consonants and their English equivalents, as much as they can be given.

b	bááh	bread	like p in spot
ch	chizh	firewood	like ch in church
ch'	ch'ah	hat	-----
d	dibé	sheep	like t in stop
dl	dlǫ́ǫ́'	prairie dog	like dl in paddling
dz	dzil	mountain	like dz in adze
g	gah	rabbit	something like k in sky
gh	hooghan	hogan	-----
h	háadi	where	-----
hw	bil hwee-shne'	I told him	like wh in when
j	jádí	antelope	like j in jug
k	ké	shoe	like k in kitten
k'	k'ad	now	-----
kw	kwe'é	right here	like qu in quick
l	lájish	glove	like l in lazy
ł	łid	smoke	-----
m	mósí	cat	like m in mosquito
n	naadą́ą́'	corn	like n in new
s	sin	song	like s in soon
sh	shash	bear	like sh in shoe
t	tin	ice	-----
t'	t'eesh	charcoal	-----
tł	tłah	ointment	-----
tł'	tł'ízí	goat	-----
ts	tash	needle	like ts in hats
ts'	ts'ah	sagebrush	-----
w	Wááshin-doon	Washing-ton, D.C.	like w in wash
y	yá	sky	like y in yes
z	zas	snow	like z in zero
zh	bízhi'	his name	like z in azure

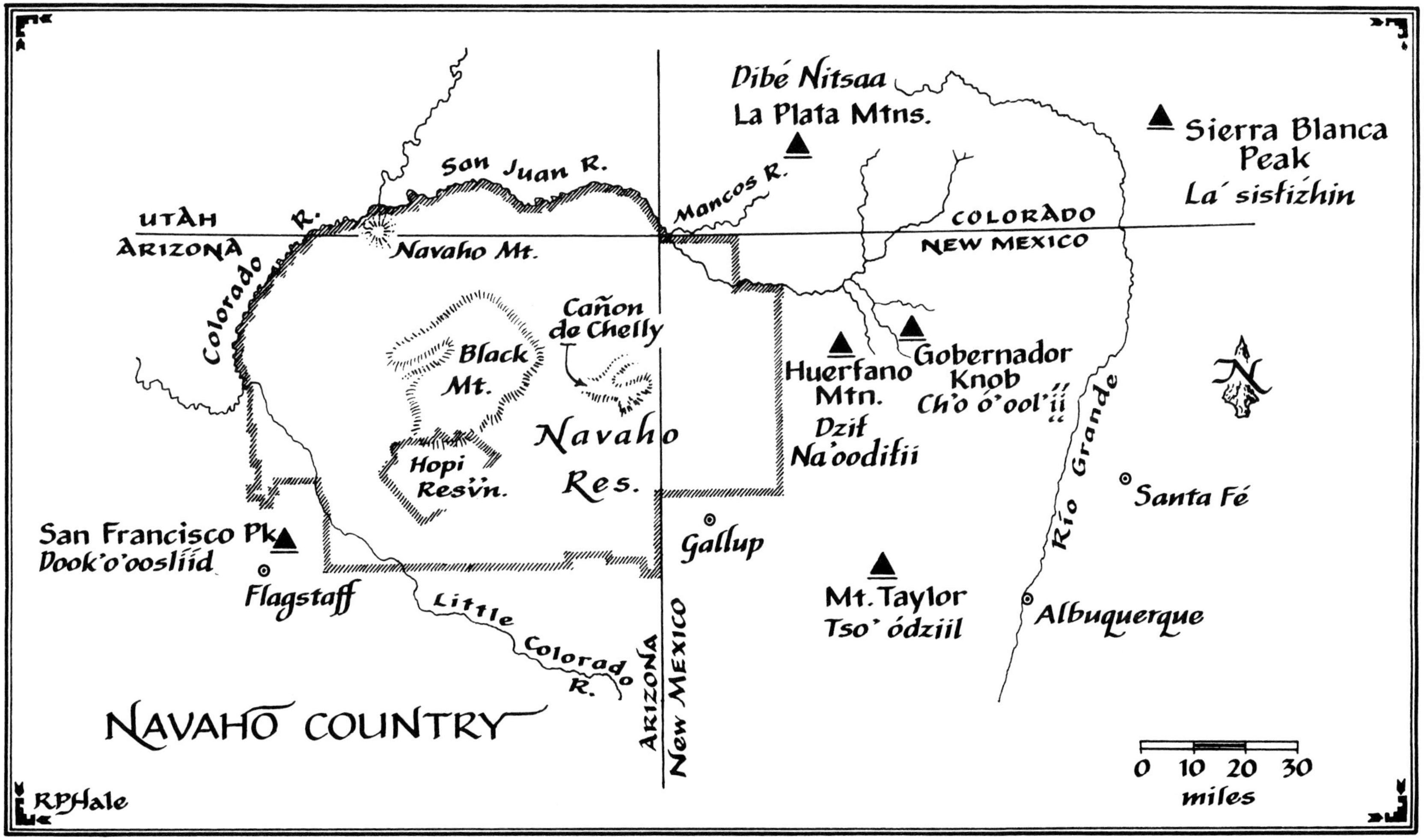
Dibé Nitsaa
La Plata Mtns.
Sierra Blanca Peak
La´ sisłizhin
San Juan R.
Mancos R.
UTAH
ARIZONA
COLORADO
NEW MEXICO
Colorado R.
Navaho Mt.
Cañon de Chelly
Black Mt.
Navaho Res.
Hopi Resvn.
Huerfano Mtn.
Dził Na'oodiłii
Gobernador Knob
Ch'o ó'ool'íí
Rio Grande
Santa Fé
San Francisco Pk
Dook'o'oosłííd
Flagstaff
Gallup
Mt. Taylor
Tso' ódziil
Albuquerque
Little Colorado R.
NAVAHO COUNTRY
ARIZONA
New Mexico
0 10 20 30
miles
RPHale

Sandpainting

Irene Nakai
Tó' ahaní

Morning:
   Let us go out into the desert, troubled friend, to
      gather red sand, black earth, white sand, blue
         clay.

Noon:
   Let us climb a rippling sand dune,
      everchanging in the celestial breezes,
                                        grain
                                         by
                                        grain.
Seat ourselves in the twilight;
Paint your troubles in the sand.

Red sand, words of anger that cut.
Black earth, screaming demons, rumbling,
         mumbling confusion.
White sand, blank walls, blank faces, titled thick
      books with blank pages.
Blue clay, blue, sticky blue, bogging blues.
Night wind blows,
Above the wind, do you hear someone knocking?
      "Open the door, it is the door of the Mountain."
Child, turn around, your painting has blown — away and
   it is Dawn!

Story of a Cricket: Spring 1978

Irene Nakai
Tó' ahaní

Little sister Eilene and I were looking, with amazed eyes, at the blooming desert flowers in the grey rock garden expanses near *Kenneth Bi Dził*. We heard a cricket, and we started to look for him. He was sitting under a flat, gray *tsé' áwozí*. Strange, it seemed, that he would be making a noise in the heat of a late spring afternoon.

Eilene took the rock off the cricket; the cricket was black and shiny. Exposed to the light, our interruption, ("pardon us") he stopped singing, and ran around looking for shade. Eilene put back his roof. The cricket took a breath and resumed his singing.

Sometimes, I see the black, shiny cricket so suited to have sung the first note of the song of creation; in dark directionless space, everyone waiting, then one chirp to make an announcement, "*K' iz* . . . something is happening. We are becoming!" *Nahak' ízii.*

Jim Darnton

The Beginning

Sandoval

Hastin Tlo'tsihee

Sandoval, Hastin Tlo'tsi hee *(Old Man Buffalo Grass), joined Aileen O'Bryan at Mesa Verde National Park in late November of 1928 for the purpose of having her record some of his knowledge. When he arrived he said to her: "You look at me, and you see only an ugly old man, but within I am filled with great beauty. I sit as on a mountaintop and I look into the future. I see my people and your people living together. In time to come my people will have forgotten their early way of life unless they learn it from white men's books. So you must write down all that I will tell you; and you must have it made into a book that coming generations may know this truth."*

Sandoval talked for seventeen days. His nephew Sam Ahkeah translated; O'Bryan recorded. It is reported that Sandoval would often stop and chant a short prayer, then sprinkle the manuscript, Ahkeah, and O'Bryan with corn pollen. The following is from The Dine: Origin Myths of the Navaho Indians *(Washington, D.C.: Government Printing Office, 1956).*

THE FIRST WORLD

These stories were told to Sandoval, Hastin Tlo'tsi hee, by his grandmother, Esdzan Hosh kige. Her ancestor was Esdzan at a', the medicine woman who had the Calendar Stone in her keeping. Here are the stories of the Four Worlds that had no sun, and of the Fifth, the world we live in, which some call the Changeable World.

The First World, Ni'hodilqil,[1] was black as black wool. It had four corners, and over these appeared four clouds. These four clouds contained within themselves the elements of the First World. They were in color, black, white, blue, and yellow.

The Black Cloud represented the Female Being or Substance. For as a child sleeps when being nursed, so life slept in the darkness of the Female Being. The White Cloud represented the Male Being or Substance. He was the Dawn, the Light-Which-Awakens, of the First World.

In the East, at the place where the Black Cloud and the White Cloud met, First Man, Atse'hastqin, was formed; and with him was formed the white corn, perfect in shape, with kernels covering the whole ear. Dohonot i'ni is the name of this first seed corn,[2] and it is also the name of the place where the Black Cloud and the White Cloud met.

The First World was small in size, a floating island in mist or water. On it there grew one tree, a pine tree, which was later brought to the present world for firewood.

Man was not, however, in his present form.

The conception was of a male and a female being who were to become man and woman. The creatures of the First World are thought of as the Mist People; they had no definite form, but were to change to men, beasts, birds, and reptiles of this world.[3]

Now on the western side of the First World, in a place that later was to become the Land of Sunset, there appeared the Blue Cloud, and opposite it there appeared the Yellow Cloud. Where they came together First Woman was formed, and with her the yellow corn. This ear of corn was also perfect. With First Woman there came the white shell and the turquoise and the yucca.[4]

First Man stood on the eastern side of the First World. He represented the Dawn and was the Life Giver. First Woman stood opposite in the West. She represented Darkness and Death.

First Man burned a crystal for a fire. The crystal belonged to the male and was the symbol of the mind and of clear seeing. When First Man burned it, it was the mind's awakening. First Woman burned her turquoise for a fire. They saw each other's lights in the distance. When the Black Cloud and the White Cloud rose higher in the sky First Man set out to find the turquoise light. He went twice without success, and again a third time; then he broke a forked branch from his tree, and, looking through the fork, he marked the place where the light burned. And the fourth time he walked to it and found smoke coming from a home.

"Here is the home I could not find," First Man said.

First Woman answered: "Oh, it is you. I saw you walking around and I wondered why you did not come."

Again the same thing happened when the Blue Cloud and the Yellow Cloud rose higher in the sky. First Woman saw a light and she went out to find it. Three times she was unsuccessful, but the fourth time she saw the smoke and she found the home of First Man.

"I wondered what this thing could be," she said.

"I saw you walking and I wondered why you did not come to me," First Man answered.

First Woman saw that First Man had a crystal for a fire, and she saw that it was stronger than her turquoise fire. And as she was thinking, First Man spoke to her. "Why do you not come with your fire and we will live together." The woman agreed to this. So instead of the man going to the woman, as is the custom now, the woman went to the man.

About this time there came another person, the Great - Coyote - Who-Was-Formed-in-the-Water,[5] and he was in the form of a male being. He told the two that he had been hatched from an egg. He knew all that was under the water and all that was in the skies. First Man placed this person ahead of himself in all things. The three began to plan what was to come to pass; and while they were thus occupied another being came to them. He also had the form of a man, but he wore a hairy coat, lined with white fur, that fell to his knees and was belted in at the waist. His name was Atse'hashke', First Angry or Coyote.[6] He said to the three: "You believe that you were the first persons. You are mistaken. I was living when you were formed."

Then four beings came together. They were yellow in color and were called the tsts'na or wasp people. They knew the secret of shooting evil and could harm others. They were very powerful.

This made eight people.

Four more beings came. They were small in size and wore red shirts and had little black eyes. They were the naazo'zi or spider ants. They knew how to sting, and were a great people.

After these came a whole crowd of beings. Dark colored they were, with thick lips and dark, protruding eyes. They were the wolazhi'ni, the black ants. They also knew the secret of shooting evil and were powerful; but they killed each other steadily.

By this time there were many people. Then came a multitude of little creatures. They were peaceful and harmless, but the odor from them was unpleasant. They were called the wolazhi'ni nlchu nigi, meaning that which emits an odor.[7]

And after the wasps and the different ant people there came the beetles, dragonflies, bat people, the Spider Man and Woman, and the Salt Man and Woman,[8] and others that rightfully had no definite form but were among those people who peopled the First World. And this world, being small in size, became crowded, and the people quarreled and fought among themselves, and in all ways made living very unhappy.

THE SECOND WORLD

Because of the strife in the First World, First Man, First Woman, the Great-Coyote-Who-Was-Formed-in-the-Water, and the Coyote called First Angry, followed by all the others, climbed up from the World of Darkness and Dampness to the Second or Blue World.[9]

They found a number of people already living there: blue birds, blue hawks, blue jays, blue herons, and all the blue-feathered beings.[10] The powerful swallow people[11] lived there also, and these people made the Second World unpleasant for those who had come from the First World. There was fighting and killing.

The First Four found an opening in the World of Blue Haze; and they climbed through this and led the people up into the Third or Yellow world.

THE THIRD WORLD

The bluebird was the first to reach the Third or Yellow World. After him came the First Four and all the others.

A great river crossed this land from north to south. It was the Female River. There was another river crossing it from east to west, it was the Male River. This Male River flowed through the Female River and on;[12] and the name of this place is tqo alna'osdli, the Crossing of the waters.

There were six mountains in the Third World.[13] In the East was Sis na' jin, the Standing Black Sash. Its ceremonial name is Yol gai'dzil, the Dawn or White Shell Mountain. In the South stood Tso'dzil, the Great Mountain, also called Mountain Tongue. Its ceremonial name is Yodolt i'zhi dzil, the Blue Bead or Turquoise Mountain. In the West stood Dook'oslid, and the meaning of this name is forgotten. Its ceremonial name is Dichi'li dzil, the Abalone Shell Mountain. In the North stood Debe'ntsa, Many Sheep Mountain. Its ceremonial name is Bash'zhini dzil, Obsidian Mountain. Then there was Dzil na'odili, the Upper Mountain. It was very sacred; and its name means also the Center Place, and the people moved around it. Its ceremonial name is Ntl'is dzil, Precious Stone or Banded Rock Mountain. There was still another mountain called Chol'i'i or Dzil na'odili choli, and it was also a sacred mountain.

There was no sun in this land, only the two rivers and the six mountains. And these rivers and mountains were not in their present form, but rather the substance of mountains and rivers as were First Man, First Woman, and the others.

Now beyond Sis na' jin, in the east, there lived the Turquoise Hermaphrodite, Ashton nutli.[14] He was also known as the Turquoise Boy. And near this person grew the male reed. Beyond, still farther in the east, there lived a people called the Hadahuneya'nigi,[15] the Mirage or Agate People. Still farther in the east there lived twelve beings called the Naaskiddi.[16] And beyond the home of these beings there lived four others — the Holy Man, the Holy Woman, the Holy Boy, and the Holy Girl.

In the West there lived the White Shell Hermaphrodite[17] or Girl, and with her was the big female reed which grew at the water's edge. It had no tassel. Beyond her in the West there lived another stone people called the Hadahunes'tqin, the Ground Heat People. Still farther on there lived another twelve beings, but these were all females.[18] And again, in the Far West, there lived four Holy Ones.

Within this land there lived the Kisa'ni, the ancients of the Pueblo People. On the six mountains there lived the Cave Dwellers or Great Swallow People.[19] On the mountains lived also the light and dark squirrels, chipmunks, mice, rats, the turkey people, the deer and cat people, the spider people, and the lizards and snakes. The beaver people lived along the rivers, and the frogs and turtles and all the underwater people in the water. So far all the people were similar. They had no definite form, but they had been given different names because of different characteristics.

Now the plan was to plant.

First Man called the people together. He brought forth the white corn which had been formed with him. First Woman brought the yellow corn. They laid the perfect ears side by side; then they asked one person from among the many to come and help them. The Turkey stepped forward. They asked him where he had come from, and he said that he had come from the Gray Mountain.[20] He danced back and forth four times, then he shook his feather coat and there dropped from his clothing four kernels of corn, one gray, one blue, one black, and one red.

Another person was asked to help in the plan of the planting. The Big Snake came forward. He likewise brought forth four seeds, the pumpkin, the watermelon, the cantaloup, and the muskmelon. His plants all crawl on the ground.

They planted the seeds, and their harvest was great.

After the harvest the Turquoise Boy from the East came and visited First Woman. When First Man returned to his home he found his wife with this boy. First Woman told her husband that Ashon nutli' was of her flesh and not of his flesh.[21] She said that she had used her own fire, the turquoise, and had ground her own yellow corn into meal. This corn she had planted and cared for herself.

Now at that time there were four chiefs: Big Snake, Mountain Lion, Otter, and Bear.[22] And it was the custom when the black cloud rose in the morning[23] for First Man to come out of his dwelling and speak to the people. After First Man had spoken the four chiefs told them what they should do that day. They also spoke of the past and of the future. But after First Man found his wife with another he would not come out to speak to the people. The black cloud rose higher, but First Man would not leave his dwelling; neither would he eat or drink. No one spoke to the people for 4 days. All during this time First Man remained silent, and would not touch food or water. Four times the white cloud rose. Then the four chiefs went to First Man and demanded to know why he would not speak to the people. The chiefs asked this question three times, and a fourth, before First Man would answer them.

He told them to bring him an emetic.[24] This he took and purified himself. First Man then asked them to send the hermaphrodite to him. When he came First Man asked him if the metate and brush[25] were his. He said that they were. First Man asked him if he could cook and prepare food like a woman, if he could weave, and brush the hair. And when he had assured First Man that he could do all manner of woman's work, First Man said: "Go and prepare food and bring it to me." After he had eaten, First Man told the four chiefs what he had seen, and what his wife had said.

At this time the Great-Coyote-Who-Was-Formed-in-the-Water came to First Man and told him to cross the river. They made a big raft and crossed at the place where the Male River followed through the Female River. And all the male beings left the female beings on the river bank; and as they rowed across the river they looked back and saw that First Woman and the female beings were laughing. They were also behaving very wickedly.

In the beginning the women did not mind being alone. They cleared and planted a small field. On the other side of the river First Man and the chiefs hunted and planted their seeds. They had a good harvest. Nadle[26] ground the corn and cooked the food. Four seasons passed. The men continued to have plenty and were happy; but the women became lazy, and only weeds grew on their land. The women wanted fresh meat. Some of them tried to join the men and were drowned in the river.

First Woman made a plan. As the women had no way to satisfy their passions, some fashioned long narrow rocks, some used the feathers of the turkey, and some used strange plants (cactus). First Woman told them to use these things. One woman brought forth a big stone. This stone-child was later the Great Stone that rolled over the earth killing men. Another woman brought forth the Big Birds of Tsa bida'hi; and others gave birth to the giants and monsters who later destroyed many people.

On the opposite side of the river the same condition existed. The men, wishing to satisfy their passions, killed the females of mountain sheep, lion, and antelope. Lightning struck these men. When First Man learned of this he warned his men that they would all be killed. He told them that they were indulging in a dangerous practice. Then the second chief spoke: he said that life was hard and that it was a pity to see women drowned. He asked why they should not bring the women across the river and all live together again.

"Now we can see for ourselves what comes from our wrong doing," he said. "We will know how to act in the future." The three other chiefs of the animals agreed with him, so First Man told them to go and bring the women.

After the women had been brought over the river First Man spoke: "We must be purified," he said. "Everyone must bathe. The men must dry themselves with white corn meal, and the women, with yellow."

This they did, living apart for 4 days. After the fourth day First Woman came and threw her right arm around her husband. She spoke to the others and said that she could see her mistakes, but with her husband's help she would henceforth lead a good life. Then all the male and female beings came and lived with each other again.

The people moved to different parts of the land. Some time passed; then First Woman became troubled by the monotony of life. She made a plan. She went to Atse'hashke, the Coyote called First Angry, and giving him the rainbow she said: "I have suffered greatly in the past. I have suffered from want of meat and corn and clothing. Many of my maidens have died. I have suffered many things. Take the rainbow and go to the place where the rivers cross. Bring me the two pretty children of Tqo holt sodi, the Water Buffalo, a boy and a girl."

The Coyote agreed to do this. He walked over the rainbow. He entered the home of the Water Buffalo and stole the two children; and these he hid in his big skin coat with the white fur lining. And when he returned he refused to take off his coat, but pulled it around himself and looked very wise.

After this happened the people saw white light in the East and in the South and West and North. One of the deer people ran to the East, and returning, said that the white light was a great sheet of water. The sparrow hawk flew to the South, the great hawk to the West, and the kingfisher to the North. They returned and said that a flood was coming. The kingfisher said that the water was greater in the North, and that it was near.

The flood was coming and the Earth was sinking. And all this happened because the Coyote had stolen the two children of the Water Buffalo, and only First Woman and the Coyote knew the truth.

When First Man learned of the coming of the water he sent word to all the people, and he told them to come to the mountain called Sis na'jin. He told them to bring with them all of the seeds of the plants used for food. All living beings were to gather on the top of Sis na'jin. First Man traveled to the six sacred mountains, and, gathering earth from them, he put it in his medicine bag.[27]

The water rose steadily.

When all the people were halfway up Sis na'jin, First Man discovered that he had forgotten his medicine bag. Now this bag contained not only the earth from the six sacred mountains, but his magic, the medicine he used to call the rain down upon the earth and to make things grow. He could not live without his medicine bag, and he wished to jump into the rising water; but the others begged him not to do this. They went to the kingfisher and asked him to dive into the water and recover the bag. This the bird did. When First Man had his medicine bag again in his possession he breathed on it four times and thanked his people.

When they had all arrived it was found that the Turquoise Boy had brought with him the big Male Reed,[28] and the White Shell Girl had brought with her the big Female Reed.[29] Another person brought poison ivy; and another, cotton, which was later used for cloth. This person was the spider. First Man had with him his spruce tree[30] which he planted on the top of Sis na'jin. He used his fox medicine[31] to make it grow; but the spruce tree began to send out branches and to taper at the top, so First Man planted the big Male Reed. All the people blew on it, and it grew and grew until it reached the canopy of the sky. They tried to blow inside the reed, but it was solid. They asked the woodpecker to drill out the hard heart. Soon they were able to peek through the opening, but they had to blow and blow before it was large enough to climb through. They climbed up inside the big male reed, and after them the water continued to rise.

THE FOURTH WORLD

When the people reached the Fourth World they saw that it was not a very large place. Some say that it was called the White World; but not all medicine men agree that this is so.

The last person to crawl through the reed was the turkey from Gray Mountain. His feather coat was flecked with foam, for after him came the water. And with the water came the female Water Buffalo who pushed her head through the opening in the reed. She had a great quantity of curly hair which floated on the water, and she had two horns, half black and half yellow. From the tips of the horns the lightning flashed.

First Man asked the Water Buffalo why she

had come and why she had sent the flood. She said nothing. Then the Coyote drew the two babies from his coat and said that it was, perhaps, because of them.

The Turquoise Boy took a basket and filled it with turquoise. On top of the turquoise he placed the blue pollen, tha'di'thee do tlij, from the blue flowers,[32] and the yellow pollen from the corn; and on top of these he placed the pollen from the water flags, tquel aqa'di din; and again on top of these he placed the crystal, which is river pollen. This basket he gave to the Coyote who put it between the horns of the Water Buffalo. The Coyote said that with this sacred offering he would give back the male child. He said that the male child would be known as the Black Cloud or Male Rain, and that he would bring the thunder and lightning. The female child he would keep. She would be known as the Blue, Yellow, and White Clouds or Female Rain. She would be the gentle rain that would moisten the earth and help them to live. So he kept the female child, and he placed the male child on the sacred basket between the horns of the Water Buffalo. And the Water Buffalo disappeared, and the waters with her.

After the water sank there appeared another person. They did not know him, and they asked him where he had come from. He told them that he was the badger, nahashch'id, and that he had been formed where the Yellow Cloud had touched the Earth. Afterward this Yellow Cloud turned out to be a sunbeam.[38]

THE FIFTH WORLD

First Man was not satisfied with the Fourth World. It was a small, barren land; and the great water had soaked the earth and made the sowing of seeds impossible. He planted the big Female Reed and it grew up to the vaulted roof of this Fourth World. First Man sent the newcomer, the badger, up inside the reed, but before he reached the upper world water began to drip, so he returned and said that he was frightened.

At this time there came another strange being. First Man asked him where he had been formed, and he told him that he had come from the Earth itself. This was the locust.[34] He said that it was now his turn to do something, and he offered to climb up the reed.

The locust made a headband of a little reed, and on his forehead he crossed two arrows. These arrows were dressed with yellow tail feathers. With this sacred headdress and the help of all the Holy Beings the locust climbed up to the Fifth World. He dug his way through the reed as he digs in the earth now. He then pushed through mud until he came to water. When he emerged he saw a black water bird[35] swimming toward him. He had arrows crossed on the back of his head and big eyes.

The bird said: "What are you doing here? This is not your country." And continuing, he told the locust that unless he could make magic he would not allow him to remain.

The black water bird drew an arrow from back of his head, and shoving it into his mouth drew it out his nether extremity. He inserted it underneath his body and drew it out of his mouth.

"That is nothing," said the locust. He took the arrows from his headband and pulled them both ways through his body, between his shell and his heart. The bird believed that the locust possessed great medicine, and he swam away to the East, taking the water with him.

Then came the blue water bird from the South, and the yellow water bird from the West, and the white water bird from the North, and everything happened as before. The locust performed the magic with his arrows; and when the last water bird had gone he found himself sitting on land.

The locust returned to the lower world and told the people that the beings above had strong medicine, and that he had had great difficulty getting the best of them.

Now two dark clouds and two white clouds rose, and this meant that two nights and two days had passed, for there was still no sun. First Man again sent the badger to the upper world, and he returned covered with mud, terrible mud. First Man gathered chips of turquoise which he offered to the five Chiefs of the Winds[36] who lived in the uppermost world of all. They were pleased with the gift, and they sent down the winds and dried the Fifth World.

First Man and his people saw four dark clouds and four white clouds pass, and then they sent the badger up the reed. This time when the badger returned he said that he had come out on solid earth. So First Man and First Woman led the people to the Fifth World, which some call the Many Colored Earth and some the Changeable Earth. They emerged through a lake surrounded by four mountains. The water bubbles in this lake when anyone goes near.[37]

Now after all the people had emerged from the lower worlds First Man and First Woman dressed the Mountain Lion with yellow, black, white, and grayish corn and placed him on one side. They dressed the Wolf with white tail feathers and placed him on the other side. They divided the people into two groups. The first group was told to choose whichever chief they wished. They made their choice, and, although they thought they had chosen the Mountain Lion, they found that they had taken the Wolf for their chief. The Mountain Lion was the chief for the other side. And these people who had the Mountain Lion for their chief turned out to be the people of the Earth. They were to plant seeds and harvest corn. The followers of the Wolf chief became the animals and birds; they turned into all the creatures that fly and crawl and run and swim.

And after all the beings were divided, and each had his own form, they went their ways.

This is the story of the Four Dark Worlds and the Fifth, the World we live in. Some medicine men tell us that there are two worlds above us, the first is the World of the Spirits of Living Things, the second is the Place of Melting into One.

Endnotes

Notes attributed to "recorder" are those of Aileen O'Bryan; those attributed to "interpreter" are from Sam Ahkeh; all other notes are from the storyteller himself. In addition to these interpretive notes, O'Bryan prepared extensive comparative notes which we have deleted. The interested reader is referred to the original publication The Dine: Origin Myths of the Navaho Indians, *Bureau of American Ethnology Bulletin No. 163 (Washington, D. C.: Government Priting Office, 1956).*

[1]Five names were given to this First World in its relation to First Man. It was called Dark Earth, Ni'hodilqil; Red Earth, Ni'halchi; One Speech, Sada hat lai; Floating Land, Ni'ta na elth; and One Tree, De east'da eith.

[2]Where much corn is raised one or two ears are found perfect. These are always kept for seed corn.

[3]The Navaho people have always believed in evolution.

[4]Five names were given also the the First World in its relation to First Woman: White Bead Standing, Yolgai'na ziha; Turquoise Standing, Dolt i'zhi na ziha; White Bead Floating Place, Yolgai'dana elth gai; Turquoise Floating Place, Dolt 'izhi na elth gai; and Yucca Standing, Tasas y ah gai. Yucca represents cleanliness and things ceremonial.

[5]The Great Coyote who was formed in the water, Mai tqo y elth chili.

[6]Some medicine men claim that witchcraft came with First Man and First Woman, others insist that devil conception or witchcraft originated with the Coyote called First Angry.

[7]No English name given this insect. Ants cause trouble, as also do wasps and other insects, if their homes are harmed.

[8]Beetle, ntlsa'go; Dragonfly, tqanil ai'; Bat people, ja aba'ni; Spider Man, nashjei hastqin; Spider Woman, nashjei esdza; Salt Man, ashi hastqin; Salt Woman, ashi esdza.

[9]The Second World was the Blue World, Ni'hodotl'ish.

[10]The names of the blue birds are: bluebird, do'le; blue hawk, gi'ni tso dolt ish; blue jay, jozh ghae'gi; and blue heron, tqualtl a'gaale.

[11]The swallow is called tqash ji'zhi.

[12]The introduction of generation.

[13]Sis na' jin, Mount Baldy near Alamos, Colo.; Tso'dzil, Mount Taylor, N. Mex.; Dook'oslid, San Francisco Mountain, Ariz.; Debe'ntsa, San Juan Mountains, Colo.; Dzil na'odili, El Huerfano Peak, N. Mex.; and Choli, also given as El Huerfano or El Huerfanito Peak, N. Mex. These mountains of the Third World were not in their true form, but rather the substance of the mountains.

Recorder's note: Although both Matthews and the Franciscan Fathers give Sisnajin as Pelado Peak, Sam Ahkeah, the interpreter, after checking, identified it as Mount Baldy near Alamosa, Colo. Also, although the Franciscan Fathers give Dzil na odili choli as Herfanito Peak, Sam Ahkeah says that it is the Mother Mountain near Taos.

[14]Ashon nutli', the Turquoise Hermaphrodite, later became masculine and was known as the Sun Bearer, Jo hona'ai.

[15]The Hadahuneya'nigi are the Stone People who live where there is a mirage on the desert.

Interpreter's note: These Stone People came from the East.

[16]The Naaskiddi or Gha'askidi are the hunchback figures connected with seeds, fertility, and phallus worship. They are said to have come from the mountain called Chol'i'i.

[17]The White Shell Hermaphrodite or Girl later entered the Moon and became the Moon Bearer. She is connected with Esdzanadle, the Woman-Who-Changes, or Yolgai esdzan, the White Shell Woman.

[18]The Corn Maidens are deities of fertility.

[19]The Great Swallow People, Tqashji'zhi ndilk'si, lived in rough houses of mud and sticks. They entered them from holes in the roof.

[20]The Gray Mountain is the home of the Gray Yei, Hasch el'ba'i, whose other name is Water Sprinkler. The turkey is connected with water and rain.

Interpreter's note: Gray Mountain is San Francisco Mountain, Ariz. Tqo'neinili, the Water Sprinkler, whose color is gray, lives there. He is also called the Gray God, Hasch e'lbai, and the Clown whose call is "do do," and whose name is Hasch e'dodi.

[21]First Woman and the Turquoise Hermaphrodite represented the female principle. Later he said: There is confusion among medicine men regarding this. Some say that the Turquoise Boy was Ashon nutli'; some say the Mirage Man, some contend that "it" was another "Turquoise Boy."

[22]Some medicine men call them the chiefs of the Four Directions.

[23]These are not the Black and White Clouds of the First World. As there was no sun, and no true division of night and day, time was counted by the black cloud rising and the white cloud rising.

[24]The emetic was believed to be either *Babia woodhousei* Gray, of the thistle family, or the root of the wild cherry. In either case, after a hot brew is drunk, copious vomiting ensues.

[25]The metate and brush are symbolic of woman's implements.

[26]Nadle means that which changes. Ashon nutli', or nadle, the Turquoise Hermaphrodite, was the first man to change, or become, as a woman.

[27]Here, and following, magic is associated with First Man.

Recorder's note: The magic of First Man was considered white magic, reason, logos.

[28]The big male reed is called luka'tso. It grows near Santo Domingo Pueblo, not far from the home of the Turquoise Boy, the little turquoise mountain south of Santa Fe, N. Mex.

[29]The big female reed is thought to be the joint cane which grows along the Colorado River. This was near the home of the White Shell Girl.

[30]Recorder's note: That the tree is here called a spruce and earlier a pine is not explained.

[31]First Man's name, Aste'hastqin, corresponds to the sacred name of the kit fox.

[32]Recorder's note: This blue pollen, tha'di'thee do tlij, is thought to be *Delphinium scaposum* Green.

[33]The Four Worlds were really 12 worlds, or stages or development; but different medicine men divide them differently according to the ceremony held. For the narrative they call them the Four Dark Worlds, and the Fifth World, the one we live in. An old medicine man explained that the Sixth World would be that of the spirit; and that the one above that would be "cosmic," melting into one.

[34]The name of the locust was not given.

[35]The water birds were grebes.

[36]The First Chief, Nlchi ntla'ie, the Left Course Wind; the Second Chief, Nlchi lichi, the Red Wind; the Third Chief, Nlchi shada ji na'laghali, the Wind Turning from the Sun; the Fourth Chief, Nlchi qa'hashchi, the Wind with Many Points; the Fifth Chief, Nlchi che do et siedee, the Wind with the Fiery Temper.

[37]The place of emergence is said to be near Pagosa Springs, Colo. The white people have put a wire fence around our Sacred Lake.

A Navajo Life Story

Tom Ration

This narrative is reprinted from Stories of Traditional Navajo Life and Culture *(Tsaile, Arizona: Navajo Community College Press, 1977).*

I am from the Crownpoint, New Mexico, area of the Reservation, and I have lived here for most of my life. I was born in 1901 at Smith Lake, N.M., just north of the Hosta Buttes. My clan is the Towering House People *(Kinyaa'áa nii)* on my mother's side, and I was born for the Water Flows Together People clan *(Tó'aheedlíinii)* on my father's side.

The Towering House clan came from near a natural feature called Towering House. My parents told me I was born not far from that place, just south of it. Long ago it was traditional custom to return to one's birthplace now and then and roll in the earth there. Today, though, almost no one practices that because many babies are born in hospitals, making it impossible. Imagine a person rolling around in the obstetrical ward! They would think that he was crazy.

My mother married my father in Tohatchi, N.M., where he had lived. My father's name was Water Flows Together With Eye Glasses. When I was four years old my parents and I often went to visit my aunt at Willow Extended Red near Tohatchi. Her husband's name was Hard Ground Man. She was my father's sister. I remember the large irrigated farmlands at Willow Extended Red because there was plenty of water there; and the people raised abundant crops.

We lived at Willow Extended Red for quite a while. At that time, Smith Lake was on public land. Navajos migrated freely in any direction they chose. Families made temporary shelters wherever they found good grazing areas which had water for their sheep.

Looking back to the first Navajo government, it is amazing to see how we have progressed; and we can give the credit to our Navajo leaders who made it possible. I remember when there were no district lines in our area. It was all open range, and we made our settlements wherever we chose. We could live in one place a short time and then move to another area with our livestock. Now we have boundaries and permanent home sites. We have grazing regulations by which we must abide. In the good old days no one called us trespassers. It was anybody's land.

Suddenly, however, early in this century lines were drawn and enforced on the New Mexico public lands. It was called the checkerboard area because some land belonged to white ranchers, some to the Navajo Tribe and some still was public land. Each Navajo land user had a permit. Those permits were documents signed by Woodrow Wilson, the President of the United States. All the natural resources found on a particular piece of land were claimed by the one who had the permit for that piece of land. No one could take it away. All trespassers who violated the law could be prosecuted. As a result, we have had many disputes about the land we live on in the checkerboard area, among ourselves and with the Anglos, also with those who live within the true Reservation.

There were times, in those days, when a Navajo sheep grower had two or three large herds of sheep. In the open country, we could see sheep grazing on a mile-wide area. That was something really beautiful, and I wish we could see something like it again.

Navajo children are very precious to their parents, and we want the best for them. I have the same feeling toward all young people, however, no matter who they are. I do not want them to destroy themselves. Life is too short to be taken for granted, or misused, especially while people are young. They have so much to live for.

When I was a boy there was no such thing as an idle day, partly because my father and mother had a large flock of sheep. Times were hard; so we all did our share of the work around our home. I brought in the horses before sunrise; after that, I herded sheep all day. I carried a tortilla, with a piece of mutton folded in it, for a snack. At sundown, after the sheep had been put into the fold, my father made me wrestle with a tree to develop strong muscles. He would say, "Train yourself to be ready for any sudden attack by a bully." A strongly developed body was very important, and that was why we yelled while we raced. We took snow baths in the winter, and we did strenuous exercises very early every morning. Those things helped us have strong lungs, good voices and clear, sound minds. I ran — fast — each morning until I was over 20 years old. And, even now, when I take a notion to have a snow bath, I still do it. When younger, I was sort of an athletic person. I liked to do gymnastics, and sometimes I acted like a Navajo Tarzan swinging on the trees. Anyone can see what I am like at 75 years of age. I still have strong resistance to illness, and I see well. Some men I know who are much younger than I are stooped, and their hair is much whiter than mine. I have a cousin, eight years younger, whose hair is pure white, and he looks aged. Many people have asked how I keep looking so young. I reply, "My early exercises account for it."

A person doesn't see many tall, brawnily-built men and women these days — as Navajos often were a generation or more ago. Now, men and women often are short and fat or large-bellied. They are lazy, and they have more to eat. The people of long ago worked hard, with less food; and they died of old age if they were not killed in battle or otherwise. They were slim and tall, and I believe they were like that because of the kind of food they ate and the exercise they got. Some died from sickness and other causes, but that number was not too high. As I said, that was the way I grew up, and it is why I kept my health so long.

As a student, I was bright, and I learned fast. I now realize that knowing how to read, write and speak English has helped me a lot. I also had the traditional Navajo education at home.

We are told that Navajo life is different from that of other tribes, which may be so. But there are many people who live in ways similar to ours. That goes for different nationalities, too. Of course, today, many prefer to follow the Anglo way of life, and their living conditions have much improved. However, building a hogan for a Navajo family may be a problem. The members have to want to live in it, and we cannot make them like it. Some prefer hogans, though. We are moving with modern progress, but there are some Navajos who still do not like to sleep on a bed or eat canned food. We also have some good and wise elders among us who share their wisdom with the young people. Our people still depend to some extent on their sheep as a source of food and income. For some families caring for their sheep comes first in priorities. Many of them also keep their Blessing Way songs for the sheep and horses, as well as soft goods and hard goods songs. When they are away from home some still chant their traveling songs and the sacred mountain songs. These songs and prayers are part of their everyday life. Blessings are fulfilled for them through these chants when they are sung in reverence.

I feel that both Anglo and Navajo education are essential and are to be studied side by side.

Our children should learn both cultures. We value the teachings that our great-grandfathers taught us from generation to generation, and we must not forget them. Men of wisdom have said, "If one knows the legends he will be blessed with goodness." That describes me.

Now, about our history and legends: Navajo elders are asked about the origin of the hogan — how it was made, and why the door always faces the east. These questions seldom are answered correctly, and I briefly will tell you why. It may be that some Navajos are afraid to give out such confidential information. They value its holiness.

Long ago, at the emergence place, it was said that Talking God performed a "No Sleep" ceremony, or vigil. At that "sing" the people could not find anyone to do the bathing of patients. Talking God gathered sand from where the ground was black, blue, red and white. He made a picture in a round, pan-like shape, with the colored sand used to design it. It became the ceremonial basket. The finishing outlet was arranged toward the east. It was very beautiful. Later, again at Huerfano Mountain (the emergence spot), the first Blessing Way was held at a place called Mating of the Corn. Here, again, the question was asked about who was do to the bathing, how and in what way it should be done. Talking God was told to go exactly to the emergence area, to the hogan there, and get what he had hidden in the far side of the hogan. He ran and brought it back. It was copied and the design has been kept. Today the ceremonial basket, with that design, is used for ceremonial baths. It was granted to the people for use in the Blessing Way "sings." Its outlet faces the east. Thus, the doorway of the hogan faces the east, too. We must remember, also, that all good things enter with the dawn from the east.

Talking God and his follower, Hogan God or Calling God, were People of the Dawn. It was said that they came at the break of day with valued possessions. That is why we were told to rise with the dawn to meet these gods so that they could present us with worthy goods. Our parents would say to us, "Wake up. What are you sleeping for? Take the ashes out. Clean around outside. We do not want trash around the hogan." It was said and done so that the Dawn People would not see any trash. They would know they were welcomed at our place and would say, "There is no wealth here. Let's go in and give them some." Trash meant there was wealth. Where a place was dirty and trashy they would ignore it and say, "Too much wealth here. Let's go to another place." The lesson is that a person was expected to keep clean and be an "early bird to catch the worm."

Also, the people used to offer their thanks at dawn by sprinkling cornmeal toward the east to thank the Good Spirit for the night's rest and to greet another pleasant day. The men offered white cornmeal at dawn and in the evening. The women offered yellow cornmeal each time. At noon corn pollen was offered to the sun because the sun preferred pollen. The offerings were made for good health and prosperity.

About the hogans, long ago there were two ceremonial types. One was a "dugout" hogan and the other was the round hogan. The hogan was made round in the way Talking God made the round basket. The main beam logs were placed with their growing ends clockwise to the east; the next one to the south, clockwise; the west, clockwise, and the north the same. During the blessing of a new hogan white cornmeal was anointed on all main beams clockwise — east, south, west and north.

Our history begins with the underworlds, where the dark world was known as the first world; the second was the blue world; next was the yellow third world, and the fourth was the white world that sparkled. Each level had its prayer sticks painted the appropriate color. The last (the sparkled or crystal world) is where we live now. Prayer sticks were granted to us by the Holy People who inhabited the world then. They were for us to use.

All the legendary stories have their significance, and it is wonderful to be able to understand them. I know that many Navajos do not have the correct idea about them because they had not heard the stories before. I always have wished that someday I could have a chance to tell my stories to big groups of young people. Now I have the opportunity — even to have the stories printed; and it makes me very happy, but I regret that the stories are not complete. An elder who tells stories usually prepares himself for at least two or three days and nights to tell one complete story. That is about how long it takes to tell whole legends in song. For instance, the story of One-Who-Wins-You would take that length of time from its beginning to the conclusion. Telling about the Cliff Dwellers or the Ancient Ones takes a lot of time, also. Another reason why I shorten my stories is because they are valuable to me, and the payment I receive for telling them barely covers the value. If someone pays the real price for a complete story, then I can say I will tell it with all the usually withheld information included. There are accounts of various kinds about the ancient ruins, like Pueblo Bonito or Pintado, Mesa Verde and Canyon de Chelly. Some stories go 'way back to California and the ocean, even to a small mountainous island, where One-Who-Wins-You was born.

Now I will tell you a real story, briefly. The location was Chaco Canyon. There was this man named One-Who-Wins-You. He was like a wizard with all gambling games. He won everything from his opponents. I do not know what he did to have such remarkable luck. Maybe it was made possible by mere instinct. He was born as a twin, but no one has told us exactly who he really was. As for myself, I think he might have been an ancient Anglo of some kind. I judge it could be because of what he said one time. The people from whom he has won practically were his slaves. They all worked very hard. They carried limestone on their backs from a rock quarry to Chaco Canyon. There, the rocks were masoned into blocks to make stone houses which had many rooms, of which we now can see only the ruins. Today, many archaeologists dig in our ruins for ancient relics. Their findings tell us that people lived there ages ago. But their research still does not really tell who the Ancient Ones were. One-Who-Wins-You lived above the Canyon. Below his home was where the slaves built the houses. The people who did the building were called the Cliff Dwellers. (There is a lot of detail to the story, but I will give only the main points.) Someone dreamed that the wizard would be a loser not too far in the future. He had a brother who was his identical twin. The only way to tell them apart was that his brother was an honest man. He lived at Bird Knoll. The people all said, "Let his own twin be his next opponent. That will change his luck, you will see." It is said that twins are extraordinary beings. In this case I will tell you the part where his brother personally encountered him.

In those days the Holy People communicated closer with each other and knew more of what was happening. Who were the Cliff Dwellers? That I do not know. However, the legend I am now telling happened during the time when all the people, no matter what descent they were, mixed themselves in sex relationships. It was told that these mixed tribes inhabited Chaco Canyon, a place used as a sort of retreat. From the activities that occurred there, new tribes were added and other races were born. But, as I said, One-Who-Wins-You might have been an Anglo man, or at least someone who was different. It was told that a real brother could win from his own brother only after having had sex relations with his sister-in-law. That was what happened when the gambling wizard's brother came to his home. The visiting brother was advised by the people not to greet his wizard brother as "My dear brother." He was not supposed to shake his hand, either. The only greeting expression was to be, "My opponent," and then to immediately sing a song from the Prostitute Way. After that the gambler would say, "Let's play a game and see who wins." The wizard knew he always won; so they started with the shinny game. One game after another the gambling wizard lost. The last was the tree-breaking game. The only possessions One-Who-Wins-You had left were his wife and children. "We will bet our wives and children," he said.

The two trees were at the far end of the race track. They got set, and the race was on. About halfway, One-Who-Wins-You shot a witch missile at his brother's feet, but he missed. That was how he had won all the races from his opponents before. However, his twin brother caught the missile and tossed it back to the wizard's feet. By that time the honest twin was ahead. Before he got to the finish line Horned Toad was running beside him. Horned Toad told the twin that of the two trees ahead one was a cane reed tree and the other was a hard oak tree. Horned Toad pointed out the oak. Usually the one who broke the tree lost. The twin was struggling with the oak when One-Who-Wins-You got to his tree and broke it without a struggle. We all know the hard oak cannot be broken; so we know that the gambling wizard lost everything he had, even his wife, children and home.

His honest twin brother had redeemed all the people, with their belongings, as well as their children and wives. Everyone was happy. One-Who-Wins-You was downhearted. He told his brother to take good care of his family, and he began to speak to the people, but they ignored him. "Send him away," they shouted. "Put him on a strong swift Black Arrow and shoot him up yonder into space," they shouted.

Ages ago the Holy People used holy arrows. The gambling wizard was placed on the arrow. Before he left, he yelled, "Even if you send me far into space I will return. I will see you, and I will be above you. Wait and see." (The words he spoke were prophetic about today's airplanes, and they help me to believe that he must have been a white man.)

One-Who-Wins-You also said to the people, "In the future there will be round objects which the people will play games with to win. They will be a reminder of me." We know that today many pieces of game equipment are round — like baseballs, volleyballs, basketballs and golfballs. People play with them to win. They all are part of the white man's games that have been introduced to us. Thus, there are many round objects which remind us of the gambling wizard who became a loser. Whatever is round belongs to him. He also said that the lightning flash would be his power, and also the wind. He added, "When I return, everything that is round will roll beneath you with the wind. We will travel on the rolling rainbow arc." Today, that is all very obvious. We travel on the highways with yellow and white stripes. A highway reminds us of the rainbow as it curves. The round objects under us are the wheels of whatever we travel in — such as trucks, automobiles, trains, bicycles and other things; and we travel with the wind. The lightning, I also know, has to do with electric current. People have lights in their homes and business places, along with all kinds of electrical devices. We have electricity everywhere today. Taking these things together, One-Who-Wins-You must have been a white man. We Navajos also call the radio "Wind that Talks." It is a white man's invention. That is all I will tell about the gambling wizard.

The stories we tell were recited by our elders from generation to generation, on down the line. They were not kept in written books.

The stories I have told for many years are educational, especially for Navajos today. People should think very carefully about what I have said and see if it means anything to them. Whether the words I have spoken are interesting or boring, I believe I have revealed some information which other consultants or elders never have told. I have done it so that Navajos will be able to know more of their culture, and then I hope they realize how important I consider the Navajo Nation's growth and development. Telling long legends is very tiresome to all concerned. It becomes monotonous and makes a listener restless and sometimes sleepy. I know that if I should give an entire story at one time anyone listening would be fast asleep before I got one-third of the way through it; and, if people took recesses, they would forget some parts of the story I had told them. All legends include songs that cannot be left out of them. So, if done absolutely right, it takes several days and nights without a rest. That was the way my elders told their stories to me, but now listeners like to rest during the day.

About our own traditional culture, those of us who have gone through hardships use our experiences when teaching the young people. We have struggled to live and it has been well worth it. We relate background so that our young people will realize how fortunate they are. If we compare the white man's culture and the Indian's culture, we find some similarities. I know this because I compared what I learned in school to my traditional education at home. One problem is that the majority of school children today have little or no knowledge about their native Indian culture. However, some are now beginning to ask questions. Years ago, the elders were vey good at telling stories to the children. Now, many of these people are gone. Also, almost all of the original Navajo scholars are gone. Probably, those who remain have told stories similar to mine.

I have lived a long time, and I am grateful to the Good Spirit. I often have considered what benefits I got from all that my parents taught me, such as exercising at dawn which immunized me to extremely cold weather. Altogether, my early life and training gave me a long and happy and healthy existence.

Now that I have talked at great length, I hope that Navajo young people and others will remember what I have said. A person who has self-respect and a well-adjusted and stimulated mind is likely to succeed. He pays attention to elders like me and keeps their teachings in his head.

I pray that I have taught my readers something that they have wanted to know.

Window Rock, Arizona 1975

Kenji Kawano A Portfolio

Window Rock, Arizona 1975

Flagstaff, Arizona 1976

Flagstaff, Arizona 1976

Window Rock, Arizona 1974

Ganado, Arizona 1974

Nancy Woodman

Ła' T'áá Bita'ígóó Njighą́ą́ Nt'éego Hahane'

Shiyaa Hazlį́į́'dę́ę́'

T'ah 'ánísts'íísígo shimá ńt'éé' 'ádin jiní. T'áadoo yiiłtsą́ą́ dóó t'áadoo baa 'áhoniizį́į' da. T'ah shį́į́ 'awéé' nishłį́ígo shimá 'ádin. Shizhé'é t'éiyá hólǫ́. Shimá sání dó' hólǫ́. Nléí shimá 'ádin silį́į́' dóó shį́į́ ha'át' éego shį́į́ shiyaa hazlį́į́', hóla.

Díí t'áadoo le'é baa 'áhoniizį́į́' dóó k'asdą́ą́' t'áá 'ałtso béédaashniih. Ts'ídá hojoobá'ígo yishááł lágo baa 'áhoniizį́į́'. Ts'ídá t'áá 'íiyisíí t'áá 'áhoodzaagóó ńléí łeeshch'iihtah nahalindi nisédzil lágo baa 'áhoniizį́į́'. 'Áádóó 'atíshi'dil'į́įdi ńléí ts'ídá t'áá 'ałtso bee 'atíshi'dool'į́įd, háí shį́į́ t'áá bił ha'doolchid shį́į́ bee. Ts'ídá t'áá 'ałtso bee 'atíshi'dil'į́į lágo baa 'áhoniizį́į́'. T'áá bíhólníihgóó ńléí t'áá ch'é'étiingóó da tsé'yaa shishjoolgo nashíiłka' ńt'éé'. Bee 'adínóotéełii ndi doo bee shaa 'áháyą́ą́góó.

T'áá 'áko ndi na'nishkaad. Shimá ńt'éé' bitł'ízí t'áá hólǫ́ǫgo yąąh 'ádin lá. 'Áko 'éí t'ah yidziihígíí bikéé' naashá. Shikee' ndi t'áá gééd dibé bikéé' naashá.

Shi'éé' ndi 'ak'áán dabizisígíí t'áá 'áhoodzaagi 'ádaalyaago ndahaazt'óodgo shik'i dah

The Story of an Orphan

Early Childhood

My mother died while I was still very small. I didn't see her, nor did I ever become aware of her, for I was still a baby when she died. I had only my father and my grandmother. I have no idea how I grew up after my mother died.

I became aware of these facts, and I can remember almost everything. I was aware of the fact that I was neglected, and I recall how I was shoved off among the trash piles. I suffered every imaginable kind of mistreatment — inflicted upon me with any and all means at anyone's disposal. I can remember how I was abused in every way. I used to spend my nights sitting huddled just any place — places like the doorway. What care I got did not even include bedding for me.

Nevertheless, my mother left some goats when she died, and I used to herd them. I had to take care of these. I did not even have shoes for my feet when I went herding.

When I was out herding, my tattered clothing, made

ndaat'a'go na'nishkaad. Sitsii' ndi hááhgóóshį́į́ ts'iilzéí bił k'ídaaz'áago naashá. Yaa' ndi k'ad shida'niiłhį́įgo. Kót'éego ts'ídá t'áá 'ałtsoní bik'ee ti'hooshníihgo shíiníłką́. 'Áko ndi t'áá 'áko ndi shilį́į' hóló̜.

Łah ha'át'éegi shį́į́ 'asésiihgo shimá sání shik'í-'oosxaal dóó t'áadoo sha'íłtsódí naaki daats'í yiską́. Níwohji' daats'í. T'áadoo 'ashání t'óó tł'ízí bikéé' tádíshááh. Tł'ízí yázhí ła' t'óó bá ná'iistso'go 'éí t'áá 'áłahji' shikéé' tádígháah. Dóó tł'ée'go t'áá shit'ah ntééh. Éí 'abínígo bá náá'iideestsoł nisingo tł'óó'góó dah diiłtį́į́ ńt'éé' t'áá 'áajį́' bił naa'adzííł-haal lá honibąąhį́į'. Dichin shį́į́ bik'ee naa'íígo'.

'Íídą́ą́' naadą́ą́ t'éiyá 'aghá nahalingo daadą́ą́ ńt'éé'. 'Áko 'éí tóshchíín ha'nínígíí łá shá 'ádajiilaago 'éí yishdlą́ą'go 'índa bikiin ch'íníyáá dóó 'á'iiłtsood.

Shimá sání nilíinii ha'át'éego shį́į́ shijoołáago daats'i, 'ayóo 'atíshíł'į́į́ ńt'éé'. Dóó 'ayóo shich'ah hashkéé ńt'éé'. 'Áko tł'ée'go da hak'az bik'ee haa'í lá doo ninish'nééhgóó yiłkááh. Łah tł'ée'go t'áá 'ákónáánát'éego t'áá bíhólníihgi nááshíshjool ńt'éé', háahgi shį́į́ yoołkáałgo t'óó báhádzidgo shi'niidlíí lágo ch'éénísdzid.

'Áko haa'í lá doo ch'ééh ntsí náánákéez da. Ts'ídá haa'í lá doo ch'ééh 'í'deesh'įįł da. Ch'ééh da tsé'yaa nááníshjoł. 'Áko shimá sání halį́į́' biyéél nichxǫ́ǫ́'í yee' hóló̜. T'ah ńt'éé' nagháí 'át'éegi si'ǫ́. Łį́į́' biyéłę́ę ńdii'áanii'

haphazardly out of old flour sacks, would flutter about me. I even went about with my hair filthy and matted with burrs, and I was covered with lice. This is how I suffered day by day. But even so, I had some goats.

Once when I did something wrong my grandmother beat me with a club, and gave me nothing to eat for perhaps two days. Without a thing to eat I continued to trail along after the goats. There was an orphaned kid which I fed, and which always followed me about. At night it would lie cuddled in my arms. One morning (during the time when I was given nothing to eat) I carried the kid outdoors to feed it, but I collapsed by the fireplace with the kid in my arms. I had fainted from hunger.

In those days corn was the main staple, so some corn gruel was made for me. After drinking it I gained enough strength to go out and feed the kid.

My grandmother seemed to hate me for some reason, and was very mean to me. She would give me awful tongue lashings. And I would crawl or roll about all night long, because of the cold. One night as I lay huddled somewhere I woke up nearly frozen to death. It was in the middle of the night.

I thought and thought about my plight, but could think of nothing to do about it. I did everything I could think of (to get warm,) but without success. I would sit huddled face down, but I couldn't get

tsé’yaa náánéshjoolii’ shinághahdę́ę́’ bik’i dah sé’ą́. ’Áko ’éí ’índa bee honeezdogo ’iiłhaazh.

T’ah ńt’éé’ t’áá ’ashhoshgo ha’íí’ą́ą́ lá. ’Ashhosh yę́ę shimá sání shiiłtsą́ą́ lá. T’ah ńt’éé’ báhóóchį́įd yiists’ą́ą́’. ‘‘Ch’į́įdiitahgóósh díníyáago ’iiníziin k’ad ni’niiłhį́. Nimáani’ísh bikéé’ díníyáago ’ánít’į́!’’ shiłníigo ’ashhosh yę́ę hashídzííłhaal.

Nahji’ náhidiishtahgo łį́į́’ biyélę́ę shąąh naalts’id. Háí shį́į́ ’íiyisíí ’át’éego shiznoodzih ńléí ’ákohgóó hooghan bits’ánishwod. ‘‘Ch’į́įdiitahgóó dínááh! Ńlááh shash da ’aniyółdlaad! Níwohdi naních’į́įdii,’’ shiłníigo ’ashízníídzíí’. Kót’éego t’áá ’ałtsoní bik’ee ti’hooshníihgo shiyaa hoo’a’.

Shizhé’é Bich’į’ Yóó’ ‘Eeshwod

Saad yę́ę bik’ee ntsinisdzáago ’aadóó ńléí náánáłahdi shizhé’é yę́ę náá’ágéehgo ’ákǫ́ǫ yóó’ ’anáshwa’ sélį́į́’. Wónáásdóó t’áá ’áájí nikidiiyá. ‘Áájí t’áadoo le’é yee shaa ’adahalyą́ągo hodeeshzhiizh. ‘Índa t’áadoo le’égóó k’é ndaazt’i’góó da t’áá yee ndashineeztą́ą́’. Dah ’iistłǫ́ ’ádaat’éii da yidashiyiił’ą́ą́’.

’Áádóó t’áá shí shiłł’ízí hólǫǫgo bikéé’ tádíshááh. ’Íiyisíí hooghan dooleełgi ndi ’ádingo

warm. Then I happened to see an old saddle that belonged to my grandmother. I picked it up and then sat down again, crouched forward, and put the saddle on top of my back. Then I went to sleep, warmed by that cover.

I was still sleeping when the sun came up, and my grandmother saw me as I slept. Suddenly I heard her give vent to her anger. "You must be going to the land of the dead, trying to bring evil this way. You must be trying to follow your dead mother," she said to me, striking me as I lay asleep.

As I leapt to my feet the saddle fell off. Then, as she cursed me with everything she could think of, I ran off to some distance from the hogan. "Go to the land of the dead! Go where a bear will tear you apart and gobble you down! Stay away, you evil spirit!" she said, cursing me. Suffering like this from everything I grew up.

Ran Away To Father

I could stand this abuse no longer, so I got to the point where I would run away and go to where my father lived with his new wife. Later on I started to live there. I got good care. They gave me instructions in clan relationships, and taught me to weave.

I went on herding my goats. I increased my goat herd even though I hadn't a home to call

'aadę́ę́' t'áá 'e'e'áhígóó nashíiłka'go kót'éego shitł'ízí t'éiyá bił náás nishkai. 'Aadóó diné shee hazlı̨́ı̨́' dóó tł'ízí t'áá hólǫ́ǫgo hoolzhiizh. Tł'ízí yę́ę t'áá náás yikah. Niha'áłchíní dó' hodideezlı̨́ı̨́'. Tł'ízí yę́ę t'áá náás yikahgo wónáásdóó táadi neeznádiin dóó níwohjį' silı̨́ı̨́'.

'Áko tł'ízí yę́ę kónéelą́ą́' silı̨́ı̨́'go kwii t'áá níłtéél ńt'éé' tł'ízí baa dahwiinít'įįd. T'ááłá'í bą́ąhílį̨įgo kót'éego tł'ízí yę́ę 'ałtso sits'ą́ą́' 'anoolkaad.

'Akwii baa yíníił biih néítłizh. 'Aadóó baa ńtsídiikééz. T'áadoo la' biniiyéhégóó ńléídę́ę́' baa naanish siisxį̨ lá. 'Índa bikéé' tádíshááhgo bik'ee t'áá 'ałtsoní 'ach'į' nahwii'ná 'ádaat'éii béé'iisis'nii'. 'Áko 'éí t'áá 'ałtso ts'ídá t'áadoo ńdaasdlı̨́'í da silı̨́ı̨́' nisingo baa ntséskees łeh. Dííjį̨́ígóó t'ah ndi 'ákót'éego baa ntséskeesgo sédáa łeh k'ad.

'Aadóó t'áá shí 'ák 'inínáádiisdzilí 'éí 'akǫ́ǫ́ t'áadoo le'é da nishóhoosht'eehgo baa nínáá-diisdzá. T'áá 'ákót'éego 'akǫ́ǫ́ díí Lók'ai'jígai hoolyéegi tsin bee kiní nichxǫ́ǫ́'í léi' shá niit'ą́. Ni'iijíhídę́ę́' tsiniheeshjíí' biniiyé ła' shá nájaa'. Bikáádę́ę́' bik'ésti'ígíí dó' ła' bá chóiséłt'e'. Kót'éego tsin bee kinígíí shá niit'ą́. Hooghan hólǫ́ǫgo 'éí yá'át'ééh. 'Índa ha'áłchíní hólǫ́ǫgo yá'át'éehgo hooghan bá hólǫ́ǫgo biyi'dóó dahiniyéego t'áadoo beełt'éhé da. Shí 'éí ńléídę́ę́' t'áá bíhólníih nahalingóó t'áá 'ałtsoní bik'ee shíiníłką́. Doo 'asohodoobéézhgóó hóyéé lá haa

my own, and had to spend the night wherever evening caught me. Later I got a man, and we continued with the goats. They increased, and as for ourselves, we began to have children. The goats multiplied until there were over 300 of them.

About the time the herd had risen to this number, goats became the subject of discussion everywhere. The result was that my goats were taken from me, and I was paid a dollar a head for them.

So once again misfortune overtook me. I began to give it thought. It occurred to me that all my work had been for nothing, and in caring for my flock I had suffered every hardship. I came to the conclusion that all these hardships had been for nothing. I still feel that way about it today.

After that I busied myself with a search for a new means of support. As a result of my efforts I had a log cabin built for me at Lukachukai. I got the lumber from the sawmill. I also got some roofing paper, and that's the way I got my house.

It is nice to have a home. And there's nothing that can compare with a home of your own where you can raise your children. In my time I spent my days without a roof over my head, and with all the consequences of such a life. It's terrible when one

’áhályą́ą doolee-łii ’ádingo. ’Índa nahodínóotįįłii da ’ádingo.

Dah ’listł’ǫ Ha’nínígíí Bíhooł’ą́ą’.

Táá’ts’áadah daats’í shináághaigo dah ’iistł’ǫ́ ha’nínígíí bíhooł’ą́ą’. ’Áádóó shinaanish silįį’ ni’. ’Áádóó bíhooł’ą́ą’ dóó t’áá sahdii bee ’ats’áníyá. T’áá shí bee ’ák’inaasdzil sélį́į’ dóó ’índa ’aadę́ę’ shinaanish nilį́įgo hoolzhiizh. T’áá yá’át’éehgo ’ásh’į́įgo hoolzhiizh.

‘Éí díishįį́góó t’ah ndi shinaanish nilį́. ‘Áko ’éidíígíí ’ákót’éego baa níyá. Haa shįį́ néelą́ą’ ’áshłaa diyogí. ’Áko t’óó naalyéhé bá dahooghanįį’ ’ahishníiłgo ’aadę́ę’ hoolzhiizh.

T’óó bik’idiit’ą́ ha’nínígíí k’ehgo shaa hoonihgo hoolzhiizh. Ch’iyáán t’éiyá bik’é nishóhoot’eehgo. ’Ákót’éego baa níyá. Jó ’éí dízdiin dóó ba’aan náhást’éí nááhaiídą́ą’ baa ńdiisdzá dah ’iistł’ǫ. ’Éí ’ákót’éego bínáshniih. Jó ’íídą́ą’ ’ániid naasháago doo hazhó’ó baa ’áhonisingóó t’óó naalyéhé bá hooghanįį’ ’ahishníiłgo baa níyá. Ts’ídá la’ kót’éego bą́ą hílį́į doolee-ł ńt’éé’ ’éí doo nisingóó t’óó ’áajį’ ’ahishníił.

’Áko k’ad ła’ ts’áadah nááhaiídą́ą’ ’éí náánáła’ beeldléí háábalii ha’nínígíí t’áá kindę́ę’ ndahaniihígíí be’deeshłííł niizį́į’. ’Áko ’éí ła’ t’áá yá’át’éehgo be’iishłaa. ’Aghaa’ígíí ts’ídá t’áá ’íiyisíí nizhónígo ’ááshłiiłgo kót’éego beeldléí bee béé’iishdlaa. Baa ńdiisdzáá dóó tseebíí ’íishłaa beeldléí.

Díí beeldléí ’áshłaa dóó t’áá ’éí bik’ehgo dah ’iistł’óníg íí dilzhǫǫhgo baa nínáádiisdzá. ’Aghaa-

has no one to care for him, and nobody to teach him.

Learned To Weave

I learned to weave when I was 13 years old, and weaving became my trade. When I learned it, I gained my independence. I got so I could support myself by my work, and I kept it up. I made fairly good rugs, and still do.

That is how I got along. I've made a great many rugs. I just take them to the trading post, where I have always just taken them out in trade.

I get food for my rugs, and that is how I get along. It is now 49 years since I learned to weave, according to my recollection. And back there in the days of my innocence I merely took them to the trader accepting whatever he offered for them.

Eleven years ago I decided to copy a blanket of the commercial type found in stores, and my copy turned out well. By processing my wool very carefully I succeeded in making a good copy of the store blanket. I started doing this, and made eight of them.

I made these, and then carried the same processing over to

'ígíí t'áá 'íiyisí dilzhǫǫhgo dóó ts'ídá nizhónígo 'ál'į́įgo baa nínáádiisdzá. Beeldléí kindę́ę́' ndahaniihígíí be'iishłaago ła' Tségháhoodzánídi shaa nahaaznii'. 'Áadi t'áá béeso hastą́diingo bik'é shaa yí'nil.

'Aadóó 'ákwii diyogí ła' 'áadi náánííłtsooz. T'áá 'ákohgo bą́ąh náá'ásdlį́į́'. T'áá béeso bik'é shaa yí'nil. Ts'ídá 'íídą́ą́' 'índa 'ákót'éego diyogí bik'é t'áá béeso shaa yí'nil. Níwohdą́ą́' 'éí łitso ndi t'áadoo ła' bik'é shílák'eet'ą́ą da. 'Éí kót'éego dah 'iistł'ǫ́ baa niséyá.

Díí k'ad kǫ́ǫ́ nihitahgóó naalyéhé yá naazdáhígíí ts'ídá 'ádin. Łitsogo ndi ch'ééh bee yíníshkeed. Łitsogo ndi t'áadoo bik'é shaa yílts'id da. 'Áko k'ad baa ntséskeesgo ha'át'éego lá 'át'éé lá díí kǫ́ǫ́ naalyéhé bá dahooghanígíí. Diyogí doo ts'ídá t'áá béeso yik'é ndayó'ááł 'át'ée da. Ha'át'éego lá 'át'éé lá. T'áá daats'í 'ákót'éego bee bá nahaz'ą́. Ts'ídá daats'í łitsogo ndi doo yik'é 'iidoołniiłgóó bee bá nahaz'ą́. T'óó nisin k'ad baa ntséskeesgo. 'Éidíígíí bąągogo dah 'iistł'ǫ́ yázhí da ła' 'ásh'į́įhgo t'áá bíyó t'áá bąąh shíni' nahalingo yóó 'ahishnííł. Níláahdi shinaanish naat'i'di bee nabik'ítséskeesgo biniinaa t'áá bąąh shíní' nahalingo yóó' 'ahishnííł hazlį́į' díí kǫ́ǫ́ naalyéhé bá dahooghangóó.

T'áá ha'át'éego da nabik'í yáti'go daats'í t'áá haada 'át'ée dooleełgo 'át'é nisingo t'áá 'ádíighahígo 'ákót'éego baa ntséskees łeh. 'Índa 'adahwiis'áágóó sáanii da'atł'óii bił nabik'í yádajiłti' laanaa t'óó nisin łeh. Biniiyé

produce very smooth Navajo rugs. Making these copies of the store blanket taught me how to work the wool and make it smooth. I sold one of my copies of the commercial blanket at Window Rock, and there they paid me sixty dollars in cash for it.

Later I took a Navajo rug there, and they again paid me the same price. And they gave me cash. That was the first time I had ever received cash for a rug. Before that I had never been handed a single nickel. That is my experience in the matter of making Navajo rugs.

There is not a trader here amongst us who pays cash. I ask for even so little as a nickel in cash, but they won't give it to me. I have never received so much as one nickel cash (at a trading post). As I now give thought to this matter, I wonder why this is true of the trading posts. You simply cannot get cash. Why is it? Could there be some law which makes it that way? Maybe there's a regulation against giving so much as a nickel cash. I'm just making guesses. It's for this reason that even when I take a little rug to the trader I feel sort of unhappy at letting it go. I put a great deal of effort into my rugs, and it is this fact which causes me to be a bit unhappy at letting them go to the traders hereabout.

I think matters such as this one are worthy of discussion. I wish that weavers all over the reservation would meet together for the purpose of discussing it.

'ahíníjiikahgo da nabik'í yádajiłti' laanaa t'óó nisin łeh.

'Áadóó da'jitł'óhígíí ła' 'aghaa' t'áá 'íiyisíí t'óó bee ndajiné. T'áá na'níle'dii nahalingo diyogí t'áá 'áhoodzaagi 'ályaago kį́įh dajiijááh. 'Éidíígíí t'áá 'íiyisíí nihits'ą́ą́' ndayiłchxǫǫh nisin. 'Éí doo 'íłį́įgóó nihits'ą́ą́' 'ádayósin. 'Éidíígíí t'áadoo 'ádaat'íní laanaa. T'áá 'át'é yee 'ałkéłk'e dókáahgo nizhónígo 'aheełt'éego da'atł'óo laanaa t'óó nisin.

'Ákót'éego da shą' k'ad haa yit'ée dooleeł ńt'éé'. 'Áko ha'át'éego da t'áá nabik'í yáti'go daats'í t'áá bihodoolnííł. 'Índa díí béeso bik'é 'ahi'nííł dooleełgi dó'. T'áá shǫǫ łitsogo da bik'é náhizhdii'aagho t'áá yá'át'ééh.

Na'nitin T'áá Shí Bíká Nikidiiyá

'Éí 'aadóó 'éí t'áá ha'át'éhégóó da 'atah 'ańdishchi' nahalingo k'ad kǫ́ǫ́ shíyoołkááł. Łah kwii Lók'ai'jígaigi 'éé' neishoodii First Aid wolyé nígo yaa naniheezh'eezh ła' 'aghaaí. T'áá 'éí dąąjį́' ch'ééhoolzhiizhgo Ch'ínílį́įgóó t'áá 'éí biniiyé ninéánihi'disht'eezh. First Aid wolyé 'éí bídahwiidooł'ááł biniiyé nihi'di'nígo sáanii díkwíniilt'é shį́į́ 'ákǫ́ǫ́ nanihi'disht'eezh.

'Áadi t'áá łáhádi damį́įgo 'azłį́į'įį' bee nihił ninááházne'. Ts'ídá t'áá na'nitin haz'ánígi 'akon. T'áá díí wóne'é haz'ánígi ndi 'eii t'áadoo le'é shéé' 'ádaat'éii da

Of course there are some weavers who merely toy with their wool, and they bring poor products in to the stores. These people really spoil things for us. They keep the sale value of our products low, and I wish they would stop. I wish that everybody would adopt the same standards and do good weaving.

If that were the case, I wonder how much better things might be. If there were any chance for us to discuss these things, maybe something could be worked out. And possibly this matter of paying in cash could be worked out too. It would be nice if the weavers got even one whole nickel in cash.

Self-Educated

Nowadays I take part in many activities. One winter the priest here gave us a course in First Aid, and that same spring we were taken over to Chinle to continue the course. There were several of us women who were taken over there for the First Aid course.

We were taught even about little things in the home — even such things as being careful about spit. "Even though you might think of that as a minor

ts'ídá baa 'áháyą́. Háálá 'éí 'ákódaat'éii 'éísh t'įįdígoígíí 'íl̨į́į́ ndi bik'ee ka hodeezt'i' ni-hi'di'níigo, 'áádóó na'ni-tin biyázhí haa shį́į́ néelą́ą' bee ndanihidi'neestą́ą'. Jó 'akon 'ákót'éego t'áá ná'nitin haz'ánígi bee bik'idizhyiitįįh łeh lá 'akon. T'áá hó 'ájít'éego dóó t'áá hó bíkatsídzíkeesgo 'akon. 'Índa ła' 'ádajiníi łeh. 'Éí 'ákó'óolyéenii t'áá 'ałtsogo yilwoł ni. Ha'át'íí yik'ídoolwołgo t'áá 'ałtsogo 'atah yilwoł dajiní 'akon. 'Áko shí 'éí doo 'ákót'éego baa ntséskees da. Kǫ́ǫ́ t'áadoo le'é biniiyé 'áłah 'aleehgo da, 'índa 'aseezį́ da t'éiyá baa 'áłah 'aleeh ndi 'ákǫ́ǫ́ yisháááł łeh. 'Áko t'áá 'ałtsogo 'anishtah łeh. Díí kwe'é haz'ą́ągi lá haa yit'éego baa hwiinít'įį́ lá nisingo 'éí biniiyé 'ásht'į́ 'akon. K'ad t'áá 'ał'ąą bił nahaz'ą́ nahalin ha'át'íi da baa dahwiinít'įį́góó, 'índa 'áda'ool'įįłgóó. Nashidínó otįįłíí 'ádinígíí bąągago, 'índa shił ch'íhodoo'áałii 'ádinígíí bąągogo t'áá shí bíkaashá nahalin, dóó t'áá shí bíka'íists'ą' nahalin. T'áá ńléí t'áá shiyaa hazl̨į́į́'dę́ę́' t'áá 'ákót'éego shídi'deesdzil ni'.

'Aadóó Bilagáana bizaad dóó naaltsoos da wólta' 'ádaat'éii 'éí doo shił bééhózin da. 'Áko ndi díí kwii Lók'ai'jígai 'ólta'ígi 'at'ééké Girl Scouts danil̨į́ ha'níigo 'éí binant'a'í níl̨į́ shi'di'níigo 'ałdó' 'áajį' 'anáshi'dilt'eehgo táá' daats'í nááhai. "Dooda, ha'át'íishą' biniiyé, shí Bilagáana bizaad doo diists'a' da,," ch'ééh dishníigo. "Jó t'óó bínítááh dóó t'áá 'éí bee ni dó' t'áadoo le'é bee bik'idi'yiitįįh dooleeł biniiyé," shi'di'níigo. 'Áko 'ákwe'é bee

thing, it can cause sickness," we were told. And we were taught many other facts. In such ways one can learn many things.

But you yourself have to take the initiative and go after it. And when you do that there are people who say, "But I don't look at it that way." When people meet here for any purpose, even just for the purpose of settling little troubles, I always attend. I take part in everything. I go just to learn how they handle such matters. Different problems require different approaches. Because there is no one to tell me about things, I look into them myself, and keep my ears open. Since the days of my childhood I have been on my own.

I do not know the English language, and cannot read it. But here at Lukachukai I was asked to be the Girl Scout Leader, and I have been in that position for three years. At first I declined, saying, "What for? I cannot understand English," but they took me anyway. They told me, "Give it a try and you will learn things." So, I took the position for a three year term. And what they told me was right. You can learn a lot of things in this way. Such

’atah náshwo’go táá’ náháhai. ’Áko t’áá ’aaníí ’ádaaníí lá. T’áá bee ’ak’idi’yiitįįh lá ’ákódaat’éí. T’áá ha’át’íhíi da t’áá há ’ada’diłdlaad naha-lin lá. Kót’éego ’ákódaat’éego na’nitin ’ahí-hiit’aah lá.

Índa ’áłah nda’ale’góó hanááł yádaati’, hastóí ’índa sáanii dahóyáanii hanáát yádaałti’go saad ’ahíjiyii’aahgo baa njigháa łeh łah. Nahodínóotįįłii ’ádingo ’ákót’éego na’nitin baa nahozhdidáa łeh lá. Kót’éego ’át’ée łeh lá łah jidilt’éhé wolyéego hahastóí ’ádingo. Shí díí k’ad ’ákónísht’éego shíyoołkááł ’akon.

’Íhoo’aah T’éiyá Bee Náás Diikah

K’ad niha’áłchíní yéigo da’íítta’ii, yéigo naaltsoos bił béédahózinii ts’ídá t’áá ’éí t’éiyá daníil’į k’ad. Ts’ídá ’áajį’ t’éiyá choo’íįłká da-diit’íį’. Shí kót’éego baa ntséskees. ’Índa da’óoł-ta’ii, naaltsoos béédahosoosįįdii ts’ídá t’áá ’ánółtso nihá baa ’ahééh nisin. Ts’ídá t’áá ’awołí bee nihik’i dayínółdzííł. Ts’ídá t’áá ’awołí bee nihidine’é bíká ’ańdaałwo’. Kodóó naaltsoos doo béédahoniilzinii, ’índa Bilagáana bizaad doo ła’ ńdadiit’áanii t’áá áwołi bee nihik’i dayínółdzííł. Kǫǫ sáanii ła’ dasiidw-lįį́’, ’índa ła’ hastóí daazlį́į́ ’akon. ’Éí ’ólta’ wolyéii baa dáádadiitih ’akon. Háajį’ shįį́ ndahidiildził ’akon. ’Éí bąą ’ádíshní díí k’ad niha’áłchíní ’ólta’ bá dahólónígíí ts’ídá baa ’ahééh nisin.

’Aadóó náasdi niha’áłchíní ’ólta’ yaa náádahidínóoséłígíí ndi t’áá ’ákót’é ’akon. ’Ólta’ wolyéii ts’ídá bá

activities seem to throw light on things you did not know. That is how one learns many things.

And when you attend meetings and hear intelligent men and women speak, you learn things. This is how you struggle to learn when you have no teacher. This is the way it is when you have no folks. And this is the way I am today.

Education Only Means To Progress

Today we look to the educated of our children for leadership. We pin our hope on them. I am in agreement with this. I am thankful for all of you who went to school and learned to read.

Help us with what you have learned, in every way you can. Help our people in all ways possible. Help those of us

bichą́ dayídéelni ’akon. Niha’áłchíní ts’ídá t’áá ’éí t’éiyá ’aghá baa ntsídeiikees. Háadi da t’áá bí yee ’ák’idadéekáah dooleeł haa da ’ádzaa léí’, jó kodi t’éiyá ’aghá baa ntsídeiikees ’akon.

Shí díí k’ad ’at’ééké t’áá naakihí sha’áłchinígo ’ádíshní. Ła’ t’áadoo hazhó’ó ’íiłta’ da. Tł’ízí t’éiyá daha’nínígíí biniinaa. T’áá tágí ghaaígo. ’íiłta’go k’ad hooghandi naaghá ’akon. T’óónee’ bi’deelchid nahalinígo ’íiłta’ ’akon. ’Áko doo shił sihgóó baa ntseśkees. Ła’ ’éí ńléí ’Ahééhéshį́į́h hoolyéégóó ’ólta’ yiniiyé sits’ą́ą́’ ’íiyá. T’áá ’ółta’ ńt’ée’go ’ólta’ bił bi-dánáhás’ni’go ’ólta’góó ’anáádzá. K’ad ’áádę́ę́’ naaltsoos ’ánéíl’į́įgo t’áá ’ahą́ą́h nahalingo naaltsoos shaa ninááhájeeh. Yę́ęni’ ńláhjí t’áadoo yéigo ’ajíiłta’ yę́ę t’áá bi’oh jiniłnah nahalin. Doo shił sih da ’áko. Kót’éego baa ntséskees.

T’áá ńléídę́ę́’ ’ólta’ béshniłgoshą’ k’ad haa yit’éé ńt’éé’ nisingo t’óó bą́ąh shíni’ łeh. Doo biká’ígóó díí ’íhoo’aah wolyéii bidááh haníinii ’át’éé lá. Doo ’ajíiłta’ dago Bilagáana da hach’į’ niighááhą́ągo hach’į’ haadzihę́ę t’áá ’áko t’óó ’ahíjí’is łeh. Bich’į’ haosdziih laanaa, bił ’ahił nahóshne’ laanaa t’óó ’íllį́įgo kodóó bee ’ádił ni’ídzíił łeh. Shí díí k’ad ’akónísht’é ’akon.

who do not know a word of English, and who cannot read. Some of us have become old men and women. We are too old to go to school, and we don't know how much longer our struggle will last. That's why I say I am grateful for the schools available to our children, and to those who will grow to school age in the future. We want schools for them. This is our main concern for our children. If our wish comes true, our children will make a living by means of their education.

My only children are two girls. One of them did not go to school very long because she had to herd goats. She is at home now, with only three years of schooling. She had merely a smattering of education. I think she had too little. The other one has left me to go to school in California. She had gone to school before and wanted badly to return. She often writes home to me. But when she writes, there's no one at home to read her letters. The girl at home knows too little English.

If I had kept them in school since they were small I wonder how they would be. I'm sorry I didn't do so. This matter of education is something to be sought after. If you do not go to school, and a white man comes up to you to say something to you, you can only stand and rub your heels together. You just stand there wishing you could talk to him. That's the way it is with me

Ch'índahanii 'ólta' dajiníí ńt'éé' hastóí 'índa sáanii da lá t'ah nahdéé' ndajiskaii. 'Ana'í binahagha'ígíí biniinaa 'áłchíní doo 'ádahalyą́ą da ndahaleeh dajiníí łeh ńt'éé' 'akon. Doodago shį́į́ 'ádajiní nisin shí baa ntséskeesgo. 'Ana'í binahagha' lá dooda ni jó dajiní 'akon. Shí 'éí t'áá 'ałch'ishjí shił yá'át'ééh dóó t'áá 'ałch'ishjí baa 'ahééh nisin. T'áá 'ałch'ishjí shił nilį́įgo baa ntséskees.

'Áádóó ńléídę́ę́' hodiyinę́ę k'ad baa'diildéehjį' hodideeshzhiizh dajiníníígíí 'éí shí doo baa'diildéeh da nisin. T'óó yíní dilyinee wolyéego 'ákót'éego baa ntséskees. Nihidiyinę́ę t'ah bidziilgo yit'ih nisin.

Ńléídę́ę́' sodizin yolyéhę́ęni', nahat'á wolyéhę́ęni', 'índa sin dabidziilii yę́ę, 'índa hastóí sodizin bidziilii yee 'aghá dahideezínę́ę díí nihe'ółta'í danilíinii, 'índa bidziilgo 'áłah ńda'adleehgóó nihe'adiits'a'ii danilíinii ts'ídá t'áá 'éí 'át'é nisin shí. Háálá k'ad t'áá 'éí t'éiyá choo'į́ bił bíyah ńdeiigał. Ts'ídá t'áá 'áajį' t'éiyá dadíit'į́į'. 'Ałk'idą́ą́' 'ákót'éego hastóí yę́ę t'éiyá daníl'į́į ńt'ée'go baa dahojilne'. 'Áko 'éí k'ad t'áá 'éí 'ákwii násdlį́į'ii 'át'é nisin díí nihe'ółta'í danilíinii.

'Índa nihinant'a'í béésh bąąh dah naaz'ání danilíinii dó' t'áá 'éí 'át'é nisin. Bee yá'át'éehgo náás yiikah dooleełii yiniiyé nihá hojooba' 'ádaaní 'akon. 'Áko ts'ídá t'áá 'áajį' t'éiyá choo'į́įł dadíit'į́į'go hoolzhish k'ad 'akon. 'Áko baa 'ahééh nisin.

now.

The old folks used to say that schools are a waste of time. They used to say that the children become odd on account of the white man's religion. I do not believe that. They used to be really opposed to the white man's religion. But both the Navajo and the white man's religion are all right with me. I am grateful for both, and I respect both of them.

Some people say that we are getting away from the old religion, but I don't think so. I do not think that there is any cause for alarm. I think the power of our religion keeps right on.

The old prayers, customs, powerful songs, and the foremost medicine men of former times are now passing some of their functions to our scholars and interpreters — that is all that is happening, I think. For at present we look to the students and interpreters for leadership. We look only to them. But in former times people looked to the medicine men. So the educated people of today have replaced the medicine men of past times in this sense.

And our councilmen too have taken over some of the functions that once belonged to the medicine man. They are all striving for something good which will show us the way forward. I am thankful.

'Áko ńléídę́ę́' diyin yit'ihę́ę t'ah ndi t'áá łáhági 'át'éego náás yit'ih nisin. Doo ninit'i' da nisin. 'Éí bąągo da'íínółta'íi, 'índa Bilagáana bizaad béédahosoosįįdii, 'índa nihinant'a'í béésh dah si'ání danihi'di'níinii ts'ídá t'áá 'ánółtso wołí bee nihik'í dayínółdzííł.

And I think that the Navajo religion goes on just as it went on in the past. I do not think it has come to an end. So you who are in school — you who know English — you whom we call our councilmen — work hard for us.

Betty John

Hasdá'jíí'eezh

Łah shį́įgo táá'ts'áadah shinááhaiyę́ędą́ą́ k'adą́ą́ e'e'aahgo chaha'oh biyaagi shádí ba'áłchíní at'ééké yázhí dóó ashkii yázhí bił naháshtą́ Baa shił hózhǫ́ haashį́į́ nííłtsogo óhólnííh shąąh niilyáago. Ałtso ch'aa'i'iisdee' nidáá'góó ashdla' yiskáąjį́'. Shicheii éí hooghangi hwoł nahísóótą́ądoo nihi'dooniid ńt'éego bik'is yikéé' dah diilwod. T'áá sáhí nahísíítą́ągo táá' yiską́ągo ch'iyą́ą́n nihits'ą́ą́' dínéezhchą́ą́'. Ts'ídá haa'ashį́į́ doo ntsíníkéézda. Dibé doodago éí tł'ízí yázhí daats'íła' diyeeshxééł nisin. Ndi shimásání doo bił yá'át'ééda doo nisin. Náábiiskání ch'iiyáán nihits'ą́ą́' ásdįįd. Áłchíní sits'ą́ą́' ada'niicha, ch'iyáán áníléeh daaníigo. Áko Naalyéhé báhooghandi t'éiyá ch'iyáán hólǫ́ ndi béeso éí bá'ádin. Áłchíní ch'ééh daachago t'óó da'iiłhaazh. Shí éí t'óó tsídékééz. Shimá diyogí yázhí k'adą́ą́ niítł'óhąą baa tsídékééz. Shimásání dóó shimá shináál atł'óogo t'áá áłts'íísígo shił bééhózin. T'áá'áko ałtsoh ninítł'ǫ́. T'óó tsxį́įłgo hasht'eeshłaa dóó ła' oobąąs léí' bikéé' iihiijéé'.

The Rescue

One summer when I was 13 years old, I sat in the shade house at dusk with my older sister's little girls and her little boy. I was proud of the responsibility bestowed upon me. Everyone had gone to a squawdance for the next five days. We were told that my maternal grandfather was to stay at home with us; however, the very next day, he took off after a friend of his. We stayed by ourselves for the next three days. By that time, our food was running low. I schemed, but only in vain. I thought that I would possibly butcher a sheep or even a kid goat. Then, I thought to myself that my maternal grandmother would not approve of that. The next day, we ran out of food. The children started crying from hunger and kept asking, "Why don't you cook for us?" There is food at the trading post, but there was no money for it. The children at last went off to sleep after crying in vain. Then I started scheming again. I started thinking about the small rug that my mother was close to com-

Kindi diyogí yázhíyę́ę dízdiin bą́ąh azlį́į́'. Áádóó áłchíní yázhí t'áá deiinízinígíí ńdayiizláá'. Áádóó biláahjį' índa ak'ą́ąn dóó nímasii dóó atsį' dóó awéé' be'abe' naháłnii'. Hooghangóó iihnín áánéíijéé'. Nihił dahózhǫ́ǫgo t'óó ahayóígo ch'iyáán íishłaá dóó da'iidą́ą́'. Nihił dahózhǫ́ǫgo da'iilghaazh. Biiskání t'ahdii ch'iyáán lą'í yidziihgo nidáá'dę́ę́' niná'iisdee'.

Kódeet'įįdígíí diné doo dayoodzą́ąda azhą́ shicheii nihits'ą́ą́' yóó'eelwod ndi t'áá sáhí kót'éégo áłchíní yázhí hasdéíí'eezh. Áko t'áá'íyisí diné shaa ąhééhdaniizį́į́'.

pleting. I knew a little about weaving just from observing her and my grandmother. So I began weaving it and completed the rug very quickly, and I hurriedly touched it up for finishing. We all hitched a ride in a wagon going to the trading post. At the trading post, I sold the rug for $40.00. Henceforth, the children were able to pick whatever they wanted at the store. Thereafter, I bought some flour, potatoes, meat, and milk. We caught a ride back home. We were very happy, so I cooked lots of food, and we feasted. We went to sleep very filled and contented. The next day, there was still some food left when everyone returned from the squawdance.

No one could hardly believe the experience we had or what we did, or the fact that our maternal grandfather had gone off and left us by ourselves. They were all very grateful to me for handling the crisis very well by myself and the fact that I saved the children from starvation.

Bridge Perspective

Irene Nakai
Tó' ahaní

i must be like a bridge
                    for my people
i may connect time; yesterday
      today   and tomorrow — for my people
            who are in transition, also.
i must be enough in tomorrow, to give warning —
       if i should.
i must be enough in yesterday, to hold a cherished secret.
Does it seem like we are walking as one?

Sunrise Flight into Acid Rain Cancelled

Irene Nakai
Tó' ahaní

I woke up my mother, father and little cousin around one-thirty in the early morning. My luggage was packed and already in the trunk of the car. Around two o'clock, we bumped down the short dirt road drive to the highway. From there it was a smooth two hours' cruise to Cortez, from where I was to catch my plane to Denver. My mother drove, I sat beside her, and my cousin Victoria and my father were in the backseat. Once in a while, someone spoke, sang a song or told a story. It was a novel experience, traveling in the predawn darkness. Only one car passed us on the road and it was going the opposite way.

We arrived in Cortez in a seemingly short time and got some gas at a truckstop. We also had some coffee and sweet rolls in the adjoining cafe. The cafe had only two other customers when we entered and it was very quiet. Sitting across from me, my mother looked sad so I told her a funny story and she smiled.

At five-thrity, we left the cafe and drove to the airport. I checked in and had my luggage tagged. I barely had time to wash my face again when suddenly it was time to go. I went through security check, came back through and hugged my mother, father, and cousin: "goodbye and I will be back, soon." I remembered my horse and told my cousin to take care of him while I was away. As I walked through the glass door, and past the armed security guard, I was also going through a "time warp."

On the plane I sat at the far end, in the smoking section, although I do not smoke. I had heard from my sister that that part of the plane offered a better outside view, she was right. The stewardess mumbled her well-memorized jargon about airbags and emergency exits as the plane ambled down the runway. Minutes later, we were over Mesa Verde. Down below, there were the still-bald spots from the forest fires of 1970, a drought year. The sun was peeking over the horizon, lighting the eastern slopes of the high mesas of junipers and pinon pines, and already behind, in the northwest lay the Sleeping Ute Mountain, Dzil Naajinii. Looking south over Dinétah, my people's homeland, I saw it enveloped in an ugly, green cloud — the dreaded smoke from the Four Corners Power Plant in New Mexico. In mourning, I also saw the furrowed alkaline hills north of the power plant. There were also the septic-green pools of dammed water, not sparkling like living water. South of Farmington, on the mesas, I saw for the first time the green hay fields, the product of an optimistic and colossal irrigation project. I questioned, "Would those fields be irrigated with an acid rain? Would the well-known sandstone pillars and mesas of Dinétah be drenched with the same deteriorating rain and would we wake up one day, in a flat dead land? No! No, it must not be." There was only mourning in me as the plane lifted off again, from Farmington, into the north, the mountain country of Colorado.

The mountain country scenery was more pleasant but it was remote, now, National Forest/Private/No Trespassing land. Somewhere over central Colorado, we flew over aspen forests and high mountain meadows over-run with cloud shadows. The forests were bright green clumps, the texture of a shedding pony's back. Another time, while over some still snowy mountains, I looked down and noticed the gray-dusted-no-longer-white snow. Shortly after the gray snow, the little plane left the mountains, and Denver and the plains came into view. The cityscape was the same rather monotonous domino trails of squat buildings arranged in rows and patches of small green lawns — paradoxical tributes to a once free Earth.

My black horse runs fast; one ear back, one ear forward and his mane tangled by the wind. I would whistle to the meadow larks, mountain bluebirds, and all the tsídii in the sagebrush and the junipers, and we had talked.

Back in Denver, the plane descended, bumped along the runway and taxied to a stop. Slowly, I collected my carry-on bag, tennis racket, and purse, and walked down the steps of the plane and up again into an eight o'clock already-busy terminal. There was a breeze blowing, warm air bouncing off the paved-over Earth. No, it must not be. It shall not be.

male rain

Agnes Tso

He comes
  riding on the wind
    kicking up dust
      bending the trees
        blowing flakes of rain
He flees past my window
  to a distant rumble

In-laws beware of him
who mocks the braves
as his features are majestic illusions
his knife the cutting cold
and his soul a drifter

female rain

she pregnant with rain child
comes
  quite
    softly
      and gently
in the night

At dawn she gives birth
  to little droplets of rain
    and for days on end

awakening

male rain has come and gone
female rain is fading in the distance
father sun is here
and mother earth is awakening

Navaho Inn

Nia Francisco

riding by a bar called "nn"
where broken wine bottles trickle
down sun-baked face of earth
where barb-wire-type scar crawls
over a navaho swollen nose
trickling tears down swollen lips
over chapped cheeks at home alone
as casted silver buttons/visions
fade into stoned grave flower images
where a mirage of *yei bii che*
quivers in brown red eyes of mine
sadness, emptiness in a voice
as a beggar behind a woven blanket
in a photograph
of navaho times
the weakness of a spring sprout
shows in drunken men and women
only to have eyes glisten
with greed for turquoise/silver
eyes belonging to gallup independent
readers riding by a bar called "navaho inn."

Morning and Myself

Nia Francisco

i wake to see the morning
from outside our home
from within me

i walk at dusk
to greet dawn boy
    his sister
  and their mother
i say i am your grandchild
  and that i will
meet you some day

and as that i want to live
 of the flesh of earth
  of the flash of water
   of the flesh of sky

and I will always give
 the soles of my feet
  the water of my mouth
   the sweatbeads of my skin
    the tears of my eyes
     the urine of myself
      the placenta of my babies
and the cleansing water of our hair
                                        and bodies
to earth
  to water and sky
in peace i go now
in peace we will walk
and in beauty we walk

Beautifying the World through Art

Gary Witherspoon

Gary Witherspoon is a non-Navajo scholar who is fluent in the Navajo language. In the following portion from his book Language and Art in the Navajo Universe *(Ann Arbor: University of Michigan Press, 1977), he talks about one of the central concepts in Navajo art and life: hózhó.*

In the Western world, where mind has been separated from body, where man has been extracted from nature, where affect has been divorced from "fact," where the quest for and focus upon the manipulation and accumulation of things has led man to exploit rather than to respect and admire the earth and her web of life, it is not surprising that art would be divorced from the more practical affairs of business and government and the more serious matters of science, philosophy, and theology. In the Navajo world, however, art is not divorced from everyday life, for the creation of beauty and the incorporation of oneself in beauty represent the highest attainment and ultimate destiny of man. *Hózhó* expresses the Navajo concept of beauty or beautiful conditions. But beauty is not separated from good, from health, from happiness, or from harmony. Beauty — *hózhó* — is the combination of all these conditions. It is not an abstractable quality of things or a fragment of experience; it is the normal pattern of nature and the most desirable form of experience.

For the Navajo, beauty is not so much in the eye of the beholder as it is in the mind of its creator and in the creator's relationship to the created (that is, the transformed or the organized). The Navajo does not look for beauty; he generates it within himself and projects it onto the universe. The Navajo says *shił hózhó* 'with me there is beauty', *shii' hózhó* 'in me there is beauty', and *shaa hózhó* 'from me beauty radiates'. Beauty is not "out there" in things to be perceived by the perceptive and appreciative viewer; it is a creation of thought. The Navajo experience beauty primarily through expression and creation, not through perception and preservation. Beauty is not so much a perceptual experience as it is a conceptual one.

In the Western world beauty as a quality of things to be perceived is, in essence, static; that is, it is something to be observed and preserved. To the Navajo, however, beauty is an essential condition of man's life and is dynamic. It is not in things so much as it is in the dynamic relationships among things and between man and things. Man experiences beauty by creating it. For the Anglo observer of Navajo sandpaintigs, it has always been a source of some bewilderment and frustration that the Navajo "destroy" these sandpaintings in less time than they take to create them. To avoid this overt destruction of beauty and to preserve its artistic value, the Anglo observer always wants to take a photograph of the sandpainting, but the Navajo sees no sense and some danger in that. To the Navajo the artistic or aesthetic value of the sandpainting is found in its creation, not in its preservation. Its ritual value is in its symbolic or representational power and in its use as a vehicle of conception. Once it has served that purpose, it no longer has any ritual value.

Navajos take little interest in the display or preservation of their works of art, with the exception of silver and turquoise jewelry. They readily sell them to non-Indians who are looking for beauty in things. Traditionally, they put their works of art to practical use in their daily activities. Now it is more practical to sell them for money and buy stainless steel pots and other more durable but less artistic things. This practice offends the purist's view of aesthetics, but it is, in fact, not a depreciation of aesthetic value at all. It is simply based on the idea that beauty is a dynamic experience in conception and expression, not a static quality of things to be perceived and preserved.

With regard to the two different views of art contrasted above, it is not surprising that Navajo society is one of artists (art creators) while Anglo society consists primarily of nonartists who view art (art consumers). The Navajo find it incomprehensible that we have more art critics than we have artists, and more art collectors than we have art creators. Nearly all Navajos are artists and spend a large part of their time in artistic creation. All Navajos are singers, and most Navajos have composed many songs. Traditionally, over 90 percent of all adult women wove rugs and today, despite limited opportunities to learn this art, a majority of Navajo women over thirty still weave. A large number of Navajo men are skilled at silver work and sandpainting. Some women still make pottery and beautifully designed baskets. Teachers in Navajo schools find that nearly all Navajo students take a special interest in and have an unusual proficiency in the graphic arts. Navajos are also very eloquent and often poetic in their use of language.

A Navajo often counts his wealth in the songs he knows and especially in the songs he has created. A poor Navajo is one who has no songs, for songs enrich one's experiences and beautify one's activities. Songs accompany and enrich both cermonial and nonceremonial activities. There are riding songs, walking songs, grinding songs, planting songs, growing songs, and harvesting songs. There are songs to greet the sun in the morning and songs to bid it farewell in the evening. There are songs for horses, for sheep, and for various other animal species. There are songs for blessing a hogan and songs for taking a sweat bath. In the past there were even songs for bidding visitors farewell. And, of course, there are songs of love and romance. But the most powerful songs are those that are essential parts of ceremonial and ritual activities. The former type is a means by which Navajos maintain *hózhó* in their daily life experiences, while the latter type constitutes a means by which Navajos restore *hózhó* when it has been disrupted.

In white society it is the exceptional and abnormal person that becomes an artist. The artist is usually associated with marginality and nonconformity with regard to the mainstream of society. From this marginal position the artist dedicates himself almost solely to his artistic creations. The nonartist among the Navajo is a rarity. Moreover, Navajo artists integrate their artistic endeavors into their other activities. Living is not a way of art for them, but art is a way of living.

Mt. Taylor
Lee Marmon

Song of a Mountain

Andrew Natonabah
singer

Martha Austin
translator

Dził Nanit'áo baanitsíníkees
Dził Nanit'áo baanitsíníkees
Dził Nanit'áo baanitsíníkees wólághéí néíyá

K'ad Lá Sisłízhiin néíyá baanitsíníkees éí
K'ad Yoołgaiídziil néíyá baanitsíníkees
K'ad Dził Nanit'áo néíyá baanitsíníkees éí

K'ad Sį'ąhnaagháí
K'ad bik'eh Hózhǫ́ǫ́ néíyá baanitsíníkees
Dził Nanit'áo néíyá baanitsíníkees wólághéí néíyá

K'ad Tso'ódziil néíyá baanitsíníkees éí
K'ad Dootł'izh'ádziil néíyá baanitsíníkees
K'ad Dził Nanit'áo baanitsíníkees éí

K'ad Sį'ąhnaagháí
Éí k'ad bik'eh Hózhǫ́ǫ́ baanitsíníkees

Planning Mountain, you think about,
Planning Mountain, you think about,
Planning Mountain, you think about.

Now, Blanca Peak, you think about that,
Now, white shell, you think about it,
Now, Planning Mountain, you think about that,
Now, long life,
Now, by it beauty, you think about it,
Planning Mountain, you think about it.

Now, Mount Taylor, you think about that,
Now, strong turquoise, you think about it,
Now,Planning Mountain, you think about that,
Now, long life,
That, now, by it beauty, you think about it,

Dził Nanit'áo baanitsíníkees wólághéí néíyá

K'ad Dook'o'oosłííd néíyá baanitsíníkees éí

K'ad Diichiłídziil néíyá baanitsíníkees
Éí k'ad Dził Nanit'áo baanitsíníkees éí

K'ad Są'ąhnaagháí
Éí k'ad bik'eh Hózhǫ́ǫ́ baanitsíníkees
Dził Nanit'áo baanitsíníkees wólághéí néíyá

K'ad Dibé Nitsaa néíyá baanitsíníkees éí

K'ad Bááshzhiniidziil néíyá baanitsíníkees
Éí k'ad Dził Nanit'áo baanitsíníkees

K'ad Są'ąhnaagháí
K'ad bik'eh Hózhǫ́ǫ́ baanitsíníkees
Dził Nanit'áo baanitsíníkees wólághéí néíyá

K'ad Dził Ná'oodiłii néíyá baanitsíníkees éí

K'ad Yódídziil néíyá baanitsíníkees

Éí k'ad Dził Nanit'áo baanitsíníkees

K'ad Są'ąhnaagháí
K'ad bik'eh Hózhǫ́ǫ́ baanitsíníkees
Éí Dził Nanit'áo baanitsíníkees wólághéí néíyá

K'ad Ch'ó'ool'į́į́ néíyá baanitsíníkees éí
K'ad Nitł'izh'ídziil néíyá baanitsíníkees

Planning Mountain, you think about it.

Now San Francisco Peaks, you think about that,
Now, strong abalone, you think about it,
That, now, Planning Mountain, you think about that,
Now, long life,
That, now, by it beauty, you think about it,
Planning Mountain, you think about it.

Now, La Plata Mountains, you think about that,
Now, strong jet, you think about it,
That, now, Planning Mountain, you think about it,
Now, long life,
That, now, by it beauty, you think about it,
Planning Mountain, you think about it.

Now, Huerfano Mountain, you think about that,
Now, strong variety of goods, you think about that,
That, now, Planning Mountain, you think about it,
Now, long life,
That, now, by it beauty, you think about it,
That, Planning Mountain, you think about it.

Now, Gobernador Knob, you think about that,
Now, strong mixed precious stones, you think about it,

Éí k'ad Dził Nanit'áo baanitsíníkees

K'ad Sį'ąhnaagháí
K'ad bik'eh Hózhǫ́ǫ́ baanitsíníkees
Éí Dził Nanit'áo baanitsíníkees wólághéí néíyá

Yee shitsi'jį' Hózhǫ́ǫ́ baanitsíníkees

Yee shikésh'dę́ę́' Hózhǫ́ǫ́ baanitsíníkees,

Yee shiyahgidę́ę́' Hózhǫ́ǫ́ baanitsíníkees,

Yee shik'ihgi Hózhǫ́ǫ́ baanitsíníkees

Yee shinaadę́ę́' t'áá ałtso Hózhǫ́ǫ́ baanitsíníkees

Yee shizahdę́ę́' Hózhǫ́ǫ́ baanitsíníkees

Yee k'ad Sį'ąhnaagháí
K'ad bik'eh Hózhóóní shí nishłį́į́go baanitsíníkees

Dził Nanit'áo éí baanitsíníkees
Éí Dził Nanit'áo baanitsíníkees
Éí Dził Nanit'áo baanitsíníkees
Éí Dził Nanit'áo baanitsíníkees wólághéí néíyá

That, now, Planning Mountain, you think
about it,
Now, long life,
That, now, by it beauty, you think about it,
That, Planning Mountain, you think about it.

By means of it, in front of me, beauty,
you think about it,
By means of it, from behind me, beauty,
you think about it,
By means of it, from below me, beauty,
you think about it,
By means of it, above me, beauty,
you think about it,
By means of it, around me, just, all, beauty,
you think about it,
By means of it, from my mouth, beauty,
you think about it,
By means of it, now, long life,
Now, by it, beauty, me, I am, you think about
it.

Planning Mountain, you think about that,
That, Planning Moutain, you think about it,
That, Planning Moutain, you think about it,
That, Planning Moutain, you think about it.

Mt. Taylor
Dennis Carr

Navajo Literature: Other Sources

Two good general discussions of Navajo culture are Clyde Kluckhohn and Dorthea Leighton's The Navaho *(1946; revised edition Cambridge: Harvard University Press, 1974) and Ruth Underhill's* The Navajos *(Norman: University of Oklahoma Press, 1967). Gary Witherspoon's* Language and Art in the Navajo Universe *(Ann Arbor: University of Michigan Press, 1977) is a superb discussion of Navajo verbal and visual arts.*

The publications of Navajo Community College Press, Navajo Nation, Tsaile, Arizona 86556 include many of the best collections of Navajo oral literature. Navajo History *(1971), edited by Ethelou Yazzie, gives a composite account of the Navajo origin narrative.* Coyote Stories *(1968) and* Grandfather Stories of the Navajos *(1968) both contain traditional Navajo stories of special interest to younger readers. Ruth Roessel's* Navajo Stories of the Long Walk Period *(1973) gives Navajo remembrances of one of the most important events in recent Navajo history.*

Most collections of Navajo song are marbled with technical anthropological discussion. Of these, the editions of Leland Wyman are most useful and comprehensible: Beautyway *(New York: Pantheon, 1957),* The Red Antway of the Navaho *(Sante Fe: Museum of Navajo Ceremonial Art, 1965),* Blessingway *(Tucson: University of Arizona Press, 1970), and* The Mountainway of the Navajo *(Tucson: University of Arizona Press, 1975). Karl Luchert, editor of the American Tribal Religions series published by the Museum of Northern Arizona Press, has also published accounts of Navajo ceremonies of interest to those attracted to Navajo song. See* Coyoteway: a Navajo Holyway Healing Ceremonial *(Tucson: University of Arizona Press, 1979). A very well-annotated and readable edition of the Nightway chants has been published in John Bierhorst's* Four Masterworks of American Indian Literature *(New York: Farrar, Strauss, and Giroux, 1974). Those who wish to listen to sound recordings of Navajo song might get* Yei-Be-Chai Chants *(Canyon C-6069), songs sung by members of the prize-winning Yei-Be-Chai team of the 1968 Navajo Tribal Fair, or* Navajo Sway Songs *(Indian House IH-1501), forty-five Navajo sway songs from the Enemy Way ceremony. Navajo singer Andrew Natonabah sings Navajo songs and discusses their meaning with two of his children as they travel through Canyon de Chelly in "By This Song I Walk" a color videotape from the Division of Media and Instructional Services at the University of Arizona, Tucson. The videotape is in Navajo with English subtitles.*

Stories of Traditional Navajo Life and Culture *(Tsaile, Arizona: Navajo Community College Press, 1978), edited by Broderick Johnson, contains personal narratives from over a dozen Navajo men and women. While a student at the Institute of American Indian Art in Sante Fe, Emerson Blackhorse Mitchell collaborated with his teacher T. D. Allen to write* Miracle Hill: the *Story of a Navajo Boy (Norman: University of Oklahoma Press, 1967). A very full account of the life of a Navajo singer is given in* Navajo Blessingway Singer: the Autobiography of Frank Mitchell 1881-1967 *(Tucson: University of Arizona Press, 1978), edited by Charlotte J. Frisbie and David McAllester.*

Navajo artist R. C. Gorman published a story "Nowhere to Go" in Kenneth Rosen's collection of contemporary American Indian short fiction The Man To Send Rainclouds *(New York: Viking, 1974). Three early novels of Navajo life are Laura Adams Armers'* Waterless Mountain *(New York: Longmans, 1931), Oliver LaFarge's* Laughing Boy *(1929; rpt. New York: New American Library, 1971), and Frances Gillmor's* Windsinger *(1930; rpt. Albuquerque: University of New Mexico, 1976). Kiowa author N. Scott Momaday, who wrote the introduction to the new edition of* Windsinger, *gives a major section of his own novel* House Made of Dawn *(New York: Harper and Row, 1968) to a Navajo character. The title of Momaday's novel is taken from a Navajo Nightway song. Similarly, Laguna Pueblo author Leslie Marmon Silko sets significant portions of her superb novel* Ceremony *(New York: Viking, 1977) in Navajo country. Ten contemporary Navajo poets are included in Geary Hobson's expansive collection of contemporary native American literature* The Remembered Earth, *which was published in 1979 by Red Earth Press, P. O. Box 26641, Albuquerque, New Mexico. Work by a number of Navajo students is included in T. D. Allen's* Arrows Four: Prose and Poetry by Young American Indians *(New York: Washington Square Press, 1974).*

The Navajo Times *is a weekly newspaper published at Window Rock, Arizona on the Navajo reservation. It regularly includes imaginative work.*

Peter Iverson's contribution to the Newberry Library Center for the History of the American Indian Bibliographical Series The Navajos: A Critical Bibliography *(Bloomington: Indiana University Press, 1976) is an excellent resource for locating other writing by and about Navajo people.*

PAPAGO LITERATURE

Papago Alphabet

Ofelia Zepeda

Papago Vowels: The English counter-parts are all approximate.

a	wako	water
e	eda	roses
i	bit	beet
o	**ṣon**	**short**
u	**huḍ**	**boot**

In Papago all of the vowels can be pronounded **long**, that is the vowel sound is dragged out. This long sound is marked by a colon (:).

a:	ta:ñ	fa
e:	me:	There is no sound in English which is close to the Papago **e:**. An explanation for the **e:** sound might be to make the **u:** sound without rounding the lips.
i:	ki:	key
o:	to:n	bow
u:	hu:ñ	moon

Some of the vowels can be pronounced extra-short. These vowels are marked by ˘ above the vowel. These vowels occur only at the end of a word, as in the following examples:

bawı	In the case of the extra-short ı, there is of course no English counter-part. This particular sound is much like a whispered vowel, the vowel is literally aspirated.
nowĭ	
'uwĭ	
hehĕ	the extra-short **ĕ** and **ă** will vary among speakers, some speakers will aspirate the vowel, some will pronounce them fully as in the first examples of all the vowels.

Papago "dipthongs"

ai	**bai**	bite
ei	**kei**	Again there is no approximate sound in English.
oi	**koi**	boy
ui	**kui**	gooey
'	**glotal**	**stop**
	'a'an, 'on	The glottal stop is caused by a stoppage of air in the throat.

Papago Consonants: The English counter-parts are all approximate.

b	bo:l	ball
c	ceoj	church
d	dai	though
ḍ	taḍ	There is no sound in English which is close to the Papago **ḍ**. This particular sound is created by having the tip of the tongue curl up to the roof of the mouth very much like the way the English **r** is made.
g	ga:t	gun
h	hon	how
j	je:ñ	jem
k	ki:	key
l	la:mba	There is no sound in English which is like the Papago **l**, this sound is made by having the tongue curl up to the roof of the mouth and then coming down quickly to the bottom of the mouth
m	mu:ñ	moon
n	na:k	no
ñ	hu:ñ	canyon
ŋ	ca:ŋgo	finger
		priest
		suck
ṣ	ṣu:ṣk	There is no sound in English like the Papago ṣ, however the closest sound might be the **sh** in the word **sh**eep, but the ṣ in Papago again has the tongue curled up slightly toward the roof of the mouth.
t	tai	thought
w	waw	wow
y	ya:nda	yes

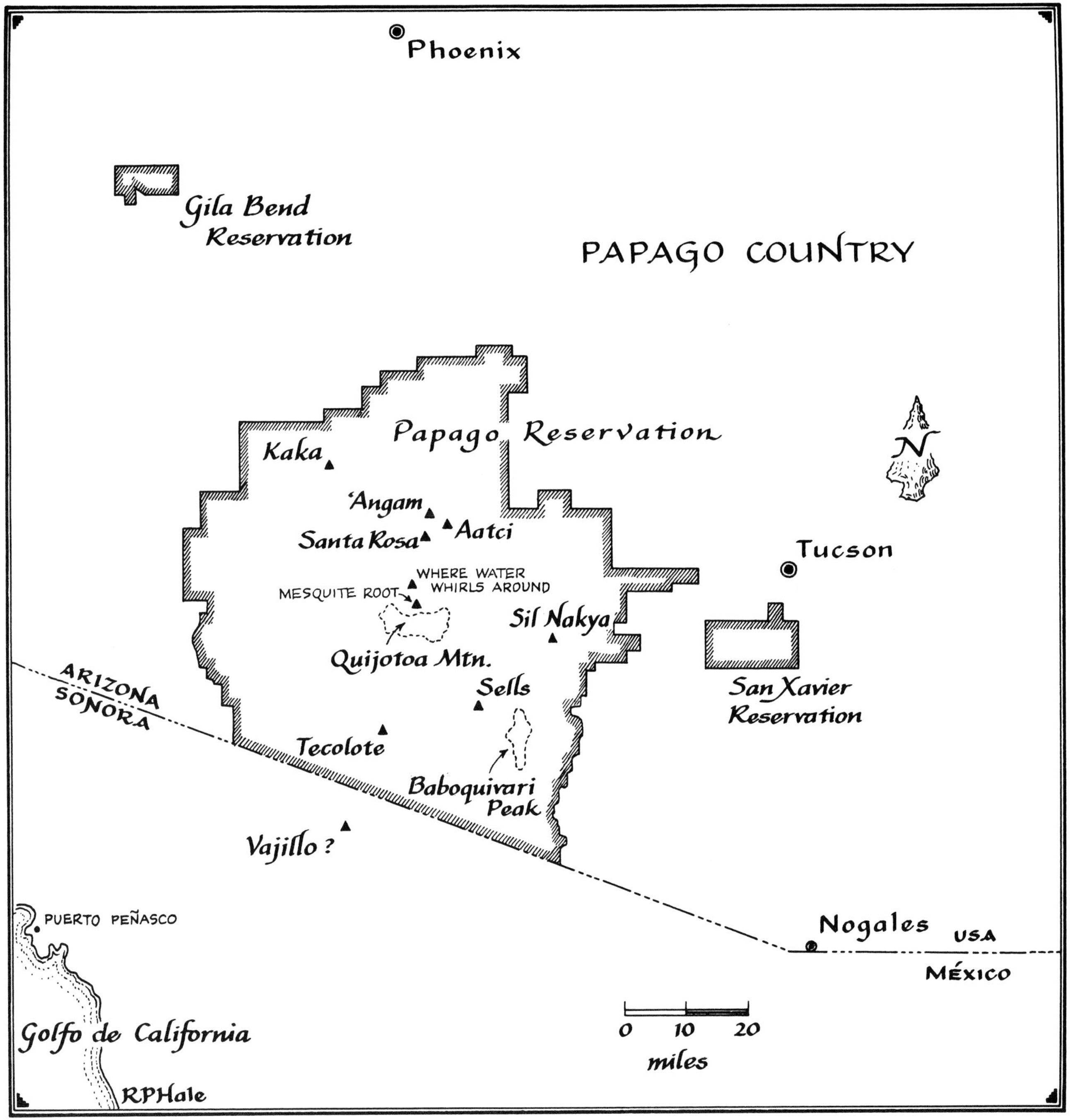
Phoenix
Gila Bend Reservation
PAPAGO COUNTRY
Papago Reservation
Kaka
'Angam
Santa Rosa
Aatci
Tucson
WHERE WATER WHIRLS AROUND
MESQUITE ROOT
Sil Nakya
Quijotoa Mtn.
San Xavier Reservation
ARIZONA
SONORA
Sells
Tecolote
Baboquivari Peak
Vajillo ?
PUERTO PEÑASCO
Nogales
USA
MÉXICO
0 10 20
miles
Golfo de California
RPHale
N

I'itoi and Ho'ok 'oks

as told by

Ventura José

I'itoi *is called Elder Brother* (Si'ihe) *by all the Papago people. He was the First Born, the first to come forth at the beginning of things, when the sky came down and met the earth:*

> *Long ago, they say, when the earth was not yet finished, darkness lay upon the water, and they rubbed each other. The sound they made was like the sound at the edges of a pond. There, on the water, in the darkness, in the noise, and in a very strong wind, a child was born. (Saxon,* Legends and Lore of the Papago and Pima Indians*)*

I'itoi *prepared the earth for the Papago people, and then he went away to his home on Baboquivari Peak. The following story tells of how* I'itoi *saved the people from the* Ho'ok 'oks. *It was told to Susie Ignacio by her great-uncle Ventura Jose who lived in Vajillo, Sonora, Mexico, and first transcribed and translated by Professor William Kurath. Papago linguist Daniel Matson passed it on to Ofelia Zepeda who has done a new transcription for this publication. The translation is essentially Professor Kurath's.*

Ṣ 'am ki: g wiapoi kc s-melidag kc s-ke:g wuḍ 'o'odham kc 'am hab masma maṣ hab cum si 'i ha-tacuid g 'o'odham g 'e-'a'alga.

Ṣ' an 'i ñei g Si'ihe, aṣ s-he:gamk 'aṣ hab 'i 'e-'a: maṣ hig 'am hu o si has ju: 'i:da wiapoi. Ñe: ṣ 'am hi: maṣ am ki: g 'uwǐ c pi gnhu aṣ s-ta-ñeidama k am hab 'a:gi "mapt 'am o hi: aṣ 'i sialimk 'ab o wa'i do'ag ṣon ab mo 'ab ṣu: dagǐ. T 'ab o jiva g wiapoi g 'e-ṣoñgiwul keickwuijc. T gahu 'o 'i ce:ka k 'ab o 'i keickwua hegai 'e-soñgiwul kut 'ab o meḍk 'an o da'ibij m-hugidan kupt o si dais. T 'am o' jiwa g cioj k o m-cu'ij mapṣ pi ṣa'i ñeid g ṣoñgiwulgaj. Kupt 'ab o 'i nammek k hab o 'a: mapt ho o wa ma: mat hekid o 'i ha-wa: g m-cu'i. T hi wa o cum ṣa pi ho:hoid k 'aṣ hab a pi has o e-to:ta k 'am hahaw o 'i s-wehokam 'el" Ñe: ṣ 'am 'i ha'icu ma' maṣ hia g ba'ag 'a'an we:naj cu'itas. Ṣ 'am wuḍ 'i ba'ic taṣ maṣ koi 'i ta'i ceṣ g taṣ ṣ 'am hi: g 'uwǐ k g 'e-ha'a mo:tk. K 'aṣ 'ab hu hebai daha maṣ' ab ṣu:dagǐ. Ṣ gahu meḍ g wiapoi. Ṣ 'abhu 'i ce:ka k 'aṣ 'ab 'i keickwua g ṣoñgiwul kuṣ 'ab medk 'in da'ibij hugidan g 'uwǐ. Ṣ 'an bek gdhu si dais. Ṣ 'am hahawa cum meliwk pi 'edagǐ. "B 'ant keickwua g ñ-ṣoñgiwul t 'i hab hi a me:, map pi ṣa'i ñeid?" "M 'am hi a pi 'am hu ṣa'i ha'icug" b aṣ kaij g 'uwǐ kc 'aṣ aṣ hehem. "Ep kia cum ñeid c aṣ pi ñ-'a'gid, 'oig 'ab aṣ 'i ñ-ma:ki" Ṣ 'am hab 'ahawa 'i kaij g 'uwǐ, "Mapt hi o a ha-wa: g ñ-cu'i ns hab o m-ma: g m-ṣoñigiwulga" Ṣ hi a cum ṣa pi 'al ho:ho'id k aṣ hab a 'am i pi has 'e-tota maṣ pi ma: g 'uwǐ. Ñe: k 'aṣ 'am 'i 'i: g wa:gaj. Ṣ hemho ha'aṣ

There lived a youth, swift and handsome, who was all that parents want their children to be. Elder Brother became jealous of him. He decided that he would do something to this boy. So he went to where lived a bold woman and said to her: "Go very early tomorrow to get water at the foot of the mountain. A young man will come, and he will be kicking his kickball. From a distance he will approach kicking his kickball; it will roll toward you and pass beside you, and you will pick it up and hide it by sitting on it. He will ask you if you have not seen his kickball. You will tease him and tell him that you will give it to him if he will mix your powder with water and drink it. He will try to refuse but will not be able to get around it, and he will drink this mix that has an eagle feather ground up in it."

The next day before sun-up, the girl went with her olla on her head to sit there where the water was. Just as the sun was coming up the young man came running from a distance. When he had come to a certain point he kicked the ball, and it rolled right toward her and rolled past her. She took it and sat on it to hide it. He came there on the run but could not find it. "I kicked my ball and it rolled this way, didn't you see it?"

"You can't find it anywhere," the girl finally told him laughingly.

"You did see it, but you didn't tell me! Come on, give it to me!"

Then finally the girl said: "Will you make a potion of this flour so that I may give you your kickball?"

gmhu a 'i ba: k si 'e-wokij. Ṣp gmhu si ce:mu ṣ 'ab 'ep si 'i:ehim c gam si 'i'ito. Ṣa'i ha'as ṣ 'aṣ we:sko 'i mu'umka k g 'a'an 'ab 'i wuwha. Ṣ hahawa aṣ cum ñei g 'uwĭ ṣki hu 'e-ba'agc. Ṣ si 'e-wokijtahim c 'm ha'ap da'a k gnhu hab 'i dahiwua. Ṣ hahawa 'i cem wu:ṣañ k pi 'edagi g 'ṣoñigwul maṣ 'am dais. Ṣ 'am hi: g 'uwĭ k gdhu jiwa 'e-ki: 'am k 'am hab 'i ha-'a:gid maṣ has 'e-ju: g 'o'odham.

Ṣ 'am him g he'ekia wuḍ 'i maṣad ṣ 'am g 'uwĭ maḍt 'i:da 'uwĭ. Ṣ a hekaj s-mai g 'o'odham maṣ 'amhu a has o cu'igk 'i:da 'ali naṣpi ṣa'i s-gewk c 'aṣ ṣa'i s-hottam ge'elim. Ṣ pi 'e-nako g je'ej maṣ has o ju: Ṣ 'am aṣ 'i cum melid k aṣ o ha-cegi'ad g 'a'al. 'Aṣ hebai o ṣa 'e-nakog k 'aṣ o mua g 'ali. Ṣ wa:m 'am 'i ge'eda k 'aṣ 'ab 'i ha-'oi g ge'egad 'a'al. Ṣ hekid 'o 'i mua g 'ali k 'aṣ do'ig o hu: Ṣ 'am 'i cum ñei g 'o'odham k 'aṣ s-'e:bid naṣpi g ge'egad hemajkam hahawa ep ha-ko'a. Ṣ am cum e-mamce maṣ has o ju: k 'aṣ 'am hab 'ahawa 'i kaij maṣ hi o 'a:gĭ g Si'ihe kuṣ has ju: k 'am o ha-'agi maṣ has o ju:. Ṣ 'am hahawa 'ep hema 'i ga:ghi g s-melidkam maṣ 'am o meḍk 'ab o ñei g Si'ihe Wawgiwulk 'ab maṣ 'ab ki:.

Ṣ 'am him g he'ekia d 'i taṣ ṣ 'am 'i jiwa g s-cu-amicuddam. K 'am hab 'ahawa ha- 'a:gi "mamt 'ab 'i bei g 'uwĭ nt 'am o ha'icu 'a:gĭ. Mṣ 'am u'apa g Ho'ok. Ṣ 'a hab ' 'ahawa 'i 'a:g g Si'ihe 'i:da Ho'ok 'uwĭ "map pi hekid ṣa'i s-ma:c maṣ hedai wuḍ m-'o:g. Mant hemuc 'i o m-'a:gĭ: Ñe: ṣ 'am 'i bei g Ho'ok k aṣ 'am ce:gĭ g tohono jewed k

He didn't want to do it, but he finally gave in when she refused to give the ball to him.

So he drank her potion. After one big swallow, he shook all over. I suppose it went all over him, and he drank and drank until he had drunk it all up. He started growing feathers all over. The girl saw that he had turned into an eagle. After repeated shakings, he flew a short distance and sat down. Finally she got up and could not find the kick ball she had sat on, so the girl went to her home and told what had happened to the young boy.

Some months later this girl gave birth to a girl child. Right away, the people found out that there was going to be something queer about this child because she was so strong and grew so rapidly. Her mother did not know what to do. As soon as she was able to walk she would fight with other children. Sometimes, when she could, she would kill the child. Later on when she grew older she proceeded to fight with the big children. Whenever she would kill a child she would eat it raw. When the people looked on this child they were afraid because now she was eating big people too. The people had a conference trying to decide what to do with this weird being, *Ho'ok* as they called her.

They couldn't think what to do, so they said they would tell Elder Brother and maybe he would tell them what to do. So they sought out a fast runner who would run up to see Elder Brother up on Baboquivari Peak where he lived.

In a few days the wise man appeared and told

'aṣ hab kaij, "Nap ñeid hegai m gmhu hab cu'ig?" Ṣ gmhu d 'aṣ 'i jegc hegai kukujgk 'am hab hia cu'ig. Ṣ 'am 'i ñei g Ho'ok 'uwĭ k s-wehoc g Si'ihe.

Ṣ hab 'am 'ahawa 'i ceha g Si'ihe maṣ o 'i 'oi g 'e-'o:g. Ñe: ṣ 'amjed hi: g Ho'ok g 'e-'o:g s-ñeidamk. K 'aṣ ' aṣ hab pi hekid ṣa'i 'ai naṣpi 'am 'i aihi kuṣ gmhu ba'ic hab 'ep o 'e-ju: g kukujegk. Ṣ heg aṣ 'i me:kohim , me:k o him k 'am 'i pi 'ai.

Ṣ 'eda 'am him k 'am 'i ce:ka m 'am hemuc 'am wuḍ Ce:dagi Wahia k 'am 'i s-mai maṣki pi hekid o ṣa'i 'ai g 'e-'o:g k 'aṣ am 'i ṣoṣa. Ṣ 'im hab ceṣ do'agt 'am k 'a hu hebai g ce:co hema ce: k 'an heg 'eda 'i ciwa.

Ṣ we:s si'alig 'ab gnhu o 'i kekiwua si waw da:m k gmhu 'a'ai o ha'icu si hewgiamad. Ṣa:kojed 'ab o s-u:wk g 'ali ṣ 'am ha'ak o me: K 'as gdhu o mel maṣ 'ab 'amjed hewgid g 'ali k 'aṣ hab o cei "Mo:si, mo:si 'ab g 'i bei g 'ali ñt o ñei." Mṣ 'am o 'i ma: g 'ali ṣ 'am hi o aṣ a'i komkcekahid c 'ab hahawa 'as o si hukidṣ wo:kt 'ab k 'aṣ 'am o wua 'e-giho 'ed k gmhu o kuswiod k hi: .

Ṣ 'an 'i 'e-'a:gid g 'o'odham maṣ 'an ha'icu memdadc d al 'i 'e:bida. Ṣ gdhu 'i mai g 'o'odham k 'aṣ gahu o 'i ka: maṣ 'ab o kaidagid ṣ gnhu o si ha-'e'esto g 'e-'a'alga.

Ṣ 'eda 'ab 'aṣ s-kaidam o medad naṣpi g ha'icu huc, ha'icu ta:tanij, ha'icu 'o:'o 'an bayokaj 'am ceckostaj ha'i 'am ep giwudaj. Ṣ ga hu hahawa 'aṣ o meḍad 'ab aṣ s-kaidam o sijkdc ab o koligid.

Ṣ 'an o 'i ka: g 'u'uwĭ k gnhu o si ha-'e'esto g 'e-

them that they were to bring the girl to him and he would tell her something. They brought her. Elder Brother said to her: "You never knew who your father was. I will tell you right now." He showed the *Ho'ok* the desert land, and he said: "Do you see that thing before you?" And there was only a mirage out in space. The *Ho'ok* looked and believed the *Si'ihe*. Then and there he told her to go after her father to try to see her father. But she never caught up with him, because whenever she got near, the mirage would be farther in front of her again. She got further and further away, but she never reached it. When she came to what is now called Green Well she found out that she would never reach her father, and she wept. She climbed up on the mountain there and found this one cave in which she made her home.

She became very old. Every morning she would stand on top of the cliff and sniff in all directions. From whatever direction she would smell a baby she would run that way. When she got there from where the smell of the child came, she would say: "Grandchild, Grandchild! You will bring the child, I want to see it." Then they would give her the child; she would hold it for a little while in her arms, then suddenly she would claw on its stomach, and she would put it in her burden basket and away she would go carrying it on her back. The people told each other that she was their greatest fear. Almost from the very first the people found out and when they heard her from a far distance, they would hide their children. They would hear her — she would be ma:mad. Ṣ 'am o jiwa k pi 'o him k 'am o wa dahak. Ṣ hebai ṣ 'am o 'i ṣoṣa g 'ali ṣ a hekaj o hatai.

Ṣ him k hebai ce:ka ṣ 'am 'i ha-hugio g si ce'ecem 'a'al k 'aṣ g ge'eged 'a'al 'ab 'i ha-'oi. Ṣ aṣ hab a g 'u'uwĭ 'a'al pi ha-'u'u c 'aṣ hegam a 'i cecoj 'a'al ha 'i ha-'u'u: Ṣ hab ha-'a:g g ha-je:j g wipiop maṣ 'am kui weco o ṣa wu:ṣ g Ho'ok kuṣ gnhu o 'e 'e-nagia 'u:s t-'an. K 'an o a 'i dahak ṣ hekid gmhu o 'i me:ko g Ho'ok ṣ gmhu hahaw o me: 'uhum.

Ṣ gdhu 'i mai g 'a'al 'i:da k aṣ hab a hekaj o cei 'ab Ho'ok wui, "U:s weco an tacu ñ-hu'ul".

Ṣ hab 'e-junhimk heba'i ce:ka kuṣ ṣa 'e-nankog g Ho'ok c 'aṣ g ge'e hemajkam mem'a. Aṣ ep ṣa'i s-e-ma:c 'ab we:s ha'icuk 'ab. Wipiat 'ab, hoatat 'ab , haha'atat'ab c we:s ha'icu maṣ hascu 'i s-ma:c g cecoj.

Ṣ 'am 'e-nanmek g hemajkam k 'am 'e-'a'aga maṣ has higi o ju: 'i:da 'oks "Kuttp o ṣa pi t-nako matt o mea kutp 'i o t-hugio t-kokdak", b 'aṣ kaij ha'i .

Ṣ ha'i 'am hab hahawa 'i cei maṣ higi o 'a'gĭ g Si'i he k o ka: maṣ has o cei. Ṣ 'an hahawa hema 'ep 'i ga:ghi maṣ si s-meldag maṣ heg 'am o medk 'ab o 'a:gi g Si'ihe.

Ṣ 'am hi a me: g wiapoi k 'ia hu he'ekia 'i taṣ pi ha'icug. Ṣ hekid gdhu 'i meliw k 'aṣ 'm 'i cum ñei g 'o'odham 'am wo'o kc d 'ali keli.

Ṣ 'am hab hi a 'a:gid mamṣ hascu 'a:gk 'am 'a:'ad.

making this noise as she ran because she wore fingernails, bones, and teeth on a necklace and some for a belt. From a far distance, when she was just on her way, they would hear her make this jingling and rattling noise. When the women heard this they would hide their offspring very securely. When she came, she would not go away, but there she would keep on sitting. Now and then a child would cry and right away she would ask them for it.

As time went on she ran out of very small children and started on the big children. She did not seize girl children but seized only the male children. The mothers told their young boys that when the *Ho'ok* went under a mesquite tree, they should hang onto a branch of it. The child would sit up in the tree until the *Ho'ok* got far off, and then he would run back home. When the children caught on to this, they would say right away to her, "I want under the tree, my grandmother."

She kept on doing this until later on she got to where, if she could, she would kill grown people. Also she knew all about things, about hunting, pottery making and basket making, and about whatever women knew or men knew. The people got together and discussed what they ought do to this old woman. Some said: "If we are not able to kill her, she will do away with us all by killng us."

There were some who said that they must tell Elder Brother and hear what he had to say. They looked for one who was a very fast runner who would run up to tell Elder Brother. The youth

Ṣ hab kaij g Si'ihe, " 'Oig me:l 'u:hum, ntp hems gdhu 'as o 'i m-'a'ahe". Ṣ hab hi 'aṣ 'e-a:g g waipoi, "ps hebai o 'i me: g ke:li."

Ṣ 'amjed medk gnhu 'aṣ cum meliw k 'am 'i ha-'a:gid, "M o hi a wo'o g 'em-nowoj c ḍ 'al 'i we:s, pi hab ṣ'ai ma:s mas hascu hab o 'i ju: ." Ṣ hab 'aṣ kia kaij ṣ 'ab hahawa 'i kekiwua g Si'ihe k 'as wuḍ 'as si wiapo'ogel.

Ṣ 'eda hab cu'ig g Si'ihe kc 'as cum has mamsma o 'e-na:to 'ab 'as cum hedai wui. Ṣ hab a 'e-a'aga maṣ g 'o'odham o ṣa taṣ wuḍ doakam c hab masma o ñei maṣ wuḍ al keli kuṣ hema s-ho:tam o ṣa mu: k 'aṣ hab masma o ñeidad maṣ wuḍ 'aṣ si wiapo'ogel.

Ṣ 'am hahawa 'e-henapai g hemajkam k 'am ka: g S'i'ihe maṣ 'am hab 'a:g g ha'icu 'e-ma:mcig.

"Man hia ha'icu hab 'elid t 'aṣ 'eda hi wuḍ o a si cikpank , ñe: 'ia 'amt o si ge'e o 'e-ñe'ic 'ia o si ge'e keihink o si 'i: g nawait. Mt gi'ikk taskaj c gi'ikk s-cuhugam 'ab o 'e-ñe'ic. T heg we:s 'oidam 'ia o memdad g Ho'ok 'Oks.

"T heg 'oidam ha'i g ku'agi o momto k 'ab o toa ceho ki:jigo 'abai mo 'ab ki: g 'oks. T hai'i 'epai o 'e'etpat 'ab o toa ki: d 'ab.

"T 'eda heg we:s 'oidam o meḍad g 'oks. Kumt g __ __kc ____ 'am o 'oiwic k 'aṇ o 'i hihimcudad c aṣ hab a o s-cegitok mam hab hi o a 'e-wuad mam 'ab si je:ñ kut 'eda g Ho'ok 'Oks pi o ma:ck mo hascu wud kut 'ab o si je:jnad"

Naṣpi ṣa'i s-je:ñk g "oks. T hab o 'e-juñhim k 'am o 'i s-ko:sim mt 'eda 'an 'i hugidan geguk c pi o ṣa'i hiwigĭ maṣ o koi. T 'am o 'i si pi 'e-nakog k

ran from there and was gone for a number of days. When he arrived up where Elder Brother was, by running, he saw a poor decrepit old man lying there. He told Elder Brother why they had sent him.

Elder Brother said: "Run back home, and perhaps I shall be there when you arrive." The young man thought to himself: "Where could you run to, old man?" Just as soon as he got back home he told them: "Your friend is lying down all exhausted. He didn't look as though he could do anything." Even as he was saying this, Elder Brother stood before them in the shape of a very young man. The *Si'ihe* was like that and could change himself to anybody.

It was told that if a person was to live a long time, he would see him as an old man, and one who would die soon would see him as a very young man. Then the people gathered together and heard that which he told them of his wisdom: "I have an idea, but it will be very hard work. Now you will have a big 'sing' here and a big dance and you will drink lots of sahuaro wine. You will sing for four days and nights. The *Ho'ok 'oks* will be on the go through all this time. During all this time some others will carry firewood to put at the mouth of the cave where the old woman lives. Still some others will make matted grass doors; they will place them at her home. During all this time the old lady will be on the go. You will make a cigarette with these ingredients, and you will pass it around, but you will remember that you must only pretend to smoke; the old lady will not know what it is, and

hahawa aṣ o ko:ṣk 'i gei. t 'eda o 'e-na:to g ki:j kut 'am ahawa aṣ o 'i ko:mk gahu o woi.

Ṣ 'am hab 'i 'i-ju: g 'o'odham maṣ hab ha-'a:g g Si'ihe. Ṣ gi'ikk taṣkaj c gi'ikk s-cuhugamk 'ab 'e-ñe'icud k heg 'oidam keihi. Ṣ 'eda ha'i 'am 'i 'e-nako k mu'i ku'agi momto k 'ab toa Ho'ok ki: 'ab. Ṣ ha'i 'am 'e'etpat 'ab 'ep to'ahim. Ṣ 'eda heg 'oidam meḍ g Ho'ok 'Oks.

Ṣ 'amhu a 'i he'es ṣ 'in 'i himcudahim k 'owick g keihindam c 'ab mamka g 'Oks. Ṣ 'ab si je:jen c gnhu si 'i howickwup, naṣpi ṣa'i si je:jeñk. Ṣ 'eda g 'o'odham hab aṣ s-'e-junim maṣ 'ab je:n. Ṣ hia cum si ha-nako g 'Oks k aṣ hab a heg we:m aṣ 'i gewkohim. Ṣ 'hebai 'i ce:ka ṣ 'am 'i si s-ko:sim k aṣ cum s-himim 'am 'e-ki: wui mṣ 'am 'i pi hiwigĭ. Ṣ gnhu (hia) 'ep kekiwup c gmhu 'ep keihin. Ṣ 'am 'i si 'ai g ko:sig kumṣ ganhu aṣ ko:m c keihinacud. Ṣ 'eda hegam a'i ko:koi ṣa'i s-ha-'e:bid, kuṣ hekid o si pi 'e-nako k 'am o cum me: ṣ 'am hu 'aki c 'ed ha'i o dadhak g 'o'odham ṣ 'am o cum meḍad kuṣ o si ha-sijkĭ g 'e-ṣaṣawkud kuṣ 'am aṣ o si melinod g 'Oks, k gadhu 'u:hum 'ep o mel maṣ 'am 'e-ne'icud k aṣ heg 'am 'ep o keihi. Ṣ waik s-cuhug c waik taṣkaj ha'i 'e-keihi ṣ 'am 'i pi 'e-nako g 'em-nawoj k aṣ hahawa aṣ ko:ṣ, mṣ gnhu aṣ ko:mc himcudahim. Ṣ 'eda hab ahawa kaij g Si'ihe, "Mo heki hu a 'i s-'ape mamt o 'i bei g 'Oks k gahu o woi ceho c-ed." Ṣ 'am 'i ge 'e-we:mt k gmhu 'i bei. Ṣ 'am ha'i ko:m k gmhu si ju:ko woi.

Ṣ 'ab a hekaj 'i ku:pahi g ceho. Ṣ 'ab o hema kei g 'etpa k 'ab ahawa o 'i to'ahi g ku'agi k 'ab hema 'ep o kei g 'etpa" Ṣ hab juñhim k 'ia hu 'i

she will smoke avidly, because she likes to smoke very much. After doing this she will want to go to sleep, but those of you who are standing next to her will not permit her to sleep. When she can't help it any longer she will sleep and fall down. Her house will be finished by this time and she will be carried and laid in it."

The people did what the *Si'ihe* told them to do. Four days and four nights they sang and during all this they danced. Some of them got ready and gathered a lot of firewood at her house. Some made doors, and they also placed them there. During all this the old woman was on the go. Every once in a while the dancers passed a cigarette around, and they gave it to her. She took big puffs and she inhaled very vigorously because she liked it so much. The people only pretended to smoke. She tried very hard to keep up with them but with all this she became tired and sleepy. Sometime later when she became very sleepy she tried to go home, but they wouldn't let her. She would stand in the dancing line, and she would dance again. When sleepiness overcame her, they held her up and made her dance.

The only thing she feared was rattlesnakes, and whenever she couldn't endure her drowsiness she would try to run home, and yet she had to cross an arroyo in which some people would be sitting; so when she passed, they would shake their rattles and she would turn right back and she would be dancing again. Three nights and three days they had been dancing, when she couldn't endure any longer, so she slept and they

wu:ṣad. Ṣ 'ab kei g ku:ḍa k 'ab mehĭ. Ṣ m heg mehek heba'i ce:ka ṣ 'am ṣoak g 'Oks c hab kaij," ñ-mo:ms si g o 'i s-ñ-ho'ige'id k 'ia ñ-do'ipiad." Ṣ 'am 'i 'ai g mehĭ ṣ 'am 'u:gk si dad'edc ' 'am si komitp g ceho. Ṣ 'am hi a cum 'e-keiṣ g Si'ihe ṣ aṣ hab a heki hu 'am wu:ṣ g ku:bs k 'aṣ 'am him gnhu 'u:gk k 'e-wisagcudk aṣ ge s-ce:dagi.

Ṣ 'am hia 'i huhug g Ho'ok 'Oks ṣ aṣ hab a 'i:da (s-)ce:dagi wiṣag maṣ 'am 'e-na:to ba'ic 'i ha-kudut g 'o'odham. Naṣpi hi pi has ṣa'i 'elid mas hedai o gewickwua k o mua ṣ gnhu 'u:gk o da'ad ṣ hebai hema hejel o ṣa himad ṣ gahujed o 'i hudun k 'am o si gewickwua k 'am o hukṣ k gmhu o da:.

Ṣ 'am 'ep cum 'i 'e-nako g 'o'odham maṣ o mea 'i:da wiṣag. Ṣ hemakojc 'im has 'am ha'icu cum 'a'aga maṣ has masma o mea. Ṣ 'am hab hia cum 'e-wua g ha'icu ha-ma:cig c aṣ pi 'am hu hab 'e-wua g ha-'a:ga.

Ṣ 'am 'i na:nko cum wuihim c 'am 'i pi 'e-nakok 'am hab ahawa 'i 'ep cei maṣ hig 'ep o cu'ij g Si'ihe maṣ has 'i masma o mea g wisag maṣ 'am ha-hugiokahim. Ṣ 'am ab 'i ha-'a:gid maṣ 'am o 'i 'e-nako g si s-haha'atadkam g gi'ikk si ge'eged hab o ha-ju: g haha'a. Ba'ic 'i ge'eged maṣpi hebai ha'i haha'aṣ hab ha-wua. Ṣ 'an ge ṣakal o ha-dadṣ 'idam haha'a. Kg ha-ci:cin 'im hab wakolim tagio o ha-'u'ul naṣpi 'ab 'amjed 'i huhuduk g wisag 'im hab ju:bin ta:gio dad'e.

Ṣ 'am hab a weho 'i 'e-ju: g s-haha'atadkam 'am ha'i si ge'eged haha'at. Ṣ 'eda hab kaij g Si'ihe

carried her and pushed her along.

Then the *Si'ihe* said: "It is time that you carry and place the old lady in the cave." A whole bunch helped each other and took her. Some carried her, and they put her in the farthest corner. They would put one of these doors, then from there they would place firewood, and then they would put another door. They did this until they reached the entrance of the cave with their doors and piles. Then they set fire to it all; it burned and burned for some time; then the old lady cried and said: "My grandchildren! Be kind to me and save me!" When the fire reached her she jumped up and down, and she cracked the top of the cave. The *Si'ihe* tried immediately to step on the crack, but a wisp of smoke had already escaped, and it became a blue hawk.

Right there the *Ho'ok 'oks* was done away with; but this hawk that was formed was bothering them far more than she had done. Because he didn't care whom he beat down and killed; and when he was flying high above, he would swoop down and beat down anyone that was walking along; then he would grab him or claw him, then fly away with him.

Once again, the people planned to kill this hawk. One at a time, certain individuals would tell their plan of how to kill this hawk. Then plans were worked out, but it didn't turn out the way they wanted it. They tried everything, but they couldn't find any way by which they could kill the hawk. So they again said they would ask the *Si'ihe* how they could kill the hawk which

maṣ 'an hema o 'i ga:ghi g 'uwĭ maṣ o s-ke:kajk k aṣ ha-ba'ic o kei 'idam haha'a. Ṣ 'am hu a 'i he'es ṣ 'an hu dad'e g wisag ha-da:m.

Ṣ hegam 'i 'e-wuwhas g haha'a k 'an ge ṣakal 'e-da:dṣ 'im ju:bin ta:gio wui 'e-cincudk. Ṣ 'am ha-ba'ic kekiwua g 'uwĭ. Ṣ hab ha'icu juñok gmhu 'a'ai melto g 'o'odham. Ṣ 'an dad'ehim g wisag c 'ab ahawa si s-wewkim 'i huduñ k gan cum si gewickwua g 'uwĭ ṣ 'eda 'e-na:tokc ṣ 'am aṣ hugid 'an wu:ṣañ k 'am hema ha-eda gei hegam si s-wegima s-toñ haha'a. S 'am ahawa si s-wehom huhug g doakagaj hegai 'ali maṣ wuḍ aṣ ṣoñgiwul c 'am 'e-na:to.

S aṣ hab a haṣ 'e-ju: g waipo'ogel maṣ 'e-ba'agc 'i'ok g wa:gaj g 'uwi?

Maṣ aṣ 'i ñei g 'uwĭ g 'o'odham maṣ 'e-ba'agc k 'aṣ ganhu me: 'u:hum k gdhu ha-'a:gid maṣ hascu has ' e-ju: ṣ 'am ge 'e-huhu'i g hemajkam k 'aṣ aṣ pi has 'e-doda.

Ṣ 'am da: 'i:da ba'ag ṣ hebai si 'u:gk g waw ṣ 'ab heg ṣa:gid ciwa. K 'aṣ 'amjed 'an ha-'oidk o dad'ed g 'o'odham c 'an o ah-kokdad. Ṣ hia cum mummu g mo:mbdam c aṣ pi 'e-nako maṣ o mea naspi ṣa'i ge'ej c 'aṣ 'ep ṣa'i s-gewk.

Ṣ 'amhu hebai s hahawa aṣ g 'uwĭ hema ha-'e:sid k 'aṣ gmhu 'i bei 'e-ki: wui. Ṣ him k hebai 'i ce:ka ṣ s-'e-mai maṣ ge maḍt g 'uwĭ, ṣ aṣ pi hekid ñeid naṣpi pi hekid weho s-'ap o 'i hud 'i:da 'uwĭ. Ṣ 'eda heg 'oidam 'an ha-oidc dad'edc 'an ha-kokda g hemajkam g ba'ag. Ṣ 'am 'ep 'e-'a'aga maṣ has hig masma o mea 'i:da ba'ag. Ṣ 'am 'i ha-do'ipia g Si'ihe k hab kaij, M 'ant 'a:ñi 'am o him k o ñei mans pi o mea 'i:da 'em-'e:bida. Kut him

was killing them off.

The best pottery makers were asked to make four big ollas. Bigger than any that they had ever made. They would put these ollas in a row. They would put their openings towards the north, because it was from that direction that the hawk came down. So the very best potters did what they were told and made the big ollas. The *Si'ihe* had told them that they should find the prettiest girl and place her in front of these ollas. It wasn't long before the hawk was flying over them. They took out the ollas and put them in a row towards the north. The girl stood in front of them. After they had done this, all the people ran away in different directions. After the hawk flew around for a while, it swooped down and tried to beat down the girl but she was watching out for him so he passed right by her and fell into one of the very red hot ollas. Right then and there the life of the child which was formed from a kick ball was really ended.

But what became of the youth who became an eagle after drinking the girl's potion? Just as she saw the young man turn into an eagle, the girl ran home and told the people what had happened. All the people ran out to that place, but they couldn't do anything.

This eagle flew away until he found a crack which was in the highest part of the mountains, and there he made his home. From there he would fly repeatedly over the people and kill them. The hunters tried to shoot him down, but they couldn't kill him, because he was big and very strong. One day, he stole a girl and took her

k he'ekia d o 'i task t ga hab si'al ta:gio g s-wepegi cewagi 'ab o ṣa'i wuwha mt 'am o 'i s-mai matki ñ-mea g ba'ag t aṣ hab a g ṣ-to:ta cewagĭ 'ab o ṣa' 'i wuwha nt 'am o 'i s-mai mant 'a:ñi mea."

Ṣ 'am hi: g Si'ihe k 'ab 'i 'ai g do'ag k 'ab cum ṣa'i ñeñeid ṣ gahu 'u:gk hia s-masma 'ab cehog mạs heg 'eda 'ab ki: g ba'ag ṣ àṣ hab a 'am wui ṣa'i pi 'apkog. Ṣ 'eda hia we:s ha'icu 'ab ab 'uliñ g Si'ihe ṣ 'am a hekaj 'i 'e-'amic mạs has o 'e-ju: .

Ṣ 'ab a hekaj wako kai 'ei waw ṣon 'ab. Ṣ koi aṣ'i he'es s 'ab wu:ṣ g wako k ga hekaj 'i cewelhim k 'i cewelhim k koi d sa'i mu'i taṣ ṣ gahu 'ai g ba'ag cehoga. Ṣ 'ab a hekaj ceṣ g Si'ihe heg 'oid g ha'icu wu:ṣdag k 'am ceṣajim k ceṣajim k gahu jiwa 'am hu 'i'maṣ pi 'ab hu ha'icug g ba'ag. Ṣ 'an daha g 'uwĭ g 'e-mạd we:m.

Ṣ 'am hab 'i 'a:gid maṣ hascu 'a:gk 'am jiwa. "Nt as hab hu'i o a cei matt 'am o 'i t-nako k heg 'ep o mea m-mad, kut hekaj pi in hu ha'icu o ṣa'i wi: 'ab g 'amjedkam 'i:da ba'ag mo ha-hugiokahim g 'o'odham." Ṣ 'am 'i s-ho:ho'i g 'uwĭ k 'am 'i 'a:gid g Si'ihe mas hekid 'i jiwiadc ṣ cum 'e-gegosidc gmhu wo'iwup c kokṣo maṣ gaswua . Ṣ we:maj kokṣo g 'alidaj . Ṣ 'am hab 'i kaij g Si'ihe, "Mat 'am o 'i koi nt 'an o hikumi'a g ha-kukswo t 'am o a koi".

Ṣ hahawa aṣ cum ka: ṣ ha'icu hab a'i kaijim maṣ g si s-gewk hewel 'ab meḍ. Ṣ hab kaij g 'uwĭ "Ḍ o hegai kc 'ab kaidkhim."

Ṣ 'eḍa gamhu d aṣ 'i hemajkam ha-ko'idag. Ha'i as heki hu 'i jejwa k ha'i hia koi jejwa k aṣ

up to his cave.

Some time passed. They found out that this girl bore a child, but no one ever saw it because she would never come down. During all this time the eagle flew around over them and killed.

They again talked among themselves and discussed what they should do to this eagle. Again the Elder Brother saved them; he said: "I will go myself and see if I can't kill this thing that you are afraid of. Some days will pass, and if from the east red clouds appear, you will know that the eagle has killed me; but if white clouds appear you will know that I have killed the eagle."

Then Elder Brother went, and when he reached the foot of the mountain he looked high up above and saw the cave in which this eagle lived, but it was hard to get to that cave. However Elder Brother knew about everything, and right away he knew what to do.

He planted a gourd seed at the foot of the cliff. And in a short time the gourd grew, and it began to grow and grow, and before many days it reached the eagle's cave. Right away Elder Brother climbed up on this plant, and he climbed and climbed; and he got there about the time when the eagle wasn't home. There sat the woman with her child. He told her why he came: "But I will say that we will try to kill your child also so that there will be no offspring from the eagle who is killing the people." The woman agreed with this, and she told him that when the eagle came he slept right after eating, while she combed his hair. The child slept at the same time.

ha'i 'am aṣkia babniopo. Ṣ si 'e-wokij g Si'ihe k aṣ 'e-ce:dagi muwalc. Ṣ 'am da'ak gdhu si ha-weco wa: hegam hemajkam ha-ko'idag. Ṣ 'ab aṣ 'i cum wa: g ba'ag k aṣ gmhu 'a'ai ha'icu si hehwgid ṣ 'eda g 'alidaj aṣ cum ñei maṣ jiwa ṣ hab kaij, "Jiwa, jiwa." Ṣ hab a hekaj cei g ba'ag, "Nat 'ia hema jiwa, 'O'odham 'an hewgid." Ṣ hab cum cei g 'oksgaj maṣ hegam hab 'u:wi maṣ 'an wo'owop. Ṣ hab kaij g ba'ag, "K hascu 'a:gk hab kaij g 'ali, "jiwa, jiwa." Ṣ hab kaij g 'uwĭ, "B 'o aṣ kaij aṣ hemuc 'i ma:cok mat hab o cec'ed hegai. B 'o a cu'ig g 'ali 'am 'i ma:cijc mat o ñeo." Ṣ hab kaij g ba'ag, "N aṣ hab a g doakam 'o'odham cu:hug hewgid." Ṣ an ahawa 'a'ai memda k 'am si ' 'u:gk 'i ha u'ulhig g ko'i. Ṣ hema gdhu si ha-weco wo'o kc as heki hu 'i si jewa ṣ 'am si 'u:gk 'i bei g ba'ag ṣ 'am si da'iwuṣ g ce:dagi muwal. Ṣ 'im hab cum 'i gewickwuahi. Ṣ gahu 'u:gk ge ta:pan g waẇ ṣ heg 'eda ab wa: .

Ṣ 'am a weho hab 'i 'e-ju: g ba'ag k 'am 'i 'e-gegesto k amhu wo'iwua, ṣ 'an hugidan wo'iwua g 'alidaj. Ṣ gmhu gaswua g ho:nigaj. Ṣ koi ṣa'i he'es ṣa'i koi. Ṣ 'am aṣ 'i cum s-mai g Si'ihe maṣ 'am 'i si koi g ba'ag ṣ hahawa 'u:hum 'ep 'e-'o'o'dhamc. K aṣ 'an a hekaj si hikumi'o g ha-kukswo g ko:kṣdam. Ṣ heg 'am a hekaj 'i mu: 'ali ṣ 'eda g ba'ag cum pi mu: Ṣ 'in has si dad'e g honaj pi 'abhu ha-mo'o kc ṣ g 'a'an aṣ s-tohama ñeñ'e k gmhu 'a'ai himto. Ṣ 'eda 'am ahawa 'i mu: g ba'ag.

Ṣ 'eda g 'o'odham 'ia hu ñeid maṣ ga hab si'al ta:gio s-to:ta cewagĭ as komal hi: ṣ 'am 'i s-mai

Then Elder Brother said: "When he sleeps I will cut off their heads, and they will die."

Suddenly he heard something that sounded like a strong wind coming. The woman said that it was the eagle coming. As far as the eye could see, there were the remains of human beings lying around in the corners of the cave. Some were already rotten, and some weren't spoiled yet, and some still showed signs of life. Elder Brother shook himself very strongly and became a blue fly. And he flew and got under the dead bodies. Just as soon as the eagle came in, he sniffed in every direction while his child cried right away: "Came, came!"

Immediately the eagle said: "Has anybody come? I smell human meat." His old lady tried to say that it was the bodies of the dead people that were lying around. The eagle said: "Why is the child saying what he said?"

The woman said: "It's only that he has learned to say that word. That's how a child is when he is learning to talk."

The eagle said: "But I smell a live body."

Then he ran around and lifted up every one of the dead bodies. When he came to the one at the very bottom, the fly flew out from underneath. He tried to kill it. High above, was a crack in the rock and the fly went into that.

The eagle really did eat and sleep afterwards, and his child went to sleep by his side. His wife combed his hair. Before long he went to sleep. Just as soon as Elder Brother knew that the eagle was asleep, he turned back into a person. Right away he chopped off the heads of the sleeping

maṣ ha-kok'o g Si'ihe. Ṣ 'eda hegam (s)to:ta cewagĭ maṣ 'ab 'i wuwha aṣ wuḍ ba'ag 'a'an maṣ aṣ s-tohama ha'as 'i wu:ṣ 'in has si s-potnim gegṣe g ba'ag.

ones. The child died right away, but the eagle didn't die at once. He flew in every direction without his head, and his feathers flew whitely far away.

The people saw that, from the east, white clouds appeared, thin and flat. Then they knew that Elder Brother had won. The white clouds that came forth were just the eagle feathers that came out whitely when the eagle came thudding down.

Tony Celentano

O'odham Ha-ñeñei Songs of the Papago People

Danny Lopez

I wish to give thanks and gratitude to the O'odham people of today and my ancestors. I owe my life to the medicinemen who saved my life when I was a sickly child. They saved my life with their given powers and with the herbs from the earth. My mother and my father spent many sleepless nights with me as I lay ill before them. They had love, care, and hope. I never knew my paternal grandparents, as they died a very long time ago, but I love them just as much as I loved my maternal grandparents whom I knew for a short time. I thank all the people who gave me their knowledge about the culture of our people. I sat with many of these wise and knowledgable people as they told about the precious ways of the O'odham *through songs, orations, and conversations.*

As a young person I did not know much about my culture but I heard the calling when I was in my mid-thirties. Only then did I think and live like a O'odham. *Only then did I learn about the beautiful and unique ways of the* O'odham. *As with everything else in the life of a human being who is devoted to a cause, there are things you must give up. While others are out enjoying life, you must be about doing your work. You even have to face ridicule from the very people you are trying to work for. Every day as I go outside and give thanks, I look at white rain clouds, the mountain ranges, the trees and cactii, as I breathe the sacred air that gives me life, as I stand on the earth that I respect, as I see the little children playing, I know that it is all worth it. Every breath is all worth it.*

I want to share a few of the traditional songs of the O'odham. *Singing is only one of the many aspects of* O'odham *culture, but one of the most important. Songs are heard during the sleeping hours of gifted people. Songs are about many things, moods, ceremonies, or just a social occasion. Some of the songs are from many years ago and some are from people who are still living today.*

I'itoi Ñe'i

These songs are from the story which tells how I'itoi *killed the Eagleman who was bothering the people. (See* Ho'ok'oks, *p. 110) The first song is sung before the killing.*

Wañ do al I'itoi
Wañ do al I'itoi
Wa:siw cuca k ab o himena

After he kills the Eagleman and the Eagleman's son, I'itoi brings all the people Eagleman has killed back to life. He stands at the edge of the steep mountain and sings this song. Then he leads them down.

Wañ do al *I'itoi*
Wañ do al *I'itoi*
Wa:siw cu:ca k ab o hununa

I'itoi Songs

Little *I'itoi* I am
Little *I'itoi* I am
With these plants I place and I climb up.

Little *I'itoi* I am
Little *I'itoi* I am
With these plants I place and I climb down.

Gohimli Ñe'i

Al wa s-ko: magi hikiwigi ma:kai
Su:nañi s-e:muina
Kia t-nanamai hihi:hime
Do k al totosagi kia ñ-ab wiwihime

Al wa s-ko: magi bamahad ma:kai
Su:nañi s-hohoimuina
Kia t-weweco hihihime
Do k al mamatod kia ñ-ab wiwihime

Song for rain

Little grey woodpecker medicineman
The water he feared
To the heavens he flew
"This is the water-foam that is on my tail," he said

Little grey frog medicineman
The water he liked
Beneath the water he went
"This is the water-moss that is on me," he said

Duajida Ñe'i

Al wa s-cucuige komkicud makaigam
Al wa s-cucuige komkicud makaigam
Jeweñe sikol bijmina
Am sikol bijmina
Am ñeida
E:na g mumkinage s-ha:sigam o cucuigam.

Curing Song

Little dark turtle medicine man
Little dark turtle medicine man
The earth is turning around.
There it is turning around
See there.
In there the sickness is difficultly there.

Celkona Ñe'i

Kums ia woiwa k wa:sañ wo:pohi
Kums ia woiwa k wa:sañ je:weñ huninan wo:pohi
Kums heg mumui huhun yuhug k wa:san wo:pohi

Corn Song

We ran to here, and we ran around over there.
We ran to here and we ran there to the edge of the world.
We took much corn and we ran over there.

A Papago Song

recorded and translated by Alice Listo

'I:da ñe'i 'at g ñ-ba:b 'am ce:c kc'am nato am ñ-je'es wehecid. Mo 'eda gmhu 'oimed mo am 'e-himcud g ge'e egiadag. Kut hab t-ma: 'a:cim 'e-mo:ms.

Kiho Do'ak

Kiho wa: To:wa:, Kihowa: To:wa:
gam hui me:k amo wa:wa:nim
Kuns iya ka:c waño pi kokosim
Kuns amoi meliwa: Kuns amoi meliwa
K we:mac am si sikola bijimi

Kiho wa: To:wa:, kihowa: To:wa:
gam hui mek amo wa: wainim
Kuns iya ka:c waño pi kokosim
Kuns amoi meliwa: Kuns amoi meliwa:
K we:mac am si sikola bijimi

Kuns amoi meliwa:
Kuns amoi meliwa:
K we:mac am si sikola bijimi

This song was dreamed up by my grandfather for my uncle who was overseas during World War II at the time. He handed it down to each one of us, his granddaughters.

Quijotoa Mountain

Quijotoa Mountain, Quijotoa Mountain,
There you stretch out,
And here I am not being able to sleep.
I wish I could go around there so I could dance.

Quijotoa Mountain, Quijotoa Mountain,
There you stretch out,
And here I am not being able to sleep.
I wish I could go around there so I could dance.

I wish I could go around there,
I wish I could go around there,
So I could dance.

Frank Lopez and the Papago Origin Story

FRANK LOPEZ is a Papago Indian makai *or "medicine man" who lives in the village of Sil Nakya ("Saddle Hanging") on the Papago Indian Reservation in southern Arizona. In the early part of summer, 1972, he was invited by administrators of Tucson's Arizona-Sonora Desert Museum, as he had been once before, to supervise the creation of a drypainting traditionally used in the Papago windway curing ceremony. This drypainting, whose function is similar to that of drypaintings among Navajo Indians, continues to be displayed inside the replica of a brush house on the museum grounds.*

It was my privilege to be present at the time Mr. Lopez and his three Papago co-workers fashioned the drypainting on the floor of the house. When they concluded, I asked him to tell the legend of the drypainting and, by extension, of the windway ceremony of which it is an integral part. He willingly did so, but in very cursory fashion. He explained that to tell the whole story would require a full night. After a short discussion, we agreed I would visit him at Sil Nakya with a tape recorder and that he would tell the entire legend.

I arrived at Sil Nakya a week or two later to discover Mr. Lopez had changed his mind about recording the story. He said it would be too dangerous for me and for everyone else. He wanted to know, however, if he could orate a substitute legend. I suggested the Papago origin story — which requires four nights for its complete telling — and he consented at once. That night, and for two other nights and one day over the next few weeks, mine was the finger on the tape recorder button while Mr. Lopez, with Papago Indian Lorentine Noceo present as interpreter and intermediary, rendered a lengthy version of the Papago equivalent of the Book of Genesis. It is an oral tradition whose beginnings are lost behind the veils of prehistory.

Being present during the telling of the origin story is among the most unforgettable experiences of my life.

The speeches and the few songs were very highly ritualized, and when Mr. Lopez began to speak he did so without hesitation. There were no ellipses, stutters, stammers, or unnecessary repetitions. Although he had neither heard nor recited the origin story for perhaps as many as forty years, his performance on this occasion was that of a virtuoso. He gazed into the space of his adobe house where we were sitting and recited as if he were reading from an unseen teleprompter. He spoke in an even, steady voice, and he gestured with his head and hands when the "script" called for such gestures. Although my Papago is poor and rarely could I understand what he was saying, I was never once bored during the several hours of the whole experience.

The finished taped product appears to be an excellent sample of formal Papago ritual oratory. The entire text has been transcribed in Papago by Papago linguist Albert Alvarez; it is being translated into English by another Papago linguist, Ofelia Zepeda. It is hoped eventually to publish the oration in both Papago and English and to illustrate it with photographs of clay figurines modeled for the purpose by Papago potter Laura Kermen.

The excerpt of Ms. Zepeda's translation published here is one selected by her for use in Sun Tracks, *and represents a very small part of the total work. It concerns vengeance warfare and some of the rituals and beliefs connected with warfare. Rich in Papago prose-poetry and in ethnographic information, it is a self-contained unit that typifies the quality of the complete text.*

My own role in this has been very minor. I was merely the expediter and technician with a tape recorder. I was, too, the awestruck listener, even as I am now the admiring reader.

Bernard L. Fontana
Field Representative
The University of Arizona

Lorentine Noceo, interpreter, and Frank Lopez, makai
Sil Nakya, August 12, 1970
B. L. Fontana

Frank Lopez
teller

'Al Wiapoi

Ñe: k 'eḍa 'am himk 'am hebai 'i cekak 'am 'i wu:ṣ hegai 'ali maḍsp heg wuḍ 'alidag mat 'am 'e-mu:kĭ mat g 'o:bĭ 'am mua g m hu mac 'am hekĭ hu 'am 'o'odhamag

Ñe: t- 'am 'i wu:ṣ hegai 'ali k wuḍ cioj 'am himk 'am 'i ge'eḍa tp 'am hu wuḍ 'i he'ekia 'i 'ahidag 'aha mo 'am hu 'i westmam wuḍ 'ahidag 'eḍa hab 'e-wua g hemajkam mañ 'am hu hekĭ hu 'am hab 'ep ṣa 'a:gahim maḍsp 'oyopojc ha'icu ga:g ha'icu mu'ajc hekaj 'e-gegusid 'am o hihi hegam hemajkam ge'egeḍ 'o'odham 'am wuḍ ki:kam 'amai 'angam 'amai 'an hab ki:dag hegai 'uwĭ maḍsp g kunaj 'am 'e-mu:kĭ

Ñe: k 'am ha-'o'oid hegai wiapoi 'am ha-'o'oidc mat 'am o hihimk hab 'a'aga mat 'e-taḍ 'ab kuṣṣad 'am he'es 'am o 'i siha hegai ceweḍ k 'a'ajid o 'i himk 'am o hebai o si-ha-'abam t-'am o 'i wu:saḍ ha'icu cu:wĭ to:bĭ matp hascu 'am o 'i wu:ṣ hebai g ge'e h'a'icu huawĭ

Ñe: k 'am o mua hegai hab o 'e-ju:k hab 'a'aga maṣ wuḍ gag'elida mat 'ab o 'al 'i 'e- ma:khi no 'i ha-ma:khi matp he'ekia wuḍ o 'i hemajkamk 'eḍa 'am o ha-wemajk hegai wiapoi maḍsp 'am 'i wu:ṣ hegai ṣ 'ab ha'icu hia 'al ma: hebai hema g to:bĭ o mŭa k 'ab o ma: 'o g cu:wĭ o mu'ak 'ab o ma: hab o cei 'am o himk ga hu o jiwa k 'ab o ma: g e'-je'e nt 'ab o a m-ñei

Ofelia Zepeda
translator

The Boy Who Gets Revenge

Ñe: after some time that child was born, the one who was the child of the one who was killed by the Apaches, over there where the Papagos used to live;

Ñe: the child was born a boy, and, as he grew up, when he was about ten years old, it was the way that the people — as I already said — that they would go out and walk around and look for something, kill it, and with that they would eat; the older men would go out, the ones who lived there at *'Angam*, and that is where the woman lived, the one whose husband was killed;

Ñe: the boy would go along with them [the hunters], and they would shake the dirt, and from both sides something would come out; sometimes, when they were lucky, they would take out a jackrabbit, a cottontail, whatever it was that came out, and sometimes it was something big like a deer;

Ñe: they would kill it, and they would do that thing that is called *"gagelida"* where they would give out the meat to however many people were there; and that boy would be with them, and they would give him some of whatever they caught; sometimes a cottontail rabbit was killed, and they would give it to him, or a jackrabbit, and they would kill it and

hudunk

Ñe: hab masma pṣ 'am hab wud a'i ha-ce'idag hegam 'o'odham

Ñe: k 'oi a 'am himk 'aḍsp 'am ba'ic 'am ṣa'i ge'eda tp 'am hema 'am hab 'ep kaij c 'am ha'icu 'ep mu'ak 'am 'ep 'ma:kk 'am hab 'agid c 'am hab a 'ep kaij o ma: g 'e-je'e n t 'ab o a ñei huḍunk

Ñe: hab kaij tp 'eḍa 'am hahawa ṣa cegĭto ha'icu 'am hab 'i kaij ga hu jiwaki mas hascu 'a:gk c hab cec'e 'idam 'o'odham hema ha'icu 'am o m'u'ak 'am o ñ-ma:k hab o cei gḍ hu o jiwak 'ab o ma: g 'e-je'e nt 'ab o a ñei hudunk

Ñe: hab cec'e s-hascu 'agc hab cec'e

Ñe: b a ṣ kaij hegai 'oi a 'am hab 'i kaij hegai je'ej mas hascu 'agc hab kaij 'ıdam 'o'odham c 'eḍ 'an a cem s-m-ma:c map has masmakaj wuḍ hejel wi'ikam cem pi 'am hu hab ṣa'i cu'ig mas hab o kaijid s-hemsi s-m-ho'ige'id c ha'icu 'am hab m- ma:k g ha'icu 'e- mu'a s-t-ho'ige'id k o kĭ 'eḍa hab a pṣ cu'ig n o kĭ 'am wuḍ a pṣ has 'elidadag

give it to him; and then they would say to him, "Go home, and when you get there give this to your mother, and we will see you there in the evening;"

Ñe: and that is what these people always said to him;

Ñe: and as time went on, and the boy got older, someone again said it; someone killed something and gave it to the boy and said to him, "Give this to your mother, and I'll see her in the evening;"

Ñe: the boy thought of it this time; and when he arrived home he said: "Why do they say that? These people, when they kill something and they give it to me, they tell me, 'When you arrive at home give it to your

Ñe: mother, and I'll see her in the evening.' See, that is what they always say;

Ñe: and why do they always say that?" that is what the boy said; and so his mother told him why these people always said that to him: "They know why you are the 'only child,' but there is no reason for them to be saying these things; perhaps they feel sorry for you, and that is why they give you the things that they have killed; they feel sorry for us, and yet it is a feeling of reverence,"

Ñe: hab masma 'am hab kaij 'ab hahawa si 'i kak'e g 'e-je'e mas has 'e-ju hascu has 'e-ju: 'am hebai ṣ 'am hab hahawa 'a:gid mat hab masma hab 'e-ju: mac gamai hu ki: map 'eḍa kia wo'o koi 'an hu wuḍ hemajkam t- 'am 'e-mu:kĭ g m-'o:g b 'amjeḍ pi ha-'o:g 'am mua g 'o:bı g m-'o:g heg 'amjeḍ 'am hab cem cu'ig mat o s-m-ho'ige'idad g m- hajuñ ḍ 'o m- hajuñ 'idam pi 'am hu hab cem ṣa'i cu'ig mas hab o kaijid

Ñe: that is what she said; and then he seriously asked his mother what really happened to her a long time ago; and so the mother finally told him what happened: "Over there, where we used to live before you were a person yet, your father was killed, and from then on you have had no father; the 'Enemy Indian' killed your father, and from then on it is the way that your relatives should feel sorry for you; they are your relatives, and it should not be the way that they should be saying these things."

Ñe: matp 'am hab 'a:gid hegai je'ej hegai wiapoi mas has 'i masma hab 'e-ju: g 'o:gaj

Ñe: after the mother had told the boy what happened to his father,

Ñe: t- 'am a'i pi 'ap'et hegi 'i:bdaj cegıtodaj maḍsp 'am 'i ka: he'gai 'e-o:g mat has masma 'am 'e-mu:kı hegai 'o:gaj

Ñe: his heart felt very bad, from thinking of it, after he heard how his father was killed;

Ñe: k hab a 'e-ju: k 'am 'i ma:si 'am cem s-gegusidam t ṣ 'am 'i pi 'e-gegus hegai wiapoi k 'am wu:ṣañk 'an a pṣ 'i himhi hab masma m o 'am hab a 'e-wua mat hebai hema 'am o pi 'ap 'i t-ta:t t-hajuñ mu:kig o kayok 'am hab o ta:hadag mat hasko himk hebai 'am a pṣ o wo'okad mapt hab masma hab 'e-ju: hegai 'am a hekaj 'i pi 'am hu cegĭto k ha'icu s-'e-hugima su:dagĭ s-'e-'i'ima si'alim 'am wu:ṣank ha'ap hi: 'am a ha'ap 'e:p ju:pin wui 'am hebai ke:k g ho'idkam 'eḍa 'ab hahawa ps 'al ju: g taṣ k ha'ap 'am 'e:keg t ṣ 'am himk 'am wo'iwa 'e:kĭgo ṣ gḍ hu'i si wo'iwa kupal wo'iwa masma hab 'e-ju:kc mo hekĭ hu pi ha'icu 'eḍa 'am pi

Ñe: that is what happened; when it was morning they tried to feed him, but he would not eat, and then he went outside and just sort of walked around, the way one does when one does not feel right, perhaps when one hears of a relative dying and one feels like walking somewhere and lying down; this is what happened to the boy, and that is why he did not think of eating anything, of drinking any water; in the morning he went out and walked toward the north where the cactus was standing; then when the sun was a bit this way and made a shade, he walked over and lay in the shade; he lay down; he lay face down; and it

'eḍagĭ hegai je'ej 'am hahawa 'i 'oidahim 'am
'a'ahe k 'am ñeid matp hab 'e-ju:kc 'eḍa am
hab a 'ep cu'ig matp 'am a s-'amicud mo hascu
'am 'i ñeidacug c hab 'e-ju:kc

Ñe: k 'am a pṣ 'i ñeidok gm hu hi:

Ñe: k 'am hab cu'igkahim k 'am himk 'am 'i
da:m ju: 'atp ha'as 'am 'ep 'e:keg mo 'am hab
'e-wua mat 'im hab o 'i ju:k 'im hab o 'e:kegk
'am ha'ap 'ep bijimk 'am 'ep wo'iwa

Ñe: k 'am 'ep wo'okahim 'am hab a'i 'ep ju:kc

Ñe: k 'am himk 'im hab 'i ju: g taṣ 'im hab
ha'ap 'ep 'e:ka si'alig wui tp 'am ha'ap 'ep himk
'am 'ep wo'iwa t 'am himk 'im hu hud g taṣ t-
'am hahawa 'i wamigk 'am hahawa himk gḍ hu
jiwa 'e-ki: 'am t-'am 'ep cem ma: g ha'icu hugĭ
t-'am 'ep pi hu: 'e:p ṣu:dagĭ 'am cem wasib tṣ
'am 'i 'ep pi 'i: 'e:p

Ñe: k 'am hab 'e-juñhimk 'am 'i cem ñeidacugk
'ab hia 'i cem si s-ba:bagid hab 'elidc matp hab
masma hab 'e-'elid mat g bihugigkaj 'am hu has

happened that his mother was missing him, so
she followed him; she found him and saw the
way he was and was also that way; she understood what he was seeing and why he was
that way;

Ñe: after she saw him, she went back;

Ñe: after he was like that for a while, it
became noon, and the shade moved the way it
does in the afternoon — the shade will be this
way; and so he went around and lay down
again and that is the way he was;

Ñe: the sun went this way, and the shade was
on this side toward the dawn; and so he went
that way and lay down again;

Ñe: the sun went down, and he got up and
walked home; there he was given food again to
eat, but he didn't eat it again; they drew him
water, and he did not drink it again; and that
was the way he was behaving; they watched
after him and tried to make him slow down,
thinking that perhaps the hunger would do
something to him, or perhaps the thirst would;
and yet he knew what was going to happen
because he saw something;

Ñe: he went to sleep and when it was morning
he went out again, and again he walked to the
place where he lay down;

o 'e-ju: 'o g tonomdagkaj k 'eda 'am a s-'e-ma:c
mat has o 'e-ju: 'am a ñeid 'aḍsp ha'icu

Ñe: k 'am ko:ṣk 'am 'i ma:si t 'am 'ep wu:sañk
'am a heg wui 'ep hi: maḍsp 'am hebai wo'iwup

Ñe: k hab a masma ge taṣ heg 'oidc g 'e:keg
hab 'e-juñhimk 'am 'i 'ep huḍuñ g taṣ g m hu:
'ep himk ga hu 'ep jiwa 'e-ki: 'ab 'am hab a
masma 'am hab 'ep 'e-ju: k 'am 'ep pi hu:
ha'icu 'ep pi 'i: g su:dagĭ 'eda hegai maḍsp wuḍ
hu'ulij 'ab 'i cem si 'i ho'igedahun mat 'ab o si
'i s-ho'ige'idk ha'icu 'ab o a hu: 'ȯ g su:dagĭ 'ab
o a 'i: pi 'am hu ṣa'i ha-ñiok c a pṣ 'am hab 'i
masma 'am hab 'e-ju:kc 'idam 'im hu a pṣ
go'olko ha'icu 'am cegĭto pi 'ap 'am hu cegĭto
'eda 'am a s-'e-ma:c mat has o 'e-ju: heg hekaj
pi ṣa'i ta:tk 'i:da bihugig ṣu:dagĭ 'i'i

Ñe: 'am hab e'-juñhimk 'am wuḍ 'i waikk
taṣkaj 'am ha'icug 'am heg weco hegai
ho'idkam

Ñe: k 'aḍsp 'am has hahawa 'i cem 'i 'e-ta:t ṣ
hab a 'am 'i 'ep 'e-cegĭto m o cem hekid 'am
hab ma:s m o ha'icu 'am wuḍ hegai 'am 'i 'e-
'o'oid g gi'ikk taṣ 'am 'am huhugid hegai gi'ikk
taṣ

Ñe: and in the same way he followed the shade
all day; and he did it in the same way until the
sun went down; and then he walked and
arrived at his house;

Ñe: in the same way he did it again; again he
did not eat, and again he did not drink the
water; and the one who was his grandmother
prayed that he would show her some mercy
and eat something or drink some water, but he
did not say anything, and he remained the
same way; these people [his grandmother and
his mother] were thinking of something else;
they were thinking of something not in the
right way; and yet he knew what was going to
happen to him; and that was why he did not
feel this hunger or the need to drink water;

Ñe: and that is the way it was happening; and
for three days he was there under the cactus;

Ñe: and as he thought about it, it was so;
when something important was going on, it
should be followed for four days;

Ñe: madsp hab masma hab 'e-ju: 'am 'i 'am hugid huḍunk

Ñe: and there he ended on the fourth day;

Ñe: k 'am 'ep himk ga hu 'ep jiwa 'eḍa hegai hu'ulij 'am a ṣa has'cu'igam wuḍ 'oks koi s-'e-ma:c mat has masma 'am hekĭ hu o s-'amic mat hascu has o 'i 'e-ju: 'im hab 'i ha'ap k 'am a s-'amicud 'i:da hu'ulij ṣ 'ab hahawa pṣ 'i ṣo:bid 'i:da je'ej mapt 'am hig a pṣ o 'i dagĭto k pi 'am hu has o 'eliḍad

Ñe: and then he went again until he arrived at his home; and his grandmother, who seemed to be a certain kind of old lady, which was why she seemed to already understand what was going to happen in a while, this grandmother understood; and she told her daughter to just leave things as they were and not to think anything of it;

Ñe: t 'eḍa 'ep jıwa huḍunk 'ab 'a:gid hegai 'e-je'e mapt 'am hig ha'ịcu o 'i ñ-ga:gĭ hascu 'an 'i ha'icug 'iks mat 'an hu o 'i ha- wo'ok s-tuhak s-tuha wuḍ o 'iksk

Ñe: the boy came again in the evening; and he told his mother, "Look for something for me. Something, if there is any cloth, if there is any lying around, some white cloth."

Ñe: k 'eḍa hab cu'ig kc pi ha'icu 'an hu wuḍ hegai ṃ-'in hema 'in hab cu'igc 'in ha'icu 'an mu'ij k a pṣ hab a 'i:da 'oks 'am a s-ma:c matkĭ has o 'e-ju:

Ñe: and yet it was the way that there were not so many things as there are today, when there are many things; and yet this lady understood that this was going to happen;

Ñe: hekaj hekĭ hu 'e-natokc hekĭ hu na:toj hegai mac 'ab a 'ep hẹkaj 'abai ga hu m o 'ab ke:k g t-ki:da 'am wuḍ a 'ep hegai 'i:da t-cuḍagĭ mat hekĭ hu 'ep na:to 'am cu:dk s hab 'a:gid mo 'am ha'icug hegai c heg 'e:p hegai 'iks s-has cu'ig 'aha nat a pṣ hejel 'am na:to heg hekaj matp 'am a s-'e-ma:c m o has 'i-cu'ig c hegai 'a'an matp heg 'am 'ep ha-kak'e has cu'ig 'an hu hema 'i ha'icug ṣ 'am 'ep 'a:gid m o 'am a ha'icug 'e:p

Ñe: that is why she had already made the cloth, and also that thing that we have over there where our house is standing; there, that thing that is in the ashes; and she had already made them, and she told him that it was there, and also that the cloth was there; I don't know how it was, perhaps she made the cloth herself because she understood what was happening to the boy; and that feather which he also asked for, perhaps there was one around, and they told him that there was one there;

Ñe: k 'am 'i 'a:gid mapt 'in o ñ-cukuj m- 'i:na 'in si gahi ñ-wuihi 'an heg 'an hekaj 'ep o ñ-wu: hegai 'iks 'i:na ñ-mo'o 'an m o hab ep 'a'aga hekĭ hu maṣ ha'icu wuḍ gewṣpaḍag mat 'in hekaj o 'e-wu: 'e-mo'o 'anai

Ñe: and he told them [his grandmother and his mother] to darken him, here, across his eyes, and to tie him with the cloth, here, on his head, where they used to call it "*gewspadag*" when they tied the head, there;

Ñe: madsp hab masma hab kaij mat 'am hab o ju:

Ñe: that is the way he said it, and so they did it for him and finished it;

Ñe: k 'am hab 'ep juñid k na:to hab 'a:g mamt 'id 'im o ke: 'ima kuṣoj 'am hegai 'a'an

Ñe: and then he told them to put the feather there at the back of his head; and so they did it for him,

Ñe: k 'am hab 'ep juñ k hab 'ep 'a:g mamt 'am o hema ñ-'owicid

Ñe: and he also told them to make an "*uacid,*" a staff,

Ñe: k heg 'am a 'ep 'e-nako hegai 'oks 'am 'ep ma: hegai ḍ ge 'al wa:pk c 'ia hu 'al 'i hug m-'i:na 'aḍsp hab a masma 'am a pṣ 'ep na:to 'ab 'e-amicudaḍag 'amjed hegai 'oks k 'eḍa hab cu'ig 'e:p mañ 'am hekĭ hu 'am hab 'ep ṣa 'em-agid hegai cewagi ki maḍsp hebai 'k ke:k g cewagĭ ki: cem hekid'am 'e-hehemapad g hemajkam we:s huḍñig 'ab 'am o daḍk ge cuhug ha'icu o 'e-jeñgidad 'aḍs has cu'ig pi ha-icu 'an hu wuḍ hegai 'aḍṣp g wiw 'an 'adsp hig a ha'icug ṣ 'am a daḍha c pi ha'icu 'ab 'i je:ñ

Ñe: and so the old lady, as she could, gave him a *wa:pk'*," a reed; and it only ended up to about here — it was sort of short; and from her knowledge the old lady made this "*uacid*"; and yet, it was the way which I told you before, about that "cewagi ki:"; wherever it, the "cewagi ki:," is standing, there the people always gathered in the evening to talk; they would sit there in the nights and discuss things; I don't know how it was back then, if there was no tobacco or maybe there was, but they were sitting there not smoking;

Ñe: k 'aḍsp 'am he'es 'i hi: g s-cuhugam t ṣ 'am hahawa himk g d hu jiwa hegai wiapoi 'eḍa hab cu'ig hab a ma:s m-'ab g t-ki: da ṣa'i ki: k

Ñe: as the night got later the boy went and arrived there; and the house was like our house here, it was a grass house standing there; the

c 'am ke:k t ṣ 'ab hahawa p ṣ 'i wa: hegai wiapoi 'eḍa g n hu daha g hemajkam kc 'ab 'al wi is ki:jig t'ab 'ab hahawa p ṣ 'i dahiwa t ṣ 'ab 'i ñei g hemajkam ṣ hab cu'ig c 'in ge s-cuk m-'i:ma

boy went inside then; they were sitting over there, and there was some room left there by the door, so he sat down there; the people looked at him, the way he was with his black marks here;

Ñe: t ṣ 'in hu g hemajkam woho 'i 'aṣ 'ab 'i ñeidok hema hasko 'ab ñeñok c hab cec'e 'at has o 'e-ju: g 'o'odham k 'eḍa heg s-ma:c hegai maḍsp wuḍ je:ñ cekcjim s-ma:c m o has masma hab 'e-wua g 'o'odham tacui 'am 'i wu:ṣañk

Ñe: and here the people laughed at him as they looked at him; and all around they were speaking and saying, "What is this person up to?"; and yet this one knew, the one that is the "*:Je:n Cekcjim,*" the "Smoke Keeper"; he knew how the people did things when something came about;

Ñe: k 'am hab hahawa 'i kaij mamt 'am hig o a'i dagito ha'as hab o a kaijid mam 'an hab kaij nam woho s-ma:c g wiapo'ogel 'am 'atp a has cu'ig k cegıtoidaj k heg 'amjeḍ 'am hab 'e-ju: k pi woho pṣ 'am hab 'e-ju: mas 'am hab a pṣ s-'e-juñim kutt 'ab hahawa o s-mai hahawa mas has 'e-'elid

Ñe: and so he said: "Why don't you leave him alone and stop saying those things that you are saying, because you don't know this boy; there must be something on his mind, his thinking; and that is why he is like this; he wouldn't be doing this just to be doing it; then we'll find out what he thinks,"

Ñe: b 'aṣ ha-'a:g ṣ 'am hahawa 'i pi has-cei t ṣ hemako wi: g 'odham mam hab 'a'aga maṣ wuḍ ban ṣ ga hu hab daha c 'aṣ s-jupij hehhem 'ab 'i ñeñeid c 'am 'ep s-jupij hehhem t ṣ 'ab hahawa si toḍwink hab 'a:g b g a pṣ 'i da:kad m- 'añ hu a 'em-'a:gid matt 'am o a s-mai matp has o 'i cei matp a ha'icu hab 'i 'elid mat heg 'am hab o 'a:

Ñe: and that is what he said to them; and then everyone was quiet except for one person whom they called "Ban," Coyote, who was sitting over there and was laughing quietly; he would look at the boy and quietly laugh some more, until he [the Smoke Keeper] jerked him and said to him: "I told you to be quiet! I told all of you that we will find out what he wants to say, or what he is thinking about, and about what he will say____."

Ñe: b aṣ kaij t ṣ 'ab hahawa pi has-cei ṣ 'ab hahawa 'i 'a:gid c 'ab si 'i:mc matp has wuḍ 'i juñij hegai 'a:gid mapt 'oi 'am o t-'a:gĭ matp has 'i masma hab 'i 'eldk hab 'e-ju: map 'am hab cu'ig

Ñe: and that is what he [the Smoke Keeper] said; and everyone was quiet, not saying anything; and then he [the Smoke Keeper] said to the boy, called to him by a kinship term, whatever he was to the boy; he said to him, "Go ahead and tell us how it is that you thought to be like this the way you are____."

Ñe: b 'aṣ kaij 'am a ps 'i pi 'am hu has sa'i kaig c 'am a pṣ 'i daha

Ñe: that is what he said to him, but the boy did not say anything and just sat there;

Ñe: k 'am hu hebai tṣ hab 'i'e-ju: k 'ia hahawa pṣ 'i wu:ṣad hegai maḍsp 'am ab ma: hegai wa:pk t-'ab owicij k 'am hahawa 'i daihim k 'ab 'i ñu'ickwa g cu:ḍagĭ k 'ab kei tṣ 'ab 'i mei tṣ hab ju: k 'ab je:jenk 'i wo:kam g ḍ hu himc ceweḍo c hab 'ep masma mat hekid heg 'am hab o 'e-juñhid t-'ab o je:jenk g ḍ hu jumal o himc k pi 'ab hu a pṣ o ma: hegai himcud k 'in daha hegai t-'ab ma: hegai

Ñe: and after a while he moved this way, and then he pulled out that thing that was given to him, that *wa:pt'*, the reed that was his staff; then he scooted down and pushed the ashes toward himself, and he stood the hollow reed there; and it started to burn, and then he moved it this way, and he smoked it; and then he slid it along the ground, which is the way whenever this smoking happens — they pass it along low and will not just hand it to someone; he pushed it along to the one who was sitting next to him and gave it to him;

Ñe: t-hab ju:k 'ab 'ep je:j t-'am ba'ic 'ep

Ñe: and he did smoke from it, and he moved it along again;

Ñe: k hab juñk 'am himcud k 'ab 'i:m hahawa 'am hahawa s-mai m o has wuḍ ha-juñ 'eḍa hab masma hab 'a:g mañ 'am hu hekĭ hu 'am hab 'a:gahim matp has 'i masma 'am hab 'i kaij g hemajkam

Ñe: and this is the way it went as each moved it along and called him [the boy] by his kinship term, and in this way he knew how he was related to them;

Ñe: k 'am hab 'e-juñhimk 'am himk ga hu 'ai hegai 'o'odham mañ hab 'a:g 'ab ṣa 'u:gk 'i 'e-bek 'am 'i:m k 'aṣ hab kaij ṣ hab wuḍ a 'al ge'elij 'ab hahawa je:jenk ṣ woho 'i howckwa 'im hahawa ba'ic 'e:p 'am hab juñhimk ga hu 'e-nam hab ju: k 'am a pṣ kei

Ñe: it happened in the way he said, the way I have already mentioned; he [THE FIRE KEEPER] took it and lifted it up and called him by his kinship term; and he said that the boy was "*'ali ge'elij,*" and then he smoked — and he really sucked on it — and then he passed it on; and it went on this way, and it reached over there; and then it just stood there;

Ñe: k ga hu 'ep ñiok hegai 'o'odham ṣ hab kaij 'a kus 'ab hab hi 'ep o 'i himc 'e:p b g a pṣ da:kad b 'aṣ 'a:g hegai matp 'am wuḍ je:ñk cekkc

Ñe: over there that person [Coyote] was talking, and he said, "I thought he was going to send it this way?" "Just sit still and be quiet," says the man who was the "Smoke Keeper,"

Ñe: t 'oi a 'ia hab hahawa pṣ cei hegai k 'ab kei hegai hahampdog m o 'am hab cu'ig

Ñe: and that was what he said; and he started the oration,

Ñe: k 'am hab ce'ihimk g m hu ku:gĭ matp 'am hebai 'i hugkam 'am taṣo 'am 'i wu:ṣ 'am we:hejed 'amai madsp 'am koksa hihimc 'eḍa heg 'am ñeidacug hegai heg 'am 'oidcug 'am 'e-ma:sidahim ha'icu 'ab 'amjeḍ

Ñe: and he spoke, and he ended it there where it was appropriate; and it came out that from where the boy slept he saw things, and that these things were made clear to him, and he understood.

Ñe: k 'am 'i ku:gĭ t-'ab hahawa 'ep 'i:m hegai t-'ab 'amjed 'i 'ep hi: g 'i:mig k 'am himk ga hu 'ep 'ai k 'ab 'ep 'i:m k 'ab 'ep 'e-'al ge'el 'a: k 'eḍa heg hab kaidam wuḍ 'i:mig mat hema wuḍ o t-'al ge'elk 'o wuḍ o t-we:nagk g 'o:gaj kut 'a:cim wuḍ o ge'ecuk heg wuḍ o 'alidajk t-nawoj mat wuḍ o 'alik p t hab o cei ñ-'al ge'el

Ñe: and it was ended; and then he [the Smoke Keeper] called him [the boy] by his kinship term, and from there it started again with the calling of kinship terms; and it went, and it reached over there, and again the kinship term was called, again they said, "*'el-'al ge'el;*" this is the kind of kinship term used when someone is our "'*alge'elk,*" one whose father is our brother; we would be "*ge'ecuk,*" "the older ones," and he would be the son of our brother, and when he is a child we would say "*n-'al ge'el,*"

Ñe: maḍsp hab kaij c 'eḍa pi wuḍ we:ngaj hegai

Ñe: and that is what he [Smoke Keeper] was saying; and yet he was not his [the boy's father's] real brother,

Ñe: t-'ia hahawa 'ep bei hegai k 'ab 'ep mehi k 'am hab a 'ep ju:k 'am himcudk 'eḍa 'ia hu 'al 'i hug c ha'akai 'o'odham ha-nako hegai wa:pk c 'eḍ 'uack 'am himk ga hu 'ep 'e-nam

Ñe: and again he took it and lit it again; and again they started passing it around, and yet it was only this short, and yet there were many people there for this reed to reach; it went around again, and it reached everyone;

Ñe: t-'ia 'i 'ep wu:ṣad hema 'i:da (hahampaḍ) t-'am hab 'ep cei 'e:p 'am a gawul kaidam 'am hab 'ep cei

Ñe: again he started the oration; and again he said it, but he said it differently;

Ñe: k gm hu 'i 'ep ku:gĭ 'e:p t-ab ep 'i:m 'e:p ṣ 'am hab a'i kaidam 'ab 'i'ime hegai

Ñe: and in a while he ended it again; and again they called him by his kinship term; they called him by the same term again;

Ñe: hab 'e-juñhimk 'am hu 'i hebai mat 'am hab 'ep cei 'e:p k 'am hema 'i 'ep wu:ṣad ce'ihimk gm hu 'ep ku:gĭ k wuḍ 'i we:s hegai mat 'am o 'ahij gi'ikk

Ñe: and this is the way it went; and after a while he said it again; and again he started the oration; and again he ended it; and when he reached four times that was all of it;

Ñe: k 'am hab hahawa 'ep cei 'e:p 'am hahawa 'i pi ha-ma: hegai k 'am a'i gokko 'am 'al ha-ma: hegai je:jena

Ñe: and again he said it, but this time he did not give it to him, and he only gave this thing they were smoking to them twice;

Ñe: k 'am i' 'ahij hegai gi'ikk ñi'okĭ

Ñe: and from there he reached four orations;

Ñe: k 'am hahawa ha-'a:gid m o has 'e-ta:tk 'ab 'amjeḍ hegai mam 'ia hab cu'ig c 'ia hemaips 'ia hemajkam n-t ṣa b a 'am o 'em-'a:gĭ mañ has 'i masma hab 'elid ha'icu

Ñe: he [the boy] then told them how he was feeling that these people were gathered here: "I will tell you what I think of things," then

Ñe: k 'am hahawa 'i 'a:gahi mat has 'i masma hab 'i 'e-ta:t 'ab 'amjeḍ hegai ñ-'o:g mat hab masma 'am mua 'idam mañ heg ha-wui 'am hab ju:kc g ñ-cegĭtodag mant 'ab o wa: hegai hab 'i ñ-tattam mamt 'ab o'i ñ-we:mt 'am o ñ-da:m cekĭ hegai ñ-'o:g mu:kig hemu hab a'i masma mant 'am o 'e-ma: g westmam taṣ mamt heg oidam 'am o 'i 'e-nakok 'ab o 'i 'e-wi:nkc 'ab ha'icu 'ab s-winam o 'i ju: 'e-ṣuṣk 'e-ga:t matp hascu 'an 'i ha'icug e-ṣonjk (kawo)

Ñe: he started telling them how it was that he came to feel this way: "My father and how he died, how he was killed by them, it is toward them that my thoughts are directed; that is why I should be wearing this; and so I felt that you should help me get revenge for my father's death; right now, it will be the way right now that I shall give you ten days in which you will get your things ready, in which you will get ready; you will strengthen things; you will fix, tighten up your shoes, your bow, your club, whatever is there;

Ñe: hab masma 'am 'i ha-'a:gid ṣ 'eḍa s-'e-ma:c c ñiok c 'eḍa wuḍ a pṣ 'ali

Ñe: this is the way he told them; he spoke very knowledgeably; and yet he was just a child;

Ñe: k 'ab hahawa ñio hegai maḍsp wuḍ ha-kownalig c 'am hab g cewed cekc hab masma 'am hab kaij mam 'idañ 'am ka: g wiapo'ogel 'am hab kaidam 'am ñiok s-'ap 'am hab kaij s-ge'ehog ha'icu 'am 'a:g 'ab 'amjeḍ mañ hab hu'i cem 'em-'elid mam 'ia hab cu'ig c 'ia ha'icug s-ge'ehokam hemajkam t hema hu hab o 'i cu'ig 'am ta:gio mat heg 'am o s-ma:ckad 'i:da has 'am 'i cu'idaj m-'am hab 'a:gas pi has cu'ig 'am g o 'i 'e-nakogk 'am 'i we:mt hegai heg hekaj m o hab cu'ig map 'am a s- ma:c mat a has 'i

Ñe: and then the one who was the leader, "the one who kept the smoke," spoke like this: "Right now you listen to the young boy and the way he spoke; he spoke very properly; he spoke of things as if he were an adult; sometimes I have felt or thought that, as you are all the adult people, that perhaps one of you would like to be like the boy, that you should know what the boy was talking about; there is nothing to it, so you all get ready and help him, because it is so that you know how

masma hab 'e-ju: hegai 'o:gaj m o kĭ 'idañ heg 'am cegĭto c 'amjeḍ 'am 'i wu:ṣad 'i:da 'e-tacui pi has cu'ig m o a s-'ap'e

it was, that thing that happened to his father, which is what he is thinking about now; and it is from that that he has let out this want; there is nothing to it, and it is all right;

Ñe: t gn hu hahawa 'i 'ep 'imc g 'i:mig no pi hekĭ hu hab 'ep ma:s mat hema ha'icu 'am o 'a:gk 'am o 'i ku:gı t-'ab o 'i:m hema 'e:p 'am a pṣ 'i cegĭto g 'i:mig heg 'amjeḍ m o cem hekid 'ab 'e-'i:m we:s huḍñig matp 'am 'e-hehemapad c 'am 'e-jeñgid ha'icu 'ab 'e-'i:m 'am hab s-'e-ma:c

Ñe: then, over there, the "*'i:mig*" went around again, because long ago it was that way, that when one spoke, when one finished, someone would call him by his kinship term; and they remember the "*'i:mig*" when they call each other by their kinship terms every evening; when they gather to talk about things, they would call each other by the kinship term, and in that way they would all know each other;

Ñe: t a woho 'am hab 'e-ju: k 'eḍa hekĭ hu s-ma:c hegai hu'ulij matkı has o 'e-ju: g ha-wiapoiga

Ñe: and they did what they were supposed to do, and already the grandmother of the boy knew what their young boy was going to do;

Ñe: t-'am himk 'am 'i ha'asa t-'am himk ga hu jiwa 'e-ki: 'ab 'am hahawa 'i 'e-wakonk k 'am 'e-kegcunk

Ñe: after it was all over, the boy walked home; then he washed up and fixed himself up;

Ñe: k 'amjeḍ 'am 'i 'oi hegai tatṣ madsp ha'akia 'am ha-to'i westmam taṣ ṭ s 'am 'i 'oidk pi 'am hu ha'icug 'ab ṣa'i 'e-nakog hegai wiapoi mat 'am ha'icu k 'am o 'i 'e-nako 'e-kawoj 'e-ṣonjk 'e-ga:t s-wohom 'am a pṣ daha ṣ hab a hab 'e-wua matp 'am 'i huhuduk 'am hihhim c gḍ hu jijwup c 'am dahajc 'am ñiok ha'icu ha'icukaj 'ab 'i ha-gewkamahun hegam s-ge'egokam 'o'odham c 'eḍa 'aigo 'atp 'am hab cem cu'ig

Ñe: and from then on he started keeping track of those days; the number that he gave them; the ten days, he kept track of them; he did not try to get ready or prepare; he should have been preparing his gun, his club, his bow, but he just sat there; when the sun went down he would walk over and arrive there and sit there and talk about things which would strengthen the adult people; and yet it seemed that it

mat hema hab masma ha'icu 'ab o 'i 'a: 'ab 'amjeḍ

Ñe: 'am hab 'e-juñhimk 'am 'i 'ai hegai wuḍ 'i we:s mat 'am o 'am hugid 'am o hugio west-mam taṣ

Ñe: t-'am jiwa hegai mac hab 'a'aga maṣ wuḍ kommo'ol m o 'in a 'oimmed mat hekiḍ o ṣa ju: 'am hab kaij mant ab hia 'i himk 'ia jiwa ṣ hab a 'ia pṣ o 'em-'a:gĭ mant pi ṣa'i ñ-nako 'am a hia cem ñ-nakog heg 'ab ñ-hahapot hab ṣ hab 'id a'i 'ab pi ñ-nakog ṣu:ṣk 'am hab hia 'i cem ñ-juñhimk hahawa pṣ 'eda hugkam 'al 'i ha-na:to k 'im hab a pṣ wi'is no ha'akia hu kakio

Ñe: nt 'ia pṣ o 'em-'a:gı mantkĭ pi 'am hu o 'em-'oi ṣ hab a hab o a'i masma hab cei mant 'am o 'em-we:majk 'em-'a'alga ha-'amjeḍ c 'e:p 'idam s-ge'egokam hemajkam maṭ hema g ciñig o paḍt kumt 'am o ga:g ñ-mu:kig matp 'an hebai hema o wo'ok k 'am o bek 'am o cuhiwa k 'an o wua 'anai s-ho:tam o ke:ga g ciñij g 'am-'aliga

Ñe: b 'aṣ kaij 'am 'i 'ap'ecud m o 'am a s-'ap'e 'am 'a:gid mat 'am o himk 'im o 'i ju: g taṣ nt o hi mt 'am o 'i ñ-'oi

should have been the other way around, that someone should have been talking to him;

*Ñe:*and that is how things were going and that was all; and the ten days were almost over;

Ñe: there arrived that which we called *"kom'ol,"* "thousand legged worm," the one that usually walks around when it rains; and he said: "I walked over and arrived here to tell you all that I am not able to prepare; I tried to get my gun, my arrows ready, but it is my shoes that I could not get ready; I was working on it, and I only have half of them finished, but there is still more left to do because of all the legs I have;

Ñe: so I came to tell you that I won't be able to go with you, but I want to say that I will be with your children and also with the grown-ups; whenever one's mouth gets disfigured or ruined, you should look for my corpse; wherever one is lying, you should take it and grind it up and apply it; and the mouth of your child will get well very quickly."

Ñe: this is what he said; after the boy had acknowledged it, and said that it was all right, then they boy said: "When the sun goes and is over there in the afternoon, I will start walking, and you will follow me."

Ñe: k hab 'e-ju: k 'am 'i 'e-'ai 'am hahawa pṣ 'ep ñei maṣ 'am ke:k hegai ga:t 'u:s ga:t c g wogṣa 'am 'ep wo'o b a pṣ 'i si ṣu:ddagĭ hegai hahapot maḍsp heg 'am a pṣ 'ep na:to 'i:da hu'ulij

Ñe: then he saw that his gun was standing there and that his quiver was lying there also, and it was really full of arrows which his grandmother had made;

Ñe: t-'am hahawa 'i 'e-ma:ck 'e-na:tok hi: 'am himk 'am he'esko 'i himk 'ab nadwa 'ab ha-ñenḍa g hemajkam — 'eda hab 'e-ju:k 'an hahawa 'a'ai 'an 'i 'e-'a:gĭ maḍsp 'an 'i hemajkamag 'an a 'e-nakog 'e-na:to ha'i k 'ab 'i ha-we:mt ga hu 'am maḍsp 'ab hebai 'i nadwa k 'eḍa ha'icu hab wuḍ hegai nawju mac hab 'a'aga nawju 'ac s-heg hascu 'a:gk hab pi 'a:gid pi cegĭto has 'aḍsp cu'ig

Ñe: after he knew all of this, he got ready and left; after walking for a while, he turned, and there he waited for the people, and then it happened that everyone told each other that the people were to gather, and the ones that were able prepared and joined the rest; then they arrived over there where the boy was, and still there was this one who was a "nawju," the ceremonial clown that we call "nawju"; "Why didn't we tell him?" "I guess we forgot."

Ñe: k gamai hu a huḍñim g taṣ 'aḍsp 'am hahawa 'i s-ha-mai mat himto g (kidayho) m o hab 'a'aga mat hasko 'am o 'i wuwha ṣ hab wuḍ kidayho 'o:bĭ we:m o himkia do t ṣ 'am hahawa da'iwuṣ k 'am medk 'im hab gei 'akĭ c 'eḍ 'am melhimk 'am hebai hahawa 'i bei g haʼicu tatk ṣ hab ma:s mam 'am ñeid m o has ma:s ga:t g nawju ḍ 'ep wa:pai t ṣ 'am a pṣ ṣa has 'i ha-ju: k 'amjed hahawa ha-hu'i ts 'eda hud g tas 'ep ge 'al kampañ 'an culscug 'amjeḍ meḍk ṣ 'am hu hebai ṣ 'eḍa 'am a pṣ kia 'e-jeñgid hahawa pṣ ka: maṣ 'ab g kampañ kolghim ṣ hab hahawa kaij hegai ha-kownalig 'i: pen 'o kĭ s-heg 'e:p pi 'am hu 'a:gid ḍsp 'am hahawa 'i s-t-ma:ck

Ñe: the sun was going down over there and he [*nawju*] finally found out that everyone had left; the "*kidayho*," that is what it is called when people leave; a "*kidayho*" is when they go to the enemy; he [*nawju*] took off and started running, and he fell into a wash, and then he ran, and somewhere along the way he picked up something's root; you have seen what kind of gun a clown has; it was a cactus rib that he did something with; and from there he really started to chase the people, and he also had a bell tied to his hip; and as he was running, somewhere, the people were still meeting and discussing things; when they heard the bell clanging, the leader said: "I forgot that we didn't tell him; I guess he finally found out about us."

Ñe: 'ab meḍaj 'ab 'i dahiwa k hab masma dahiwa m o hab masma dahiwup g nawju si s-napal daha k 'ab ñiok hab a'i kaidam 'ab 'ep ñio m o hab cec'e g nawju mat 'ab o ñio mats hab a si 'i me: woho 'ant hig si 'i me:

Ñe: he [*nawju*] ran and sat down, and he sat down the way a clown sits down; he sat in a sprawled way and talked; and he talked the way a clown talks; when he talks, he was saying that he really ran: "Truly, I did really run."

Ñe: k 'am a ps 'i 'e-jeñgid t p heg 'am hab cu'ig no pi 'am hab 'e-wua hegai 'i:da (gidahu) mat 'am hebai o 'i dahiwa hab 'ep 'a'aga mat hebai 'am o 'i nadwa hab 'a'aga maṣ ha'icu wuḍ kajiwa b 'ac 'a'aga mat 'am o ha-keihinac g '-gagt kawpu g 'e-ṣonjk 'e-lalans matp hema hascu o 'i 'edgiḍad gn hu o da:k t-'am o ñei hema m o ñe'ed t-'am 'oidc 'am hab o juñhid hegai o ha-keihinacudad

Ñe: the people went on with the meeting; I suppose that was done there because it is usually done when there is a *'gidayho*, when they go on the warpath; whenever the people sit, or when they turn in their path, there is this thing that they call "*kajiwa*," this is what they call it when they dance or *keihin* for their guns; it is to strenghten their clubs, or the lances, or whatever they may have; way over there someone will be sitting, and he will sing; he will be singing, and whatever he sings about, they will dance it out.

Ñe: k 'am 'i 'ep cem 'al dahiwa hegai nawju hahawa pṣ 'i ju: g 'e-ga:t ṣ 'eḍa hab masma s-juhujjul ga hu 'ep s-'a'asi hegai 'o'odham mañ 'am hu hekĭ hu hab 'a:g ṣ hab 'ep 'a:gid beg a pṣ da:kad pi 'am hu o ṣa'i hehhemad

Ñe: the clown tried to sit down, then he pulled out his gun; and there was someone laughing at him very quietly over there; it was that person I already mentioned before; and again they told him: "Sit still and don't be laughing!"

Ñe: t-'am hahawa 'ep 'i s-ha-wohocudk 'ab hia 'ep daha

Ñe: then he believed them and so was just sitting there;

Ñe: k 'amjed 'am hab 'e-juñhimk 'e-ju:ñhimk k 'eḍa hema g 'o'odham 'am wuḍ a gawulko himdag 'oiddam 'o'odham 'am a ha'icu k 'ab 'ab 'ep hi s-'e-ma:c 'ab 'amjeḍ 'i:da mac hab

Ñe: and that is the way it went on and on; and yet there was a person there from a different area, from a different way of life; there was something that he was very good at, this

'a'aga maṣ wuḍ wiṣag namkam 'o'odham 'am hab 'i 'e-ta:t 'am ka:k g ha'icu 'a:gaj maḍsp 'am hab kaijc 'am ha-'a:gid 'ab 'e-'o:gbaḍ 'amjeḍ 'am hab 'i 'e-ta:t mant 'am o 'i we:mt

person who we call *"wisag mamkam 'o'odham,"* the person who is the Chicken Hawk Meeter; he said: "I felt, after I heard the thing that was talked about, what he said about his father, from that I felt that I should help."

Ñe: k 'eḍa hab 'e-ce:c maḍsp 'am hekid 'i 'e-ce:cenk hab 'e-ce:c maṣ wuḍ s-'o'oi wonomim hegai wiapoi

Ñe: and he [the boy] had named himself; whenever it is that they name themselves, he named himself *"s-'o'i wonamim,"* spotted hat;

Ñe: k 'am hab 'e-juñhimk 'am ha-cu:cca g mamakai no ḍsp pi 'am a mu'ij g mamakai 'am na:nko ha-juñhim 'idam haḍsp 'am ha-wui hab 'e-'elid

Ñe: and that is the way things went; they had the medicine men standing there, because there were many medicine men back then;

Ñe: k 'am wuḍ 'i we:s g s-cuhugam mat a ha-'a'ahe maḍsp 'ab hebai 'i 'ep daḍhaiwa

Ñe: most of the night had gone by when they reached the area where the enemy was; they were sure that the enemy was near by;

Ñe: k 'am s-ha-mai m o 'ab ha'icug 'ab hebai t-'am ha'i ha-cucca gi'ikk g wi:piop b ha-'a:g mamt 'am hig o hihimk 'ab o ha-ñei mas 'ab hu a ha'icug

Ñe: they appointed four boys and told them to go over and see if they were really there and what they were up to;

Ñe: t-'am hihimk ge cuhug 'ab 'oyopohimc 'ab s-ha-mai m o 'ab a ha'icug

Ñe: they walked throughout the night and walked around there and saw that they were really there;

Ñe: t-ab hihimk 'ia hu dada k 'am ha-'a:gid m o kĭ 'ab a ha'icug

Ñe: t-'am hahawa pṣ 'i 'e-na:to k 'ia hahawa

Ñe: and again they said the *hahampdog,* the

'ep cei hema hahampdog m o 'am hab 'ep 'a:gas m o 'am wuḍ si ha-'oijj hab cu'igam g hahampaḍokĭ m o 'am 'a:gas m o s-ta-kaihogim kaij g paḍ ṣoigakam hemu pi ha'icu 'ab o 'i d dadgecuḍk gm hu a pṣ o hugio hegai

oration; this was the last oration, the one that says we will do away with this thing that is bothering us;

Ñe: k 'am 'i ha-'a:gid mamt oi o 'e-na:to tt-'am o hihimk 'ab o 'oi 'i t-nonokĭ 'am 'u:pam

Ñe: and he [the boy] told them to get ready, and we will go so that we can turn back right away;

Ñe: k a woho 'am hihi k 'eḍa hegai wiṣag namkam wo:kam 'an a ṣo:ṣonḍ'an hegai wiapoi kaij noḍspi hab 'e-ta:tk mat 'am o si 'i we:mt

Ñe: and they did go, and then this man *Wisag Namkam*, he said that he really felt that he should help him [the boy];

Ñe: k a woho hab 'e-ju:k 'am hihimk ga hu dada 'ab ha-tods hahawa 'eḍa hu'i 'am a cem ha'icug hahawa 'i 'e-wu:sadk a pṣ 'an 'e-waw cem ṣa 'i ha-himc cem ṣa'i himc g 'o'oi wonomim

Ñe: and they did it and walked over and arrived over there and ambushed them; and there were many of them; then they gathered themselves up and started walking in a line, and *'O'oi Wonamim* had them walk a short way;

Ñe: t-heg 'am hahawa na:to hegai 'am hahawa 'e-wiṣagcudk 'am himk hab aṣ masma ha-gegewk ha-ge:gewk gḍ hu'i 'e-noḍgidk gi'ikko 'ab 'i 'e-noḍgid 'am 'i ha-hugio hegam maḍsp he'ekia 'ab wuḍ 'i

Ñe: then *Wisag Namkam* made himself into a Chicken Hawk and came over; and he went, and in this way he hit them and hit them over again; then he would turn over there, and four times he turned over there, and he finished them all off, however many there were;

Ñe: k 'amjeḍ 'ab hahawa 'i 'e-no:nogĭ 'ab 'u:pam k 'eḍa 'ia hu hekĭ hu s-ma:c hegai hu'ulij hab wuḍ hu:wĭ ha'a hegai hu'ulij hekĭ hu s-ma:c mat ha'icu has ju:

Ñe: from there they turned around and came home; and his grandmother already knew; she already knew what happened over there;

Ñe: k 'ia hu ñe'e hekĭ ju 'ia hu ñe'e 'eḍa a cem koi 'am hu 'e-'a:gid t-'im hu 'i (s-ke'iḍ) hegam maḍsp 'am 'i hemajkamag hab 'a:g mas hascu 'a:gc hab kaij cem koi ha'icu 'i s-ma:cc mat hab 'e-ju:k 'am hihi g hemajkam g m hu a pṣ 'i pi ṣa:muñ hekid 'io 'o t-a:gĭ ha'icu pt hab hahaw o kaijid

Ñe: and so she was singing over here; she was already singing, but no one had told them what had happened; and over here the people were getting mad at her; and they were saying: "Why are you singing when you don't know yet what happened to those people that went? Be quiet until they have told us what has happened, then you can sing."

Ñe: b 'aṣ 'i a:g 'in hu: t p 'eḍa 'am a s-ha-ma:c 'an has meḍaj has 'am e-juñhim 'ep pi ṣa'i 'a:gid hegai 'e-maḍ maḍsp wuḍ je'ej hegai wipoi ḍsp 'an hia pṣ a ñeid hab a masma 'aḍsp 'am hab a pṣ 'elid maḍsp hascu 'i 'a:gc hab 'e-wua c eḍa g ñ-maḍ 'im hu wa: pi 'ap'ekam c 'eḍ

Ñe: that is what they said to her, but yet she knew; and she was running around doing all kinds of things; and she did not even tell her daughter, the one who was the mother of the boy; she just watched her mother and thought: "Why is she doing this when my child is in danger?"

Ñe: k 'am hihimk 'aḍsp 'ab hebai 'amjeḍ hahawa 'i kei g 'o'odham 'amjeḍ 'ab hahawa 'i meḍk 'am hahawa ha-'a:gid mat hab 'e-ju:k 'am a ha'icu has ju:

Ñe: as they were walking back, somewhere along the way they appointed a person who ran and told all the people what had happened and what they had done;

Ñe: t-'ĭm hahawa 'i s-ta-had g hemajkam hema has 'am 'e-juñhim ha'icu wuḍ koḍḍogĭ ṣ heg 'i wu:s naḍsp hab pi s-ma:c hekĭ hu hema hascukaj 'i s-ñe'imk c 'am hekaj ñe'e

Ñe: the people rejoiced then; the people were doing all kinds of things, and there was this thing "*koddogi,*" a victory yell, that was let out, because they now knew what had happened; whatever one wanted to sing, he could then sing it;

Ñe: t-'eḍa hahawa dada hegam ṣ heg pi ha'icu hegai wiapoi ṣ 'ia hia 'i 'e-ce:m tp 'eḍa 'in hu a pṣ ha-'u'a hegai maḍsp hedai 'ab 'i ha-'u'a hegam maḍsp 'ab ha kok-da g 'o:bĭ m hu a pṣ hebai 'i ha- tu'akc

Ñe: then they arrived, and the boy was not with them after they all gathered; I guess whoever was bringing the ones who had killed the enemy had put them [the boy and *Wisag Namkam*] someplace else;

Ñe: k 'am 'i 'oi g gi'ikk taṣ tṣ 'am hab 'ep 'e-ju: hegai wulda maṣ wuḍ wulda

Ñe: k 'am 'i ku:gĭ 'e:p g wulda ṣ hab a pi 'am hu (ki: ḍ 'am) 'am 'i 'oidam hegai gi'ik taṣ 'am 'i da:m maḍsp 'am ku:gĭ k 'e-wulda 'amjeḍ 'am 'i 'ep s-he:kig gi'ik s-cuhugamaj hia 'aḍsp pi mamsijid na'aḍs 'am a pṣ he'es 'aḍsp 'am hab 'i cec'e 'am hab juñhim g li:mho maṣ ha'icu wuḍ li:mho c 'id 'e:p keihina 'am o himk gm hu he'es 'i s-cuhug k 'am o ha'asa k gm hu o ko:k k o 'i huḍ 'am hab 'ep o cel ṣ 'am hab 'i masma k gm hu 'ep o ahij g gi'ikk taṣ

Ñe: for four days they did that thing that is the "*wulda*," the victory celebration;

Ñe: after the *wulda* was over, from then on, the people were happy for four nights, but their celebration did not last until morning, because they would allow a certain amount of time to do the "*limho*," victory dance; that could only go into part of the night, and then they would stop and go to sleep; and when the evening came again, they would dance again until they reached four days;

Frank Lopez, Makai
Sil Nakya, August 12, 1970
B. L. Fontana

Tony Celentano

The Egg

as told by Ted Rios
recorded by Kathleen Sands

Ted Rios is a 64-year-old Papago from San Xavier. Born and raised on the reservation, he traveled widely in the West during World War II doing defense work. At the end of the war he returned to San Xavier where he still lives. Ted, who is tri-lingual, told this story in English to Professor Kathleen Sands of Arizona State University in the summer of 1974. It is, he says, one he likes to tell to his friends. Readers should note that this story is far less formal in its content, intent, and performance than the preceding one from Frank Lopez. Whereas Frank Lopez tells what amounts to a portion of the Papago "Bible," Ted Rios' story is far more secular and conversational.

Ted Rios
Kathleen Sands

Egg.
What was that egg?
Oh, yeah, yeah, yeah, that one.
It's a good one.
He's gone,
all of a sudden disappeared.

My uncle — my uncle on my mother's side —
and this man,
they grow up together, and they're like this all the time.
Some relation —
I don't know what kind of relation,
but it's a close relation,
So, you know,
he comes.
When he got —
when my uncle got in a wreck that night and got killed there,
he knew it already.
Nobody,
nobody said anything or nothing.
He just —
I don't know how, but —
just like I say, he knew.
I know when it happened, then, see,
I know he came.

Oh, it's in the '30s sometime.
It's quite a long time ago.
He lived down there in —
by Santa Rosa in this other village.
I think they call it Ack Chin.
There's another village beyond,
before you get to Santa Rosa.
There's another village where he lived.
I don't know what happened,
but then all of a sudden somebody told me he's gone already.
Yeah,
he died.
He's the one that —
he was the one that's been curing everybody around here.
He's a good one,
and then he know everything.
And about that egg—
I guess it's before he ever came to be big —
known all over — but was like anybody else.

He fools around like all these guys.
And it's when he was in Phoenix.
That's when they try to arrest him—
Policeman tried to arrest him for being drunk or something.
They didn't know he was a smart man.
They were yelling at him and saying, "What are you, a drunk, chief?" and all that.
But he told the policeman that he wasn't drunk,
but they want to put him in jail, I guess.
They were right in the office.
Everybody came in there and came in,
you know,
like they wanted to know what happened.
He was asking the time,

and this policeman pulled out his watch,
a good watch,
a gold watch,
and he said, "It's the time right here."
And the medicine man said, "Well, let me see that,"
and it's a good time-piece—
A good watch.

The medicine man said,
"No,
I don't think so," and knocked it down on the desk there,
bang it,
whatever.
Whoosh—
everything fall apart.
"Ah, you spoiled my watch! You shouldn't do that!"
You know,
that policeman got mad.
"Oh, its still going"
You know,
the hands — I guess the hands fell off.
"It'll be going," he told the policeman.
Like this,
took it back —
"See, it's going now. It stopped, but it's going."
And you know,
the policeman still has that watch.
Put it right back.
He was afraid the medicine man might do it again.
And then everybody started coming in, you know.
They were amused by him, you know.
They really want to find out something before they take him and lock him up.
Then finally,
I think he took that egg out,
and he said, "Well, I'll show you something, too."
Set that egg down,
slapped it on the counter, but it didn't break.
They said, "What's that?"
"It's an egg.
Look at it."
That egg started moving, you know,
walking around, running just like it's kind of steep, you know.
Just when it would come to the edge where it would fall over,
it never did.
It just went right around.
And, everybody was so excited about it.
"Oh, that egg's gonna fall!" "Yeah, it's gonna bust!" "Better watch it!"

Well,
everybody was watching while it's dancing around on the table or whatever,
counter—
that's when it's going to go off to the ground—
to grab it, you know.
While they're doing that,
he walked out the door,

walked down the street,
got away.
He's gone.
So he got out of it.
Somebody told me about it, you know.
I heard it so many times, you know.
He's the one that cured my dad when he got
witched down in Pima country.
I found out he was curing somebody down in
the village,
right over there.
He was there and I told him about it.
So we went over,
came over there,
and he's the one that got that thing out,
that thorn or whatever,
got it out.
Good man—
he's very honest.

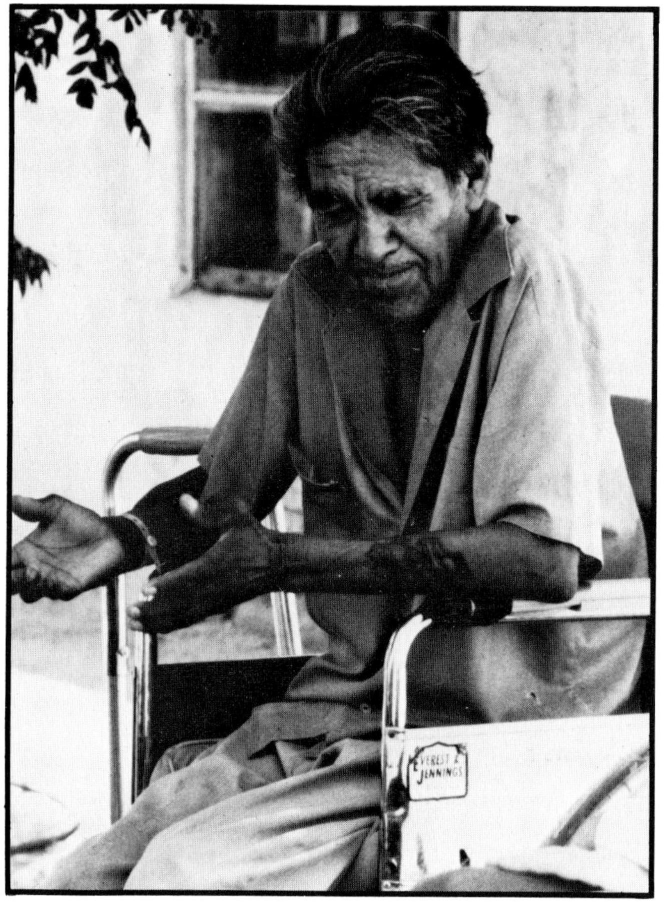

Ted Rios
Kathleen Sands

Children at Topowa

Tony Celentano A Portfolio

Juanita

Papago Woman

Children at Topawa

Boys and Chapel

Margaret

Grandfather

Ocean Power

Ruth Underhill

No one has written so eloquently of Papago life and literature as Ruth Murray Underhill, and she was honored for her writing by the Papago Tribe recently. The following is a chapter from her well-known work on Papago song, Singing For Power *(1938; rpt. Berkeley: Univ. of California Press, 1976). We include it not only for the beauty of its translations but also to indicate how much a part Papago literature is of Papago life.*

The Gulf of California is four days' journey from the Papago country, and for unknown generations the Indians have been going there to hew out some of the rocky brown substance from the shores where standing water has left it. The almost waterless journey traverses some of the most sinister country on the North American continent and the Papago name for the south is "the direction of suffering." But they have never shrunk from suffering. Instead, they have made it the cornerstone of their philosophy and the passport of dreams. The salt journey has seemed to them difficult enough and the sight of the ocean amazing enough to bring a man into contact with the supernatural.

They regard the whole ordeal as they regard war. It is an arduous duty undertaken for the sake of the kindred, and the reward is rain. The ocean, say the Papagos, their sympathetic magic marching for once with science, is the source of rain, which is brought by the ocean wind. But they go on to say that the wind will only blow if men have been to the ocean and given it gifts. And men must take back with them those white kernels which the "out-spread water" deposits on its shores and which resemble corn. In all the rituals, in fact, the salt is called "corn."

Every village, in the old days, made the journey and each had its ritual. Now there are only a few, but each of these few has an old man who is the hereditary leader. Leader and priest, in the Papago sense, are one, for the old man's chief duty is to recite the rituals and direct the ceremonies which will make the men "safe." He knows a special language which they will use on the journey, a language of roundabout phrases which the Papagos call "soft words." It would be dangerous for them to mention in bald terms the sun, the coyote, the horses, the drinking gourds, even the firewood. They will be too near the heart of power to venture such familiarity, so they learn to speak of the "shining traveler," the "burning-eyed comrade," the "friend," the "round object," and "the things piled up."

Every young man who is old enough volunteers for the journey. Once he has done so, he must go in four successive years — until the magic has been tamed. All his equipment must be new, for he cannot risk the danger that it might have come in contact with a pregnant woman or menstruant. He makes his two pairs of sandals, his net for carrying the salt (in recent days, his net saddlebags), his bridle, and his gourd water bottle.

Thus was my desire [begins a fragment of
an old ritual].
Then hastily I ate the food which my wife
had cooked.
Hastily I took my child in my arms.
"What is it?"
What has he learned that he is acting
thus?"
"The day has dawned when I must go."

The party sets out in single file, formerly on foot and now on horseback. But it has not occurred to anyone to take extra horses for carrying the salt. They load their riding horses and walk home. They ride in single file, with the leader ahead, and they do not step off the trail lest they injure the house of some animal and incur its anger. When they camp, they lie with their heads toward the sea, so that "its power can draw them on."

Camping, like all other steps of the journey, is a ceremonial act. There are three water holes in all that desert waste, where many a Spanish explorer has perished. Two must be reached on the first two nights, but no one drinks from them without permission. First they give the water a gift of eagle down and ask its help. Then they water their horses, fill their gourds, and sit in a circle. Each youth has his little pouch of corn meal, which he does not touch. The leader takes it from him, mixes the meal with a little water in his gourd, and hands it to him. The "brave" man drinks only the thin solution on top and pours the rest away. The man who turns his back so the others cannot see how much he drinks is scorned.

Now the leader takes his place in the center to recite the charm which controls the supernatural force about them and turns their hardship to power. Some phrases of this charm echo those of an ancient Aztec prayer to the rain gods. But the sonorous words of supplication for the dry earth are prefaced by a Papago scene, and from its realism one could almost draw the hut with its thatch, its center post, and the dried ashes outside. In these familiar surroundings a man has worked himself up to the emotional intensity of desiring a vision. Many a youth who knew that on a vision depended his career must have felt this half-sane restlessness that ended in frustration. The cure is tobacco smoke. Four puffs of it bring the smoker into the supernatural world, face to face with the rain god.

SALT RITUAL—PREPARATORY

(Anegam)

Food she cooked for me,
I did not eat.
Water she poured for me,
I did not drink.
Then thus to me she said:
"What is it?
You did not eat the food which I have
  cooked;
The water which I fetched you did not
  drink."
Then thus I said:
"It is a thing I feel."

I rose and across the bare spaces did go
  walking,
Did peep through the openings in the scrub,
Looking about me, seeking something.
Thus I went on and on.
Where there was a tree that suited me,
Beneath it prone and solitary I lay,
My forehead upon my folded arms I lay.

There was an ancient woman.
Some lore she had somehow learned
And quietly she went about telling it.
To me she spoke, telling it.
Then did I raise myself upon my hands;
I put them to my face and wiped away the
  dust,
I put them to my hair and shook out rub-
  bish.

I rose. I reached the shade before my house.
There did I try to sit: not like itself it
  seemed.
Then did I make myself small and squeeze
  through my narrow door.
On my bed I tried to lie: not like itself it
  seemed.
About me with my hand I felt,
About the withes that bound the walls I felt
Seeking my jointed reed [cigarette].

Then thus I did.
Within my hut I tried to feel about with my
  fingers.
At the base of my hut, in the dirt,
I tried to feel about with my fingers
Seeking my jointed reed.
I could not find it.
To the center of the house did I go crawling
  [the roof being low].
And the center post
Seemed a white prayer stick,
So like it was.
At its base did I go feeling in the dirt

Seeking my jointed reed.
I could not find it.

There did I seize my flat stick [for hoeing];
I leaned upon it.
I made myself small and squeezed out the
door.
Lo, I saw my ashes in many piles.
Already were they all hardened and all
cracked.
I sat down and with the hoe I went to
breaking them.
Among them, somehow, did I find my reed
joint.

Then did I scratch it.
Lo, there still tobacco lay.
There beside me then I saw
Near me, lying, a shaman ember charred.
Long ago had it grown moldy and full of
holes.
I took it up and four times hard did shake it.
Within, a spark burst out and brightly
burned.
Then the reed joint did I light and to my lips
I put it,
And somehow tried to move toward my
desire.

[*The speaker begins "throwing words."*]
In what direction shall I first breathe out?
To eastward did I breathe.
It was my reed smoke in white filaments
stretching.
I followed it and I went on and on.
Four times I stopped, and then I reached
The rain house standing in the east.
Wonderful things were done there.

All kinds of white clouds thatch it.
All kinds of rainbows form the binding
withes.
The winds upon its roof fourfold are tied.
Powerless was I there.
It was my reed smoke.
Therewith did I go untying them.
Quietly I peeped in.
Lo, there I saw
Him [the rain-maker], my guardian.
Yonder, far back in the house, facing away
from me he sat.
My reed smoke toward him did circling go.
Toward the door it caused him to turn his
eyes,
And set him there.

Then did I say:
"What will you do, my guardian?
Younder see!
The earth which you have spread thus
wretched seems.
The mountains which you placed erect now
crumbling stand.
The trees you planted have no leaves,
The birds you threw into the air
Wretchedly flit therein and do not sing.

The beasts that run upon the earth
At the tree roots go digging holes
And make no sound.
The wretched people
See nothing fit to eat."
Thus did I say.

Then did the bowels within him crack with pity.
"Verily, nephew, for so I name you,
Do you enter my house and do you tell me something?
The people are afraid, none dares to enter;
But you have entered and have told me,
And something indeed I will cause you to see."

"But let me reach my house, then let it happen."

Then in his breast he put his hand and brought forth seed:
White seed, blue seed, red seed, smooth seed.
Then did I fold it tight and grasp it and rush forth.
I saw the land did sloping lie.
Before I had gone far, the wind did follow and breathe upon me.
Then down at the foot of the east there moved the clouds
And from their breasts the lightning did go roaring.
Though the earth seemed very wide,
Straight across it fell the rain
And stabbed the north with its needles.
Straight across it fell the rain
And stabbed the south with its needles.
The flood channels, lying side by side,
Seemed many,
But the water from all directions went filling them to the brim.
The ditches, lying side by side,
Seemed many,
But the water along them went bubbling.
The magicians on the near-by mountains
Went rushing out, gathering themselves together;
The storm went on and on.
It reached the foot of the west, it turned and faced about.
It saw the earth spongy with moisture.

Thus beautifully did my desire end.
Thus perchance will you also feel, my kinsmen.

The Papagos have worked out a peculiar form of delivery for this speech. The peoples who vary their music by the use of different instruments have not explored the possibilities of the human voice alone. But the Papagos, whose instruments are the kitchen basket turned upside down for a drum or the drinking gourd sealed up with its seeds for a rattle, have utilized every change of tempo and of accent. While the speaker is approaching the vision, his sentences must be in a monotone moving toward the verb at the end, which is on a high note, tremendously accented. It is a style, like a tune, which is used for all introductions. But when the magic part of the speech is reached and the man is speaking to the god, he begins "throwing words." It is a panting, on one note, where each syllable stands out separate and accented, like the monotonous chugging of an engine. In all the "wise speeches," made on the salt journey, their magic part is pronounced in this way.

On the afternoon of the third day, they reach the third water hole, the last they will find. It is at the base of Mount Pinacate, famous in legend, from whose top they can see the ocean. The thirsty men do not touch the water until they have raced each other to the top of the mountain. There the desert people stand and look at "the outspread water." They stretch out their hands to gather in some of its power and they rub their bodies. Then they give to the mountain the eagle down they have brought:

Speeches like these, recited year after year by the old men, are the patterns for dreaming. The young man, exhausted with hunger and effort, awaits his vision with these pictures in his mind. He will see Coyote as surely as the monk of the Middle Ages saw the saint whom he had made his patron.

It is on the morning of the fourth day that the travelers reach the barren sands where the spring tides have left salty ponds. Even these have evaporated, leaving an expanse of saline crystals, "the ocean's corn." No matter how great their thirsty hurry, the men do not gather them immediately. The leader must plant in the salt field a stick topped with eagle down, speaking in friendly fashion: "We do not come to harm you; we come only to gather salt." Then the young men run four times around the salt bed, and at last they all fall to, to load the horses. They explain to the salt, as the Papago always does when helping himself to the fruits of the earth: "We take you because we need you. Be light now, do not weigh heavy, because we must carry you home to the women."

This is the practical part of the labor, but the magic part, which has brought the young men on this long journey, is still to come. When the salt is gathered, they walk into the sea, strewing corn meal as the ritual bade them, on the advancing waves.

To the desert people, this braving of the breakers has an element of horror. Old men, who made no great matter of death and starvation, have told me with pride how they walked in up to their necks. My statement, that I had swum gaily beyond the breakers in two oceans, was the height of unwisdom. They regarded it as a lie.

A man holds corn meal in his left hand and throws it on the waves with his right. If he has done any evil, or if his wife is "dangerous," the sea will not take his offering. But if it is accepted, perhaps then and there he may see a vision. A flight of white gulls may beckon him into the ocean depths, where he will learn wonders, or perhaps a strange sea coyote will come walking on the water and speak to him. But many wait for a further trial, and when they emerge from the water, they run for miles on the beach. Running is the well-known way for a youth to prove his strength and manhood, and running beside the waves is something like the vigil of the oldtime knight beside his armor. This is the most strange and sacred act of a Papago boy's life. Perhaps a cave in the rock opens, and he is asked in to learn the secrets of healing from the sea magician. Perhaps a flock of white cranes overhead calls him into the sky to race with them, or on the shore he sees a set of magic gambling sticks made from shells cast up by the sea.

The oration tells how the leader waits, lonely and tired, beside the campfire, until the last of the runners has come in. Then, long before dawn, the whole party starts back, for it must make each of the water holes for a night's camp. The neophytes are now in a sacred condition. They must not walk with the rest of the party, lest the power with which they have come in contact prove too strong for the others. They walk behind and they practice the ancient ceremonial taboo used by most Southwestern Indians: they do not touch their bodies with their hands. Each has a slender stick given him by the leader with which he may rub his dry, sun-bitten skin. They must never look back toward the ocean, for then it might call them. Some villages forbid them to speak at all. There are tales of men who have fallen into a pit and, because they must not cry out for help, were left behind to die.

But when they reach the home village, they make a triumphant entry. The old women help themselves to salt, and the boys swing slabs of wood on long strings to simulate the sound of rain. That night, everyone gathers in the council house. The neophytes sit to one side with the trophies they have brought from the seashore — white shells or scraps of seaweed, "ocean clouds," which will act as magic charms for the rest of their lives. In the center is the basket of "sea corn." Each pilgrim has contributed to it some of his precious load, for

"This did I do on your behalf,
All you my kinsmen."

To, it is my own offering,
Which I have carefully made and finished.
I have come bringing it and thus I do:
I offer it.

See it and do for me increasingly.
Grant powers to me:
Great speed in running,
Great industry,
Great skill in hunting.

Grant powers to me:
Great lightness in running,
Great industry.

I will take them,
I will journey back
And I will attain my desire.
Not hard will it be to turn homeward,
Not hard to reach my land.

With the power from the ocean already upon them, they go back for their last drink in twenty-four hours. From here on, it is a race of endurance to get the salt and to return. They ride that night as far as human beings may, but they do not sleep until the leader has recited to them the supernatural experience of the morrow. They are to enter the "outspread water," they who perhaps have never seen water more than three feet deep — never except in rain streams which dry in a few hours. They are to step into the appalling element and bring out a blessing.

SALT RITUAL IN CAMP—THE MARKING

(Anegam)

Thus was fulfilled my desire.

Toward the west a black road did lie.
Then upon it did I tread and follow it.
Four times did I camp and then did reach the
wide-spreading water.

Already had arrived the woolly comrade
[Coyote];
Around us four times did he go circling;
And lo, already the white clay was mixed for
me,
The owl feather for painting laid upon it.

To him did Coyote pull the young man and
set him there.
With the clay across the heart he marked
him.
Back he turned and on the right shoulder
marked him.
In front he crossed and on the left shoulder
marked him.
Back he turned and on the back he marked
him.
Then well he purified him.

There was corn meal, made from flat-headed
corn.
I sprinkled a handful and again a handful,
As I ran into the wide-spreading ocean.
Though dangerously toward me it crashed
I did not fear,
But I walked near and cast the sacred meal.

There followed another wave.
I did not fear.
I walked nearer and cast the sacred meal.
Though dangerously it roared, combing and
falling,
I did not fear.

I cast the sacred meal.

There followed a fourth wave.
Dangerously it roared;
It foamed, it rolled over me, it broke behind
me,
But firm I stood and sought what I might
see.

Then did I come forth
And along the beach begin to run
And somewhere there did come upon
Coyote, our woolly comrade,
Our comrade with burning eyes.

Dangerously he turned upon me,
But I ran toward him and did not fear.
Nearer I came and cast the sacred meal.
Then did he run, did run and run
Till at last he only walked.
And I did follow. And did come upon him.
In a circle did I run and come behind him.
I did not fear, but cast the sacred meal.

Again he dashed away.
I followed and did overtake him.
Then wild he barked and, crouching, turned
to bite.
I did not fear, but cast the sacred meal.
Then he stood still and said:
"Verily, nephew, you will take away
All my powers together,
And more and more a seer you will be
Of mysteries."

He took me then, he took me.
He made me stand
Beside the wide-spreading ocean.
Under the spray that rose like smoke, he
took me.
Across on the other side he brought me out
To a pool of water, thick as cactus juice;
He set me before it.

"Ready, nephew!
Now, if you are brave
You will drink all and you will take away
All my powers together."
Then down I threw myself;
I drank and drank,
I drank it empty, then I scraped the dregs,
Folded them up, and carried them away.

Then next he took me
To a pool of water thick with greenish scum.
He set me before it.
"Ready, nephew!
Now, if you are brave
You will drink all and you will take away
All my powers together."
Then down I threw myself;
I drank and drank,
I drank it empty, then I scraped the dregs,
Folded them up tight, and carried them
away.

Then next he took me
to a pool of yellow water
And set me before it.
"Ready, nephew!
Now, if you are brave
You will drink all and you will take away
My powers with the drink."
Then down I threw myself;
I drank and drank,
I drank it empty, then I scraped the dregs,
Folded them up tight, and carried them
 away.

Then next he took me
To a pool of bloody water.
And set me before it.
"Ready, nephew!
Now, if you are brave
You will drink all and you will take away
My powers with the drink."
Then down I threw myself;
I drank and drank,
I drank it empty, then I scraped the dregs,
Folded them tight, and carried them away.

Then he stood still and said:
"If you shall take away
All my powers together,
Then more and more a seer you shall be
Of mysteries."

Then he went taking me
And reached a land
Which lies before the sunset.
There abides the bitter wind;
Not slowly did we go.
About the wind's house, dust lay scattered
 wildly.
Not slowly did he go and bring me there.
Then leaping up did I stretch out my hand,
I grasped the wind and slowly bent him
 down,
Till blood drops trickled from him.
Then from that house I seized
A leather shield and a short club,
A well-strung bow and smooth, straight-
 flying arrow.
These did I bind together,
And did return whence I had come.

That water did I reach
Which was thick like cactus juice,
And there a magician sat.
Coyote made me stand before him, saying:
"What will you do for this, my nephew?
I have brought him here."
Then forth he brought his white magic
 power
And placed it in my heart.

Then did I reach
The pool of water thick with greenish scum.
There a magician sat.
Coyote made me stand before him, saying:
"What will you do for this, my nephew?
I have brought him here."

Then forth he brought his green magic power
And placed it in my heart.

Then did I reach
The pool of yellow water.
Therein a magician sat.
Coyote made me stand before him, saying:
"What will you do for this, my nephew?
I have brought him here."
Then forth he took his yellow magic power
And placed it in my heart.

Then did I reach the pool of bloody water.
Therein a magician sat.
Coyote made me stand before him, saying:
"What will you do for this, my nephew?
I have brought him here."
Then forth he brought
His red magic power
And placed it in my heart.

Then back Coyote took me, whence we
came
And reached the wide-spreading ocean.
Under the smokelike spray he carried me
Even to that place where I had run along the
beach,
And there he left me.
Then down I fell, but rose, and toward the
east came running.
There sat our leader, head upon his breast.
He had not slept.
Straight to him walking, into his hands I put
The power I had won, tight pressing it.
Then I saw emerge
The sun, the gift of God.
Then up I looked, I followed the road.
I camped four times and reached my land.

The powers I had won, beneath my bed I
placed.
I lay upon them and lay down to sleep.
Then in a little time mysteriously there came
to me
Beautiful drunken songs,
Beautiful songs for the circling dance,
Beautiful songs for the maiden's dance,
Wherewith the maiden I might cozen.
My songs the stay-at-home youths did learn
and sing,
Scarce permitting me to be heard.

With my songs the evening spread echoing
And the early dawn emerged with a good
sound.
The firm mountains stood echoing therewith
And the trees stood deep rooted.

But no one can receive it until it has been purified and blest, like its bearers. The leader recites again the sacred phrases. They are the old, beloved ones, but their combination seems, on this occasion, to be reduced to its beautiful essentials.

It was mysteriously hidden.
Wanting it, I could not find it.

Behind my house post did I thrust my hand.
I could not find it. . . .
I went out the door. There my ashes were
piled high.
[With a stick] hard I struck them
And out I took it — my reed cigarette.
Burned out, it seemed.
I scratched, and at the end
Charred blackness lay.
Four times I struck it,
And out a great spark shone.
I lit it in the fire, I put it to my lips, I
smoked.
Then at the east a wind arose, well knowing
whither it should blow.
The standing trees it went shaking,
The rubbish at the foot of the trees it piled.
A shining cloud toward the sky upreared
And touched it with its head.
All kinds of clouds together rose
And with it they did go.
Although the earth seemed very wide,
To the very edge of it did they go.
Although the north seemed very far,
To the very edge of it did they go.
Although the south seemed more than far,
To the very edge of it did they go.
Pulling out their white breast feathers did
they go.

Then on it the old men in a circle sat
And held their meeting.
Then they scattered seed and it came forth.
A thick root came forth;
A thick stalk then came forth;
A fair tassel came forth
And well it ripened.
Therewith were delightful the evenings,
Delightful the dawns.

Then came the songs describing the thick root, the thick stalk, and the fair tassel. They are the same as the songs which sing up the corn, but a few breaths of the ocean wind sound among them:

Now I am ready to go.
The ocean wind from far off overtakes me.
It bends down the tassels of the corn.
The ocean water hurts my heart.
Beautiful clouds bring rain upon our fields.

The outspread water!
Running along it,
I seized the corn.

The outspread water!
Running along it,
I seized the squash.

The music is made with the Papagos' most solemn ceremonial instrument. They turn over the willow kitchen basket, so tightly woven that it can hold the liquid porridge. On that, as a sound box, the musician rests a stick of hard wood, cut into notches all along its length. Then he scrapes another stick along the notches. It is a sound which our modern ears associate with the Negro dance orchestra, but the Papago does not use it for dancing. "Scraping" is our only word for translating a term which stands for the music of growth and which comes from the same root as "wind" and "the flapping of wings."

The singing lasts until the morning star appears, and then the old men purify the neophytes and welcome them back into the ranks of ordinary men. This is always done by blowing tobacco smoke over the man whose holiness is to be ended. The old man who blows the smoke says, "Hail, my kinsman," and then wishes for the boy prowess in hunting or running or whatever his ancient mentor has achieved. The boys are now almost men, but they dare not enter into their new state without a period of solitude and fasting. Each goes home to camp outside his own house, like a hermit, to eat sparingly of corn-meal gruel, and for sixteen days to wait for further visions. But he may come forth a man with a destiny; or so it seems to the fathers of eligible girls, and they often wait on his parents during the young man's seclusion. For no matter which vision has been his, he will emerge a "ripe" man to take his place with the warriors and councilors. He has helped to bring rain.

Jim Darnton

Papago Legend of the Sahuaro

Susie Ignacio Enos

While a student at the University of Arizona, Susie Ignacio Enos published this story in the first issue of the Arizona Quarterly *(Spring 1945). She introduced it with the following statement:*

> *This little story of the Sahuaro is long but I have tried to tell it in exactly the same way that one can tell it in the Indian language. There are songs that the coyotes and the rabbits sing. There are songs that the people sang when they tasted the fruit and after they again found the plant. There are songs that the mother sang. All these I do not know. So I have written them as part of the story. It is harder to translate the songs and one almost has to have a different language in these songs.*

In comparing the style in which this story is told to the stories of Ted Rios and Frank Lopez printed in this section, readers will note that Susie Egnacio Enos has edited this story heavily. She offers us here a literary, rather than a word-for-word translation of the Papago story.

Once there was a little Aw'awtam baby who lived with her mother and father, and her name was Sugu-ik Oof. She was called this by her mother because she was always happy.

Now it happened that when she was about a year old, her father, who was very fond of her, died. Before he closed his eyes in sweet sleep, he said to his woman, "Bring Sugu-ik Oof to me." When the mother had brought the child to him he said, "The Wise Man of the Aw'awtam has appeared to me as a young man, but here I lie and am about to leave you, so it is that since Sugu-ik Oof is a girl she will be different from woman. She will be great as her father should have been. She will live forever to the end of times. She will be known by races of people from far and near. She will be queen of the Taw haw naw Juwut (desert lands). Generations of Aw'awtam will be saved from starvation because of her and her family."

When the young father had spoken he closed his eyes in peaceful sleep.

Years came and years went and Sugu-ik Oof grew in beauty and in size. When she was ten years old she could not stand the loneliness of her life any longer, for her mother had to go into the village nearby to get food for them both, every day. The little girl was left all alone day after day.

So one day Sugu-ik Oof said, "I will go after my mother for I am very lonely at home by myself."

The little girl set out on her journey, although she knew not where her mother could be. Off in the distance were the Gihau mountains.

"My mother pointed out the Gihau mountains to me so I shall go toward them; maybe that is where she is."

Sigu-ik Oof walked and walked for a long time before she saw any kind of life. In the distance a coyote approached her.

"My friend, Coyote, will you tell me where I can find my mother?"

The Coyote, with sly eyes, said: "Yes, Sugu-ik Oof, I will tell you where your mother is if you will give me one of those gourds you are carrying."

The little girl handed one of the gourds to the Coyote very anxiously.

"Over the Gihau mountains you will find a village and there you will also find your mother," the Coyote said and went on his way.

Sigu-ik Oof walked on and pretty soon she met a rabbit.

"Be very kind to me and tell me where I can find my mother," the little girl again asked of the animal.

So the rabbit looked at the gourds very fondly and said, "If you will give me one of those gourds you are carrying, I will tell you where your mother is."

"My mother gave these to me and I like them very much, but I will give you one gladly." So she did.

"Beyond the Gihau mountains you will find

your mother in the village," said the little rabbit and ran off on his way.

Again Sugu-ik Oof started walking. By now she was very tired and hungry. The mountains to which she was walking seemed so near and yet when she walked toward them they seemed to get farther away.

When the sun was turning toward the west, she met a little bird who spoke very kindly to her.

"Sugu-ik Oof, why are you this far away from your home? It is getting late and shadowy. Your mother will be unhappy if she doesn't find you at home."

"Little Gray Bird, I am looking for my mother. Can you tell me where she is? I will give you one of these gourds if you tell me," the little girl replied.

"I shall be very happy to tell you. I will even show you the way to the village, but I cannot take you clear to the village for there the little Aw'awtam boys shoot arrows at me and throw rocks," the little gray bird told Sugu-ik Oof.

"I am very happy because you have been very kind to me. Some day you will be rewarded for what you will do for me this day. Shall we go?"

The two traveled on and on, over rocks and down slopes they went; the little bird ever flying by Sugu-ik Oof showing her the way. When the shadows of evening began to fall they had climbed over the mountain.

The little gray bird said, "Now, I will leave you but from here you can see the village where your mother is." And so the bird left Sugu-ik Oof.

Sugu-ik Oof walked down to the village where she saw a group of children playing.

She went up to them and asked, "Can you tell me where I can find my mother?"

The children didn't seem to hear her for they did not answer her. She waited for their answer and once more asked, but they still would not answer her.

Pretty soon Sugu-ik Oof began to chant a song. The children still did not pay any attention to her. She chanted on and on. When finally the children looked at her, they saw that she had sunk halfway into the ground. At this the children became frightened. They all started screaming for help. Some of them rushed to the place where they knew her mother worked and they quickly called her. In the meantime one of the little boys pulled her by her hair thinking he could save her, but it was no use, for he only pulled the hair off from the top of her head. They could not help her for she had sunk deep into the ground and was no more. Her mother came running but she was too late. No amount of tears could bring the little girl to the surface of the earth.

Sugu-ik Oof's mother used to visit the place where her daughter had sunk and she would place food and water there because she believed that her daughter's spirit still lingered there.

A whole year went by, and it was the same season the next year. When Sugu-ik Oof's mother went to place the food and water at the spot, she noticed a queer plant had come up in the very place where her daughter had gone. So the woman began to water the plant, and to take care of it, till it grew into a tall and stately plant. No one had ever seen any plant like it. People came from far and near to see this peculiar plant that had grown where Sugu-ik Oof had sunk.

"What use can a plant like that be to us? It has too many stickers and we cannot eat it," many of them were saying.

Years went by and Sugu-ik Oof's mother had grown old and feeble but she was faithful to her plant and daughter for she still took care of it. One day after the coldest time of the year had just passed, when it had grown so high that it soared higher than the highest plant in the desert, the stately plant began to show signs of budding. The whole village was excited over this but Sugu-ik Oof's mother was even more excited.

The buds grew and grew and when the desert flowers just began to peep out of the ground, the queer plant bloomed forth into a beautiful white flower. After the flower had gone a fruit formed and this grew from a green to a red fruit.

One day when the flowers had gone to seed and the desert began to swell with the summer heat, the fruit of the stately plant burst showing forth a scarlet red. When it had fallen to the ground Sugu-ik Oof's mother ate some of it after she had seen the birds eat it when it was still on the plant. She tasted that the fruit was delicious and so she gave some to the other people and they too liked it.

Every year after that the *hash'an*, as the people began to call it, bore the same flower and fruit. The birds liked it so well that as soon as the fruit began to show signs of ripening they would gather on the plant and eat of it. The Aw'awtams liked it too and so were angry at the birds who could reach it more easily, so the children began to shoot the birds with their bows and arrows and they threw rocks at the birds to chase them away.

One day at the time of the ripening of the fruit the children ran out to get at the fruit before the birds, but they found that the *hash'an* had disappeared. With great excitement they ran and told the other people, who ran out to see if what the children were telling them was true. They were sad for their delicious fruit had disappeared. They became alarmed, for they believed it to be the work of evil spirits. Thereupon a great council was called at which were present the wisest men of the villages far and near. Smart medicine men were there too to give their aid.

After many nights of council they decided that everybody that was able, man, beast and fowl, should go out and hunt for the plant.

The hunt started. The birds hunted in the air as far and as high as they could go; the animals that live mostly under the ground dug holes — deeper than they had ever dug before to hunt there; the men and animals alike hunted all over on the surface of the earth. The search lasted for days and days until one day they began to come back one or more at a time and began to unfold strange adventures concerning their search. They had seen many strange and beautiful things but they had not seen their plant.

Finally all but one returned. The one who had not returned was a small gray bird who had only one eye. The Aw'awtam children had hit him in the eye when he was trying to eat some of the *hash'an* fruit.

Those who were gathered there began to make fun of the little bird. "Oh, he has only one eye and he probably got lost somewhere. Anyway he couldn't have found the plant with his one eye." On they talked in this way about the poor little gray bird.

Several days went by. One day the keen-eyed eagle said that he saw a tiny speck in the sky in the very far distance. Maybe it could be their friend the little Gray Bird. And so it was. It wasn't long when the little bird came all tired out and hungry for he came so fast to tell the news. He told that he had found the *hash'an* high on the west side of a high mountain.

A group of people got together and made their way into the mountains to see for themselves.

When they reached the place sure enough the *hash'an* was there where the little gray bird directed them. The *hash'an* was asked why it had tried to disappear and this is what it said:

"Years and years ago when I was a little girl in the form of an Aw'awtam, I was hunting for my mother and a tiny gray bird like the one who found me was kind to me and willingly helped me to the village where my mother was. It was then that I promised that one day the little bird would be rewarded for his kindness. Now I am a *hash'an,* I can help the birds. They will be the first to eat of my fruit when it is ripe. When I stood near the village the Aw'awtam children used to shoot and throw rocks at the birds when they tried to eat of my fruit, but I didn't like that. If the birds couldn't eat of my fruit then no one else could."

So it was decided there between men, beast and fowl that all should eat of the fruit of the *hash'an,* the tallest and most stately plant on the desert of this country.

Sahuaro
Jim Darnton

Thoughts by My Mother's Grave

Ofelia Zepeda

Mac 'am gegok hihañ t-'am we:sko 'an aṣ 'i s-ma:sk matk ju: wenog kiko'i ha-taṣ c-ed, natkpi 'e-padc hegam tatpial hihosig mat g ñ-wepnag ha-nanto. Hegam hihosig mo 'i cem s-wepegĭ aṣ cem 'alo s-to:ta. We:s g koklo:na matk 'an ha-na:nagia kokoḍst 'an 'as s-wipionaghim 'ab 'al na:nagia. Tk g gi:gĭ kakanjul ba 'e:p ha-padc g ju:kı ck ni hema sa'i tas mei, natkpi we:s g kakanjul ha-haha'a ba'i si ṣu:d g ṣu:dagĭ-kac.

Matt 'am ṣa'i s-'ap ha'icu 'i tua koḍṣ webig c 'amjed 'am ṣa'i gegokahim nt ce: mok am aṣkiap daha hegai ha'a mant g ṣu:dagĭ b 'ab wa'ig k 'am dai ñ-je'e wehejed, 'an hugidan 'i:da ha'a g kostel an wo'o kc g ha'icu hugĭ 'am 'eda ka:c c wud hegai ha-icu hugĭ mat g ñ-wepnag 'am ha-to'i kiko'i ha-taṣ 'ed. Tp 'amai hasko ba 'e:p g spearmint ki'iwi am hema ka:c napi g ñ-'o:g s cem hekid 'am hema cecka ñ-je'e wehejed napi s-ma:c mo g ñ-je'e s-na:k 'i:da ki'iwi.

Mac 'am 'aṣkiap 'oyopo 'amai hiha'añ t-'am 'ant 'am hema mehĭ g kanjul k 'am dai. Nt 'amjed 'am ṣa'i cekto mo has 'i masma wenog

One could tell that it had rained on All Souls' Day by the appearance of the once colorful wreaths of crepe paper flowers that my big sister had made. The wreaths were now almost white, with only just a faint color left on them; all of the poor wreaths sagged from the cross at the head of my mother's grave. The jars of candles had also been ruined; water had filled up in them before they had had a chance to burn down very far.

I noticed that the jar of water which I had placed at the head of her grave was still there. There was also a sack of food there, it was some of what my sisters had prepared for the feast on All Souls' Day. There must have been a package of Wrigleys spearmint gum there somewhere, since my sisters say that my father always brings a pack of spearmint gum for my mother; it was her favorite kind of gum.

While I stood at the grave, I lit a candle and set it at my mother's grave. While standing there I could not help but think how quiet it was going to be this Christmas without my mother. It had always been her custom to

mo 'in 'aṣkiap ha'icug g ñ-je'e. T ge pi 'ap 'i n-ta:c mant 'am 'i cekto mat pi o ṣa:munk Noji Wi'na 'ed 'am t-ki: 'am. Napi wuḍ 'i cem ñ-je'e cipkanadag mat o tatmalt k ge cuhuk 'oidk o ha-gegos g hemajkam, k 'amjed ge taṣ 'oidk o piastad g 'a'al c noumko'i ha-wehejed. Kut 'am wecij 'ahidag c-ed ba'ic 'i pi o ṣa:munk, napi ba 'e:p wud ñ-je'e cipkanadag mat ge'e ha'icu o hihido k we:s o ha-gegos g hemajkam k 'amjed ge cuhuk 'oidk o piast kc g pipna:da kc kaskaslo:n o ha-hahai, c b 'ep cece'e mat pi hedai o ṣa'i koi natts pi 'enga o ñei g ke:li 'ahidag mat 'an o bic k g wecij 'ahidag 'ab o 'i-wa: .

Pegi, we:s 'idam ha'icu mant 'am 'i cekto 'at hia pi 'ap 'i ñ-ta:c, tp ba ma'i s-'ape mat b masma b ha'icu 'e-ju:. Hemu mat hab o 'i wa: 'i:da wecij 'ahidag ntp mu'i ha'icu a woho pi o 'edig. Tp hab a mo ṣa'i ha'as atp we:s ha'icu maṣ 'o'i s-'ape k nt 'am 'aṣ 'o'i himad c s-'ap mo cektod g ñ-je'e.

make red chili tamales and to feed people all through the night. On Christmas day she would entertain and play music for the children and the drunken friends and relatives that happened to come by.

On New Years it would be even quieter, since it was also my mother's custom to have plenty of food for all the people during the night. She also made sure that there was a piñada and other party favors for everyone. She used to always make sure that no one fell asleep before midnight; she tried to make sure that we all saw the "old year leave and the new year come in."

It was mainly these two times which I thought of while standing there by the grave; I figured with the coming of the new year there would be many things which I would miss mainly due to my mother's passing. But I supposed that things will be all right as the times passed. I will continue to go on my way with only these simple, but good, memories which my mother has left in me.

Tony Celentano

From This World

Geri Felix

from this world you walk to the east
where the sun rises and there is new life

no one speaks your name until one year has passed

my elders tell me not to forget you
i never will
i hear you in the distant night's wind

i see you in my dreams
i know you are always with me
and i am not afraid

it is said the journey to the sky world is a hard one
and there is work to be done

in one year's time your tracks on this world
must be covered
memories cling and pictures fade

no sign of you is left
one year has gone by quickly
i still feel your presence near
once again you must leave us
to start your long, long climb

tears swell my vision
my throat is coarse and dry
i can hardly speak
i hate to say — good-bye
i am told not to cry
my tears blow out your candle
tired you stop your climb
my tears no longer sad ones
as i realize
you are always with me
and i am not afraid.

Papago Literature: Other Sources

The works of Ruth Murray Underhill are the most reliable, readable sources on Papago literature and life presently available. Singing for Power: The Song Magic of the Papago Indians *(Berkeley: Univ. of California Press, 1938) is once again available in paperback, as is* Papago Woman *(1936; rev. ed. N.Y.: Holt Rinehart & Winston, 1979), an autobiography of Maria Chona. Chona's life also serves as the basis for Underhill's novel* Hawk Over Whirlpools *(New York: J. J. Augustin, 1940).* The Papago Indians of Arizona and Their Relatives the Pimas *(Washington, D. C.: GPO, 1941) and* People of the Crimson Evening *(Washington, D.C.: GPO, 1951) are very helpful, pamphlet-length, introductory works. They are unfortunately not widely available. More scholarly discussions of Papago life are given in* Papago Indian Religion *(New York: Columbia University Press, 1946) and* Social Organization of the Papago Indians *(New York: Columbia University Press, 1939).*

Underhill's work with Papago orations has been continued by Professor Donald Bahr of Arizona State University, in collaboration with various Papago experts. With Underhill, Baptisto Lopez, Jose Pancho, and David Lopez, Bahr has recently published Rainhouse and Ocean: Speeches for the Papago Year *(Flagstaff: Museum of Northern Arizona Press, 1979). With the help of Juan Gregorio, David Lopez, and Albert Alvarez, Bahr wrote a bi-lingual study of Papago religion* Piman Shamanism and Staying Sickness *(Tucson: University of Arizona Press, 1974). Bahr has published a third bi-lingual study of three ritual speeches titled* Pima and Papago Ritual Oratory *(San Francisco: Indian Historian Press, 1975). The study contains some sharp critiques of what is published as "Indian literature." An example: "We invent 'Indian literatures' just as 19th century medicine showmen invented Indian Herbal Remedies."*

Long out of print, Harold Bell Wright's Long Ago Told: Legends of the Papago Indians *(New York: D. Appleton, 1929) is an early collection of Papago narratives available in some libraries. More recent, reliable, and bi-lingual is Dean and Lucille Saxton's* Legends and Lore of the Papago and Pima Indians *(Tucson: University of Arizona Press, 1973).*

Frances Densmore gathered a collection of Papago songs in Papago Music, *Bureau of American Ethnology Bulletin 90 (Washington, D. C.: GPO, 1929). Frank Russell's* The Pima Indians *(1905; re-edition Tucson: University of Arizona Press, 1975) contains large selections of Piman stories, songs, and speeches.*

A number of good sound recordings of Papago song are available. Two from Canyon Records are Papago Dance Songs *(Canyon C-6098), which includes sixteen Chelkona and Keihina dance songs recorded at Santa Rosa village, and* Traditional Papago Music, Vol. 1 *(Canyon C-6084), which includes social dance, toka game, diagnosis, curing, and saguaro wine ceremony songs.*

Some prose and poetry written by Papago students is given by T.D. Allen in her collection Arrows Four: Prose and Poetry by Young American Indians *(New York: Washington Square Press, 1974).*

Byrd Baylor's Yes Is Better Than No *(New York: Charles Scribner's Sons, 1977) is a fictional account of a group of urban Papago people living in Tucson.*

The Papago Runner *is a monthly newspaper published by the Papago Tribe and edited by Stanley Throssel at Sells, Arizona.*

YAQUI LITERATURE

Yaqui Alphabet

Felipe S. Molina

a	as in English **father**
e	as in Spanish **peso** usually, but also as "a" in English **date**
i	as in English **meet**
o	as in Spanish **poco**
u	as in English **moon**
b	as in Spanish **adobe** frequently, but also as in Spanish **baca**
ch	as in English **church**
d	as in Spanish **decir**
f	as in English **foot**
g	as in English **go**, but varies to "w" as in English **word**
h	as in English **hard**
k	as in English **kick**
l	as in English **led**
m	as in English **met**
n	as in English **nice**
p	as in Spanish **pan**
r	as in English **rest**
s	as in English **see**
t	as in Spanish **tengo**
w	as in English **word**
y	as in English **yes**
'	the glottal stop, as in English in the hiatus between **an apple**

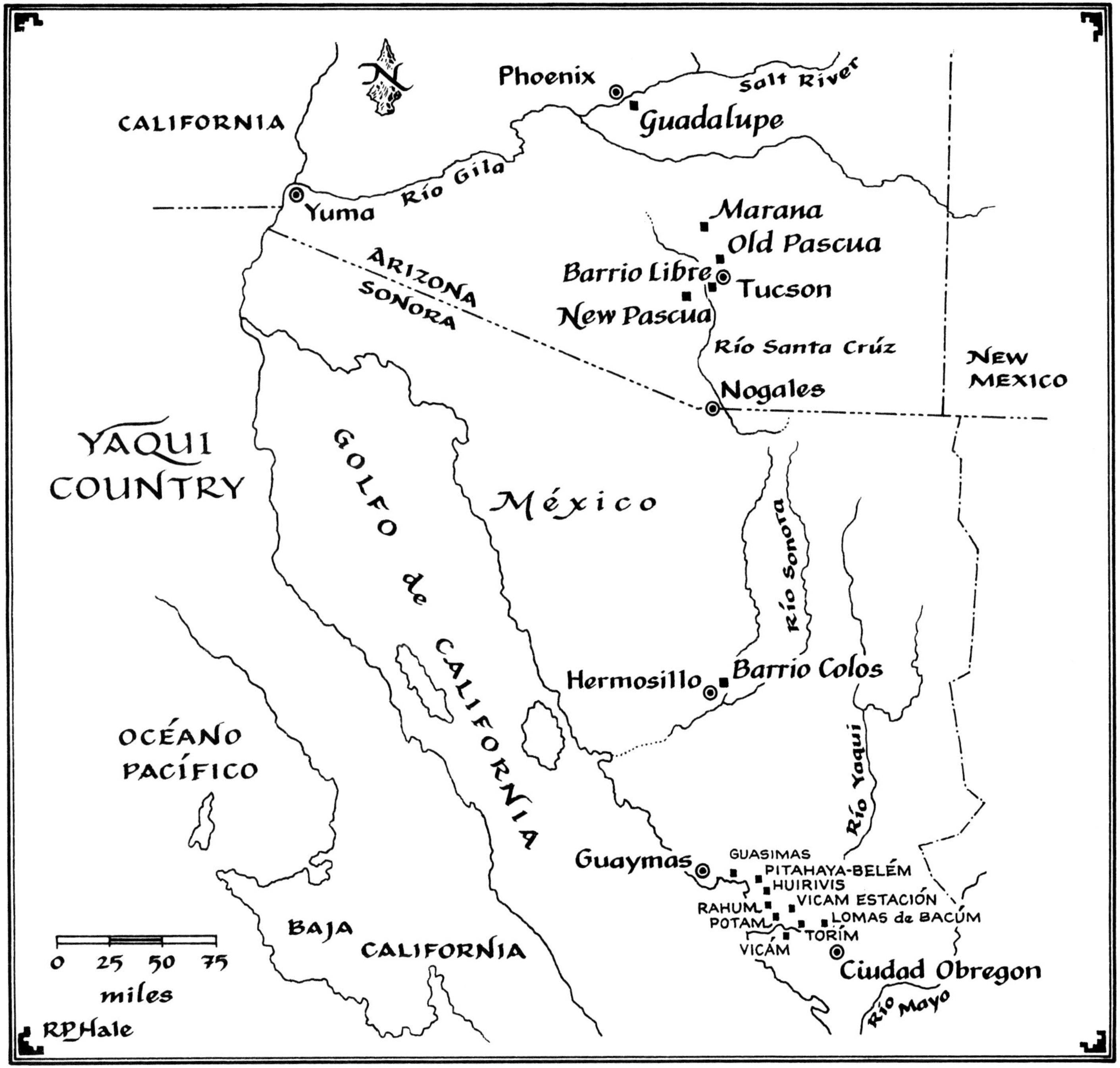

YAQUI COUNTRY
CALIFORNIA
Phoenix
Salt River
Guadalupe
Yuma
Río Gila
Marana
Old Pascua
Barrio Libre
Tucson
New Pascua
ARIZONA
SONORA
Río Santa Crúz
Nogales
NEW MEXICO
México
GOLFO de CALIFORNIA
Río Sonora
Hermosillo
Barrio Colos
OCÉANO PACÍFICO
Río Yaqui
Guaymas
GUASIMAS
PITAHAYA-BELÉM
HUIRIVIS
VICAM ESTACIÓN
RAHUM
LOMAS de BACÚM
POTAM
TORÍM
VICÁM
Ciudad Obregon
Río Mayo
BAJA CALIFORNIA
0 25 50 75
miles
RPHale

Yaqui history is preserved in the memories of the people, the Yoeme. *Yaqui leader Anselmo Valencia told the following two parts of Yaqui history to his niece Mini Valenzuela Kaczkurkin in 1976. Mr. Valencia presently serves as head of the Pascua Yaqui Tribe and is a religious leader in the village of New Pascua.*

Surems and the Talking Tree

as told by Anselmo Valencia

It has been many centuries, in times long gone, that the Yaquis were not as they are now. They were Surems, a very little people that lived in el Cerro Surem in Sonora. The Surems were a peaceful, quiet people who couldn't stand noise and violence. One day, the people noticed a tree that seemed to be making noises in a strange language. This tree was one big, ash-colored Palo Verde, which was growing in the middle of the region, on Omteme Kawi.

While the villagers gathered around, the leaders attempted to communicate with the talking tree. However, it was of no use, not even the most important leader could interpret the message. During this time, a very young girl, Yomumuli, kept tugging at her father's hand and whispering that she could understand the talking tree. At first her father ignored her, then he became angry at her insistence.

"All right, you will do it in front of the village, and then you will be punished publicly for your foolishness."

So Yomumuli sat down close to the tree and translated word for word what the prophetic tree foretold for their future. It warned of the coming of the white man with armor and new weapons; it told of the coming of much strife and bloodshed against these intruders and others, and of much suffering for a long time among the Surems, but that they would eventually overcome their adversaries. It told of the coming of modern man's trains, "A road will be made of steel with an iron monster on it." It told of much much more to come, then it said, "There will be much suffering for years, much noise, and confusion. You must decide what to do. For those among you who cannot stand noise, you have a choice of leaving if you do not want to face such a future."

So, the Surems divided into two parties, and those who could not stand such a future walked away. Some say they walked into the sea and live there still. Others say they turned into black ants and live underground under the hills. Those Surems who stayed eventually grew taller and changed into the Yaquis as they are now, and they were strong enough to fight off the Spaniards when the time came.

Christianity

as told by Anselmo Valencia

It has been a very long time, the people say, that a band of Spanish conquistadores rode toward Yaqui territory in Sonora. These Spanish soldiers were the "white invaders" predicted by the Talking Tree many years before, in the time of the Surems. They were armed and dressed exactly as foretold by the Talking Tree.

The Yaquis gathered to meet them. One of the Yaqui leaders drew a line along the ground, knelt and kissed it reverently, saying, "Up to this line and as far as the eye can see in these three directions, is Yaqui land. No invaders will be allowed to enter." They asked the soldiers to return from whence they came.

When the Spanish soldiers tried to do battle with the Yaquis, there was such fierce fighting, that the Spaniards had to retreat hastily. They had never met such valiant fighters, they said. Thus, the Yaquis drove back the white invaders, exactly as predicted, and they were well satisfied with that day's work.

Over 70 years later, some Mayos (cousins of the Yaquis) who had been converted to Christianity, came to the Yaquis and told them about the Spaniards who were peaceful and carried no weapons. The Yaquis asked that these peaceful ones be brought in, but that no armed man could enter their territory. They were converted easily because when the missionaries called their God "Our Father in Heaven," pointing upward toward the sky, then the Yaquis thought that here were others who shared their beliefs about *"Itom Achai Taa'a*, Our Father Sun." And then, too, the missionaries' cross looked almost like the Yaqui sun symbol. The missionaries came and stayed on, converting the Yaquis to Christianity. Up to that time, the Yaquis had been sun-worshipers with their own ceremonies and dances, among them the Deer Dancer, Pascola, Coyote, Raccoon, and Naji (water-fly) dances.

The Yaqui converts asked questions about the man on the cross — who was he? Why was he crucified? Who were these people that had crucified him? They took the Christian beliefs and dramatized them, acting out all the events in the Passion of Christ, *Cuaresma.* Yaquis were probably told that those that followed Jesus were both good and bad. Thus, they had the Matachinis, angelitos, and church group to represent the good. The missionaries allowed the Yaquis to include their own nature beliefs with Christianity. That was the only way they would have been allowed to stay. The ceremonies of the people, the Pascolas and Deer Dancer, were seen as being good.

But the evil ones were made to look as ugly as possible. The name of these evil ones Fariseos (Pharisees) is *Chapayeka* in Yaqui. *Chapa* means long or flat, and *Yeka* means nose, so *Chapayekas* are long-nosed Pharisees as the Yaquis saw the Spaniards. These evil ones take the worst punishments during Lent because they persecuted Christ. But the evil ones are given a chance to change their ways on *Sabado de Gloria* when Christ rises and enters heaven.

Yaqui Deer Dancer
South of Tucson, Arizona
October 20, 1976
James S. Griffith

Maso Bwikam
Yaqui Deer Songs

Felipe Molina

We believe that our ancestors the Surem *could actually talk with the animals that lived in the wilderness. According to many of our traditions, the* Surem *spoke to* saila maso, *our brother the deer, because they needed him to survive in this world. Before they set out to hunt, the* Surem *held an all night* pahko *(fiesta) in honor of the deer. They wanted to ask the deer's forgiveness for having to kill him. We still perform that ritual, the deer dance, today, even though we no longer go out to hunt deer in the way our ancestors did. The ceremony is an important part of our inheritance. It reminds us of what it is to be a* Yoeme *(Yaqui).*

Deer songs are sung during the pahko; *the deer dancer dances to them. These deer songs are ancient songs that are passed down from generation to generation. The songs tell about the animal world that surrounds Yaqui land. They are sung for the deer and most of the time are about things the deer sees in the wilderness. Many good deer dancers can actually dance the meaning of the song, and these dancers are greatly respected because they help the Yaqui people to see the close connection all living things have in common on earth.*

We Yaquis are a spiritual people. We believe in other worlds. One of these other worlds we call the sea ania, *the flower world. This place is beneath the dawn in the east. It is the home of our brother the deer and is filled with flowers* (sewam) *and other things of natural beauty. Many of the deer songs talk about flowers* (sewam) *because we consider them to be sacred and beautiful.*

The early deer singers never wrote down the songs, but instead they memorized all the songs that needed to be sung at the pahko. *Many ancient songs have been forgotten, but there are still several hundred songs circulating in the Yaqui world. Today young deer singers often record the songs on tape recorders to learn them more quickly. Several older deer singers teach and give their songs to young singers so that the songs will not be forgotten after they die. The following songs were given to me by Guadalupe Molina who lives at Vicam, Sonora, Mexico. Don Lupe, as he is called, was born in 1889 and has sung deer songs since he was fifteen. He learned many of his songs as a young man from his uncles while he served with them in the army in Veracruz.*

I have added a few comments to each of my translations of Don Lupe's songs to express some of the feelings the songs create in me when I hear them.

Sewa Yotume

Sewa yotume sewa yotume
Sewa yo machi hekamake sika
Machi hekamake hekawapo chasime
Yo yo machi hekamake sika

Ayamansu seyewailo betana
Yo aniwata bebepa
Mekka hikat chasime
Ta'ata aman weche betana
Husyoli kala lipapati ansime
Empo yo machi hekamake sika

Growing Flower

Growing flower, growing flower,
Flower went with the enchanted dawn wind.
With the dawn wind's air you are flying,
With the enchanted, enchanted dawn wind you went.

Over yonder, on the side of *seyewailo*,
On the top of the enchanted world,
You fly so high.
Beautifully, endlessly, you go sparkling.
You went with the enchanted dawn wind.

When I look at the sky in the morning before dawn after a fiesta, I think of this song. The growing flower in it is the light of the sun pushing back the darkness of the night until it disappears to the west.

Dennis Carr

Huya Aniwa

Empo sewa yo huya aniwa
Empo yo huya aniwa
Baewa sola boyoka
Empo yo huya aniwa
Baewa sola boyoka huya aniwa

Ayamansu seyewailo huyata naisukunisu
Yo huya aniwapo
Husyol machi hekamake husyolisi
Baewa sola boyoka huya aniwa
Empo yo huya aniwa
Baewa sola boyoka huya aniwa

Wilderness World

You are an enchanted flower wilderness world.
You are an enchanted wilderness world.
You lie with see-through freshness.
You are an enchanted wilderness world.
You lie with see-through freshness, wilderness world.

Over yonder, in the middle of the *seyewailo* wilderness,
In the enchanted wilderness world,
Beautiful with the dawn wind, beautifully
You lie with see-through freshness, wilderness world.
You are an enchanted wilderness world.
You lie with see-through freshness, wilderness world.

This song reminds me of the flower world in the early morning hour when the sun is coming out. I can see the dew on the blades of grass and the many leaves on different plants. Animals of the wilderness are just becoming active at this hour. In this song the animals see the peaceful and quiet morning. They see the freshness on the ground when looking towards the east when the sun is rising over the mountains.

Dennis Carr

Sewa Huli

Sewa huli haikunsa husyolisi sewa temula ne se muteka teki
Haikunsa husyolisi sewa temula ne se muteka teki sewa huli

Ayamansu seyewailo saniloata naisukunisu
Masa'asai sewata sewa nat se weche betuku
Huyolisi sewa temula ne se muteka teki
Haikunsa husyolisi sewa temula ne se muteka teki sewa huli

Flower Badger

Flower badger, where have you kicked me in a beautiful flower way
into a lying pillow?
Where have you kicked me in a beautiful flower way into a lying pillow,
flower badger?

Over yonder, in the middle of a *seyewailo* grove,
By the *masa'asai* flower, at the bottom where the blossoms fall,
You have kicked me in a beautiful flower way into a lying pillow.
Where have you kicked me in a beautiful flower way into a lying pillow,
flower badger?

Deer songs are sometimes difficult to understand unless they are explained by the singer. When I asked Don Lupe about this one, he told me it was about a badger and a sidewinder snake. The badger grabbed the sidewinder and killed it. Then the badger kicked the snake into a colorful pillow among the falling blossoms under the masa'asai. *The* masa'asai *is called the Queen's Wreath by some Anglo people.*

Dennis Carr

Neo'okaim

Inim bwiapo, sewa bwiapo
Kabesu ne yo yumalika noyoka
Tua kabesu ne yo yumalika noyokama

Ayamansu seyewailo huyata naisukunisu
Senu yo huya bakuliat ne hikatne yestekai
Imne yo aniwau ne takawaka katekai
Aniwaiti naikim ne yo yumalika katekai
Tua kabesu ne yumalika noyoka
Tua kabesu ne yo yumalika noyokama

Mockingbird

On this earth, flower earth,
Nobody talks quite like me.
Really, nobody talks quite so enchantingly as me.

Over yonder, in the middle of the *seyewailo* wilderness,
On top of one enchanted tree branch, I landed.
Here, with my body towards the enchanted world, I sat.
With the world's four I sat quite enchantingly.
Really, nobody talks quite like me.
Really, nobody talks quite so enchantingly as me.

This is a song which is sung only on Easter Sunday morning. It sings for the happiness on earth when Jesus arises from the dead. All the birds sing in happiness on Easter Sunday. The mockingbird wants to tell all the world that he is singing with happiness in his heart. When I hear this song I think of the mockingbird's pride in his songs. To the Yaquis the mockingbird sings more beautifully than any bird in the desert.

Dennis Carr

Pascola

As he performs, the deer dancer is accompanied by other dancers called pahkolam. *In Yaqui that name means "the old men of the fiesta." In English, the* pahkolam *are often called pascolas, a corrupted form of the Yaqui term. The* pahkolam *have many roles during a fiesta. They open and close the fiesta with sermons; they serve as hosts during the long night passing out water and cigarettes to the crowd; they perform jokes, stories, and even little skits to entertain the people.*

Most of the jokes and stories the pahkolam *use to entertain the people are very short, but sometimes they tell longer ones. "Tesak Pascola's Watermelons" is a pascola story. It was recorded in the Rio Yaqui area in Sonora by Ruth Giddings and first published in her book* Yaqui Myths and Legends *(Tucson: University of Arizona Press, 1959).*

Yaquis are a spiritual people. They believe that there are other worlds where they can gain supernatural powers. One of those worlds is the yo ania, *the enchanted world. In the* yo ania, *they believe, one can pick up a talent like dancing or singing or playing a musical instrument without having to practice. The masks of the* pahkolam *suggest their connection with the enchanted world. "The Enchanted Pascola" tells of one pascola's encounter with the enchanted world. It was told by Mrs. Carmen Garcia, born in Sonora in 1901, before she died in 1971. Mini Kaczkurkin recorded it.*

Tesak Pascola's Watermelons

recorded by Ruth Giddings

Well, gentlemen, this horse of mine became very old. I let him out for a few days so that he might rest. But one day I saddled him again, to take a little turn through the monte. I traveled almost a whole day, and in the afternoon I took off the saddle. I noticed that he had a sore on his back. I turned him out. On the following day I went in search of him. I found him, lassoed him and, after cutting myself a ripe watermelon, I jumped on his back, opened the melon and rode along eating my watermelon. I came to the river and let him drink and bathed the sore on his back. I got on again and commenced eating watermelon and throwing the seeds away. Soon we came to a well and I got down. I took a little fine dirt and put it on my horse's wound, then set him free in my pasture. I went back to my house and forgot about my horse.

About four or five months later, I went in search of him. The pasture wasn't very big and didn't have much underbrush in it. It is well fenced. My horse had no means of getting out, no place to hide. Nevertheless, I could not find him. I was there an entire week without once seeing him. The following week I went in search again. One day I passed near a forest I had not seen before and stopped to contemplate the branches. It was not mesquite, nor *batamote*. As I looked, I heard a horse sneeze — brr — burr.

I went up to those branches and saw that it was a watermelon vine. I looked again and saw that the vine had grown out of the sore on my horse, aided by the dirt which I had placed on it. Some watermelon seeds had fallen into the wound.

Well, I took my horse to my house and cut many watermelons, good-sized and ripe, off of him. I sold them, and gave them to my neighbors. Later, I cut the trunk of the watermelon vine off and cured my horse.

When he died, I gave him a fiesta and did mourning for six months.

There you have it, Señores.

The Enchanted Pascola

as told by Mrs. Carmen Garcia

Some time ago there was a Pascola who, when he first started out, was a very terrible performer. He was clumsy and unable to dance gracefully. He did not even know how to chat with his audience. The people only kept him on because they pitied him. One day he was requested to dance at another pueblo, so he set out alone, the others having gone ahead.

As he was traveling along, the Pascola heard the most beautiful music coming from the hills. There was a small cave there, and he heard the musicians playing so beautifully, so very beautifully, that he wanted to dance right then and there. Then he said within himself, "But, what use is that beautiful music to me, I am so ungraceful."

And he stood there, listening, and wishing with heart and soul that he were more graceful.

At this point, a goat came out of the cave, a goat so frisky that it could not stand still. This one went toward the Pascola, who stood and waited for it. The goat stood up on its hind legs leaning its forelegs on the Pascola's chest, and licked the Pascola's face — first on the mouth, then on the ears, and finally on the throat. He stood back and stared at the Pascola; this one waited calmly. The goat zoomed off and, turning very sharply, came charging at the Pascola, but the Pascola, with arms crossed, waited calmly. The animal stopped short, and raising its hind leg, urinated on him. Then the goat galloped off and disappeared among the rocks, and the music stopped.

The Pascola, wondering over what he had seen, continued his journey. He began to think of many good jokes to entertain the people, and his feet itched to dance right then and there. Thus, he arrived at the Pueblo, where all was in readiness. He dressed and began his entertainment when — *cosa rara!* — the once ungraceful Pascola danced as no one had ever done before. And he became so popular that to this date, no one has rivaled him. It is said that that goat was an enchanted Pascola. At any rate, the much-loved Pascola loved to dance beautifully at many fiestas.

Juana, Marana Village
Dorothy Fannin

In Yaqui, tales are called etehoim. *They may be told by just about anyone at anytime, but often they are told to young people by their grandparents as lessons. Yaqui writer Mini Valenzuela Kaczkurkin remembers:*

Our grandparents were refugees from the Mexican government when they came into southern Arizona. They thought that their homes here were only a temporary shelter before they returned to the Rio Yaqui area in Sonora. However, the wars went on for so long that many of their temporary shelters became permanent homes for our elders. They recounted these stories among themselves as they relived the old days and ways. During a hard day's work, our grandparents would worry and wonder about their homeland, which was still in the hands of the enemy, about their Yaqui brothers who were deported to places from which they would never return, and about those true Yoemen *still holding out in the mountains of Bacatete. After such a day, our grandparents would sit outdoors on warm evenings in Tucson and on ranches in the surrounding area, resting before the battle that would recover their land.*

Then any event – a shooting star, a streak of bad luck, a newborn child – would start off an evening of "Do you remember . . .?" as they recounted etehoim *and talked of things that happened before the wars. Their children, our parents, would gather outside along the fringes of the group to listen to stories of the supernatural, of laughter, pain, and hope, all the voices from long ago. Later, when the last battle was fought and the Yaquis were promised the return of their lands, many traditions left with them. Those* Yoemen *who stayed continued the* etehoim, *but as time passed many details were forgotten.*

Ku Wikit

as told by Mrs. Carmen Garcia

A long time ago, among the Yaquis, there lived a bird who was poor. He was so poor, in fact, that he wore the shabbiest, drabbest coat of feathers. Now, being a vain bird, he was ashamed to show himself before anyone, so he kept to himself and knew no one. But, he used to look at the other birds, each with colorful feathers, and he was very jealous of them.

One day he thought of something. He began to pluck out his feathers, one by one, painful though it was. At last there he stood, a poor, naked little bird, suffering from the cold weather. Owl was passing by, and *Ku Wikit* called to him, "My brother, please to do me a favor, and I will help you as long as I live. Help me to dress myself by lending me a few feathers of yours, even if only part of my body is covered. I am suffering from the cold."

"Well," the owl answered him, "Worry no more about your coat of feathers. I will lend you some, and I shall ask also that the other birds lend you one feather apiece. Thus you may clothe your entire body."

"Gracias, you are good," said *Ku Wikit* to the Owl. "And when I grow many more feathers, I shall return a feather to each one who has lent me one."

That is how the Owl sent a messenger all around to the birds, asking them to please come to a council early the next morning. There was much talk, and then all wanted to see *Ku Wikit*. At their request, *Ku Wikit* presented himself, but with much shame at his nakedness.

Upon seeing him, everyone felt very sorry for him. And everyone gave him one feather, until his coat of feathers was complete.

After giving them thanks, *Ku Wikit* left to take a look at himself in a spring filled with crystal-clear water. Here is where many birds with beautiful plumage often came to visit and admire themselves. When *Ku Wikit* arrived, all surrounded him in admiration, exclaiming at his beautiful, unusual plumage. He had great splashes of colors — yellow, red, blue — the colors of the rainbow, it looked like. No one recognized him as the naked, poor bird. They now called him the bird of a thousand colors.

Ku Wikit rushed to look at himself, and they were right — he was more beautiful than any other! Of course, this didn't help his vanity any. In fact, he became so conceited, constantly talking and talking about his looks, and admiring himself, that no one could stand him and didn't want to be near him. And to this day, *Ku Wikit*, the parrot, is a non-stop talker that people want to shut up. And he's still admiring his coat of a thousand colors.

The Snake People

recorded by
Ruth Giddings

Long ago there lived a Yaqui by the name of *Habiel Mo'el*. He was an orphan, but he had many relatives all over the Yaqui country. This man did not enjoy hunting as most young Yaqui men did. Instead, he liked to travel from house to house and from pueblo to pueblo, attending fiestas and eating and chatting with his friends and relatives.

The only weapon he ever carried was a big, thick club. He lived at the foot of the hill, *Mete'etomakame*. One day he started out for *Hekatakari* where there was to be a little fiesta. When he came to *Maata'ale*, the monte became too thick for passage, and he turned around and went to *Jori*. From *Jori*, he cut across towards *Bataconsica*, where an arroyo empties into the Rio Yaqui. Travel there was very difficult, for the undergrowth was extremely dense. He crawled on his belly under branches, crawled over them, or pushed past them.

When he came upon a sort of clearing, a big snake appeared, crawling across his path. *Habiel Mo'el* hit the snake right in its middle, but it vanished into the underbrush before he could strike it again. So he continued on his path toward the ranchería at *Hekatakari*.

Suddenly, what had been nothing but thick monte stretching before him became a large Yaqui pueblo with many people in it, moving about their business. *Habiel Mo'el* felt very strange. As he walked between the houses, a *cabo* from the *guardia* came up to him, and greeted him.

He told *Habiel Mo'el* that his chief would like to see him at the *guardia*. So the two went over there. Inside, on the front bench was seated the head *kobanao*. On the next bench,

Habiel Mo'el was told to seat himself. The other *kobanaom* were seated on the other benches. To one side a young girl was sitting. About her waist was a bandage of leaves.

The head *kobanao* spoke to *Habiel Mo'el*, "We have brought you here to ask you why you beat a girl this afternoon as you were traveling along between *Jori* and *Bataconsica*."

Habiel Mo'el was very surprised. He replied that from *Jori* to this place he met no one on his journey. "I did not beat any girl," he said.

"You struck a girl this afternoon, and you are liable to punishment. Why did you do this?" insisted the *kobanaom*.

Habiel Mo'el could not remember having done so; and he repeated this. Then he explained where he had come from and his route, saying that he had seen no girl on the path. He respectfully asked their pardon, but insisted that he had done nothing at all.

The head *kobanao* turned to the girl, who was seated to one side, and asked her if this were the man who had beaten her.

"Yes," she answered. "And he is still carrying the stick with which he beat me and almost killed me. That is the man."

Habiel Mo'el said that he had never seen the girl before and that he remembered nothing of it. He again asked their pardon, but disclaimed guilt. The *kobanaom* considered the matter among themselves.

Then the head *kobanao* said, "We will pardon you this once, since it is your first offense. But after this, when you are traveling, never harm anyone at all who may cross your path offering you no danger. You may go this time."

Habiel Mo'el thanked them and left the *guardia*. As he went out, he found himself in the middle of the monte with no sign of a village.

He traveled on toward his destination. It was dark when he arrived at *Hekatakari* and the house of his relative. He greeted the little old man whose name was *Wete'epoi*.

They sat down to a meal of *pitahaya* and *Habiel Mo'el* told *Wete'epoi* about his strange experience concerning the appearance and disappearance of the large Yaqui pueblo, and of his accusation.

The old man listened and then said, "You have done a great wrong. All animals, as well as people, have their authorities and their laws. You hurt a snake which crossed your path, doing you no harm. The authorities of that group took action against you. You must never again do that thing. The chiefs of the snakes met when the girl complained. They turned into people to punish you. I will give you some advice. Never hurt any snake, coyote, or any kind of animal which is just crossing your path and offering no harm. If a snake lies coiled in the path, kill it. You are defending yourself then. But always kill it completely, never let it get away or it will complain and its chiefs will punish you."

The Yaqui Curandero

as told by Mrs. Carmen Garcia

A poor, old Yaqui man had twelve sons. When the thirteenth son came along no one wanted to take him as a god-son. Yaquis believe that the god-parents are obligated to christen three children in a row from that family, and thirteen sons was just one too many.

The father became very angry. "I go now," he said, "and the first person I meet shall be my *compadre*."

He went toward the mountains and saw a man coming toward him. He was a tall and distinguished-looking person, *muy simpatico.*

"Where do you go?" the stranger asked the father of the thirteen sons.

"Anywhere."

"You go in search of someone to serve as your *compadre*?"

"Yes, how did you know?"

"I am the devil, and I will serve as your *compadre*."

"I am but a poor man," said the father. "You are for the rich who can make deals with you. *Vete*." And the devil went off in a whirlwind, which is how he travels, in those dust devils.

The father of the thirteen sons went on traveling and met a second man. This man was tall, slender, and dressed all in black. In his hand he held a sword. This one said to the father of the thirteen sons, "And where do you go, my good man?"

"I go in search of someone who would be my *compadre*."

"I will serve you, if you give me your son when I ask. He will grow up to a very good healer, the best *curandero* of all."

The father asked him, "And who are you?"

"I am Death."

"Well, as you take from the rich as well as from the poor, and make all equal, you shall be my *compadre*." This the father said, "Be at the church this coming Sunday for the christening."

Thus it was that Death appeared at the thirteenth christening.

When the boy reached his thirteenth birthday, his god-father appeared and said to the father, "I told you I would make this boy into a great healer. Leave him to me for instruction, as you promised."

Since that was the agreement, the father had to let his son go. The boy and his god-father entered into a hill in the forest, and into a large room. There were other rooms, all as big, and in each room there were flowers and rows upon rows of candles burning.

These candles were the lives of all people, the boy's god-father said to him. If the candle was tall, and just beginning to burn, that person had a long life to live. If the candle had burned half-way, that person had only half his life left, and if the candle was nearly gone, that person was going to die soon.

Death showed his god-father an herb. "This herb is used for curing." Death taught the boy: "Each time you visit a sick person, I will be there. When you see my form at the head of the sick one, you will use this herb to cure him. But when you see me at the foot of the sick one, then you know he must die. Give him no medicine."

So the boy went out to cure, and in a short time he was a good *curandero*, the best. Word of his skill went out and since he always asked a great deal of money, he was rich by the time he was thirty years.

Finally, it happened that a very rich man who was very sick called the *curandero* and said that if he could cure him, the *curandero* could marry his daughter.

When the *curandero* saw Death standing at the rich man's feet, he knew what he must do. But then he looked at the young daughter and, infatuated by her beauty and the thought of being her husband, he quickly turned the rich man about so that Death now stood at his head. The *curandero* administered the medicine, while his godfather looked on — black and angry.

The rich man got well, and the young girl was very happy. "Now, let us go to the church," she said to the *curandero.*

The wedding was held, complete with Pascolas, but before the fiesta could start, Death appeared at the door of the church. To his godson he said, "Well, I see that you got yourself married."

"Yes," replied the godson, and he thought within himself, "What can he do to me? After all, I am his godson."

"Come with me," said Death and he held his godson so firmly that the young man could not resist. They went back to the cave of the candles. Some of them were just beginning to burn, others were half-gone; still others flickered weakly or lay about, extinguished on the ground.

"See, these are the Yaqui men's lives," Death said. His godson begged to be shown his own candle.

"This is your candle," said Death, pointing to one burned not even halfway down.

And Death blew it out.

How The Mountains Were Created

as told by Paula Castillo to her son Felipe S. Molina

Hakwo ketun Itom Ae Mariata into Jesusta inim bwiapo am ho'ako ian um Hiak bwiapo wa huya ania kaita kawekantea. Senu taa'apo Jesus Itom Aetau o'omtek hita betchibosu humaku'u. Jesus Itom Aeta tehwak ke apo au hoarata tosimbaetia. Itom Ae intok hiokot au hia ka sim'i'akai. Apo ala haibu au tuten huya aniau bicha webaekai. Itom Ae into aa asoawa sak tuhta nuteriak. Itom Ae uka sak tuhta bemela, ka haitimachi tahorimpo aa bihtariak hunakbea ili kutat a sumak Jesusta henomet a weiyane betchibo.

Jesus bea bota nuka huya aniapo weamak. Haiki taeweimpo apo huya aniapo weamka hunaksanbea ume tahorim siutitaitek. Hunama ili siutiapo u sak tusi yeu wotitaitek um bwiau kom bicha. Huna sak tusi hunak bwiau kom wotekame san ume kawim ian itom bicha'um.

When Our Mother Mary and Jesus lived on Earth in the present day Yaqui country the wilderness was without mountains. One day Jesus got mad at Our Mother for some reason. Jesus told Our Mother that he was going to leave home. Our Mother tried to discourage him from leaving. His mind was already set on going so he readied himself for the departure into the wilderness. Our Mother prepared her son some lunch, which was *sak tusi* (cornmeal). Our Mother put the *sak tusi* in a new clean cloth and tied it into a bundle on a stick so that Jesus could carry it on his shoulders.

Jesus left on his journey and wandered in the wilderness. For many days he traveled in the wilderness and his cloth bundle began to tear. From this small tear the *sak tusi* began to spill out onto the ground. So all the *sak tusi* that fell to the ground at that time are now the mountains we see today.

The Evil Eye

Mini Valenzuela Kaczkurkin

The evil eye
   Is a common fact
In Yaqui life.

This evil eye
   Can dwell in anyone,
Young or old.

Sometimes, the one
   Possessing the power
Is not aware.

He causes damage
   By desiring something
He cannot have.

If humans or food
   Or plants are desired
By such a one,

The human gets ill,
   The food goes sour,
The plant will die.

Neutralize such power
   By touching the object
You admire.

Romana, Marana Village

Dorothy Fannin A Portfolio

Delores, Marana Village

Estefana and Josephine, Marana Village

Micaela, Pascua Viejo

Pascola Dancers, Fiesta de Gratitud, Pascua Pueblo

Ramon Gomez with his mural at Pascua Viejo

Daniel Leon with his mural at Pascua Viejo

Benina and Julia, Marana Village

Diane, Berta and Marcelina, Pascua Viejo

Let's Make Thunder

Mini Valenzuela Kaczkurkin

"Let's make thunder,"
As the cloud makes thunder,
Say the Pascola Dancers.
Thunder brings the rain.
So we understand
What the Pascolas mean to do.
In imitation of rain,
They're going to shower
The spectators with bowls of water.
So we who know, walk away,
Before the Pascolas
Make thunder as the clouds make Thunder.

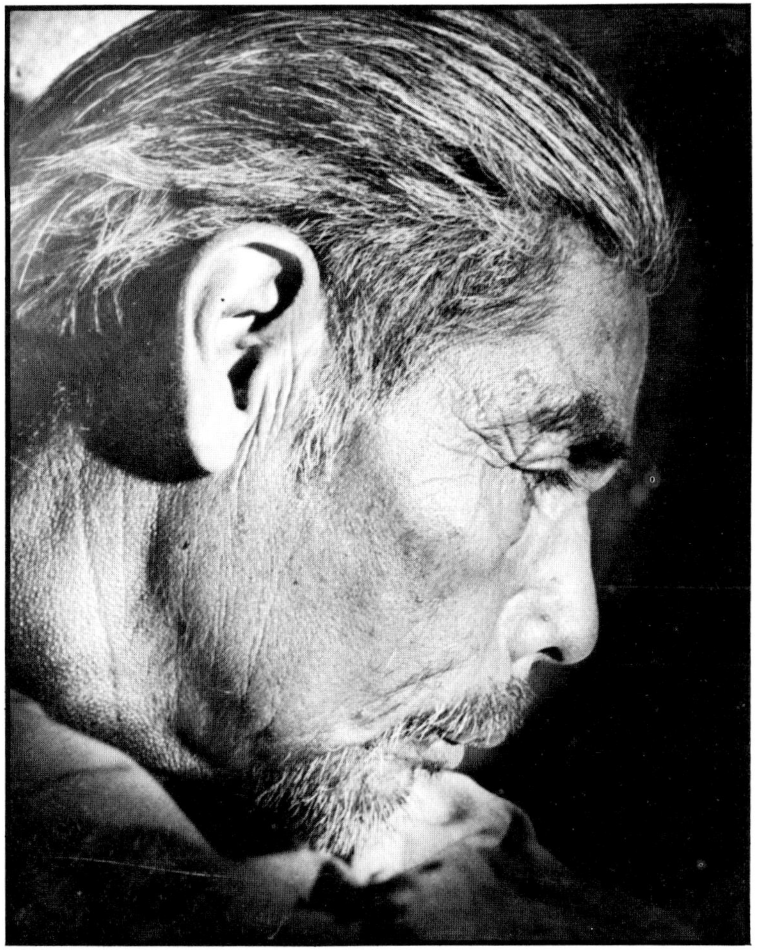

Refugio Savala, Pascua Village c. 1955
Arizona State Museum, University of Arizona
George Iacono

Refugio Savala is a Yaqui poet and translator. Born in Sonora, Mexico in 1904, he was brought by his parents into the United States during the height of the persecution and deportation of Yaquis by the Mexican government, hence his name, Refugio — refugee.

As an adult Refugio Savala worked with a number of students of Yaqui culture, among them Edward Spicer and Muriel Painter. At Painter's encouragement he began to write. The three pieces we print here grew out of that association. "Growth: Merging of Labor and Love" is a portion of an autobiography Savala drafted in the 1950's and 60's. Recently edited by Kathleen Sands, it was published this year by the University of Arizona Press as The Autobiography of a Yaqui Poet.

"The Legend of Skeleton Mountain" and "The Singing Tree" are pieces of Savala's early work which are literary translations of stories from Yaqui oral tradition Both stories were published in the first issue of The Arizona Quarterly *(Spring 1945).*

Mr. Savala resides in a nursing home in Tucson where he spends much of his time translating the Old Testament into Yaqui language.

Growth: Merging Labor and Love

Refugio Savala

How things are natural in the wild
When the flowers streams and the light
And the trees offer the shade so mild,
And protect the feeble bird aflight
Like the mother's tender love for a chld,
Add to pleasure the most sensual delight.

After my father had been away six months, there was a stepfather for us three children. With our new father we got a new sister named Eloisa, and she claimed she got a mother, a sister, and us two brothers. Our new father was not a railroad man. Best of all, he was not a drinking man. He was a big man, a heavy-set six-footer who worked adobes by contract. In this work, he made men of us two boys. He ran the molder for four bricks of prepared mud, while my brother Fernando ran the wheelbarrow. I would prepare the mud with straw and dung. We got thirty dollars for a thousand bricks. In a week's work we also put time into laying out the adobes for the sun to dry them and into stacking them for delivery.

Then the time came for our father to work out of town up on Cañada del Oro, which is on the west end of the Catalina mountain range. He was given a big green wagon with a horse team to take the whole family, and we loaded all our possessions and headed up north toward the Catalinas. We came to a park, the last grocery store, then crossed Rillito River. No bridge was put up in those days, so we went across the river, but there was no water, so the crossing was on the sandy riverbed. Then we came up to the top of the hill. Then we reached Oracle Junction, and taking the road to the right, we started into Llano Toro [Bull's Plain], a cholla forest with cattle roaming. They were decorated with cactus spines all over, even their faces. Our father knew the desert, and when we came to a ranch at Toro Cañada creek, he told us that it was the old post where the stagecoach took relief coming into town. In those days ore from the mining camps was hauled by mule train, and these we saw in town. They stopped for the mules to drink at the city water trough.

Our destination was reached when we came to Rancho Samaniego. The Cañada del Oro was flowing with a torrent of clear water, very beautiful. Our father was not working Sundays, so he told us about the way he came to Arizona. He crossed from Mexico at Douglas, going through Cochise County to Willcox on to Bowie and on to Safford, San Carlos, and Globe.

In our camp, we had a large tent to live in. The foreman had a Mexican wife, so he could talk Spanish. They lived in a building made of lumber. Our father told us we did not have to work, so we became again two playmates, but the ranch foreman's wife soon put us to work with her own boys as *wok bake'om* [walking cowboys], herding the cows to the corral early in the morning for milking. We drank much milk every morning as *wok bake'om*, and we had dinner with the foreman's family at noon. What we liked very much was the *kuahada* [cottage cheese]. This is the cheese which has not been put in the molder. This woman made the molders so big that when the cheese came out, it was about the size of a *tampaleo kubahi* [Pascola drum].

Every day after being *wok bake'om*, we had all day to go places. Going upstream, we found a good swimming hole. This was one pastime for us, and so was walking into the canyon to see the spring water flowing into the main stream. This canyon was deep, the walls on both sides solid rock. In the solid rock bottom, we found little bowls made by hand by the Indians of this river, for the purpose of catching rain water to drink when water was scarce. My father called them *tesa akim* in Yaqui.

Truly, we were enjoying ourselves here more than in town.

The study of Cañada del Oro was of much profit to me. I learned all about ranch life since both my parents had great experience. I learned the Yaqui names of plants and fowls and about taking bees for wild honey. The *siba wikit*, cliff bird, is a day bird and sings at dawn. *Kauruakte'a*, a night bird, sings all night.

The perfume flower plant is the Spanish *vinodama* [*kuka* in Yaqui]. You can sense the perfume from a long distance. My father told me how the Indians knew God by this perfume.

Before the white man, the Yaquis saw God in this creation. They saw him in the firmament's heavenly bodies, his spirit in the perfume of the *sewam* [flowers]. They would say, "*Wame'e bwere chokim iefforing* [Go the planets when our earth is suspended], For there is nothing covered that shall not be revealed" (Matthew 10:26). The Yaquis, not having any Bible study, many times tell whole chapters of the Gospel, as my own father gave me the definition of the fifth commandment: "Thou shalt not kill; do not be unjust, unkind. Do not take little animals to be a nuisance. They are made to be with us. Rather be a life saver. If you see a fly in a bucket of water trying to save itself, stick your finger in the water, let it crowd up, and snap it into the air. Here you save one life as precious to God as yours."

My father also told me of an aged Pascola Dancer who gave, in a fiesta closing sermon, a verse from the seventh chapter of Matthew, "Enter ye in at the strait gate" (Matt. 7:13). In telling the deceitfuless of the broad road he said, "But the road to heaven is a narrow footpath in the ground, narrow for not being much in use, for there be few that find it." The name of this Pascola Dancer was *Wahu Chahi* [Falcon], and the sermon was given at Mesquitalito in Tucson.

Another story he told was of Peo, which means Pedro. Peo was a big liar and deceiver all over the eight villages of the Río Yaqui. One day a priest came riding a mule. He met Peo and asked him to fool him as he had heard. Peo said, "Father, I have to get my book with which I do my tricks to deceive people, but wait here and I'll go get it." The priest said, "Take my mule and go get the book." So Peo took the mule but did not return to the priest again. This man told his lies so realistically, he even fooled himself. He told one person in Guaymas that a whale was lying on the sand at the seashore. The word was passed all over town. He saw the people running to see the whale, and when he was told about it, he started running also to see it. When he arrived where the people were, there was no whale. There was confusion, and people asked who had said there was one. Peo himself was asking the same question.

All these stories were told in Yaqui by my father in Cañada del Oro. Then the time came for us to go back to town. We had to go home because my mother was pregnant and also because the work was finished. When my father was dismissed, he was given the same green wagon and horses. I was exceedingly sorry to leave, but we said goodbye to our ranch friends: *"Adios, hasta la otra visita con el favor de Dios."*

When we pulled out of the canyon, we were again on the Llano Toro. Up here we saw the canal which brought water by force of gravity from up the river so that Llano Toro was made a farmland. They raised wheat and barley. It was wonderful, for the river water was turned up on the hills without a dam. We were on the same route as we came on, passing the *cuesta* [hill] and the old post. Then we started going around the west end of the Catalina Mountains. The huge mountains seemed to be standing at the same distance, but Tucson became visible. There was no hurry, and my father never used the whip on the horses because they went fast enough at ease until we arrived home. We caused a sensation with the neighbor kids. They asked me if we saw genuine Indians, and we told them that we were the genuine Indians up there.

The Legend of Skeleton Mountain

Refugio Savala

In the pleasant shade of a ramada, a boy who was almost a man reflected his face in the water in the olla as he dipped the gourd cup to drink.

It was in summer. A drowsy old man sat on a buckskin stool with his back resting against the wall of the carrizo that formed the jacal of his abode. The old man had just risen from the noon siesta. The adventurous boy asked his grandfather: "That mountain yonder is so beautiful and high — why is it called **Otom kawi**, Skeleton Mountain?"

The old man sighed and replied: "In olden days a monstrous bird was invading our eight villages and a person was lost every evening. The victim was followed and always was found on top of that mountain. Piles of bones were found there and skulls of victims who were carried away by the great fowl.

"Now there was a young woman who was greatly loved by her parents. She was about to be a mother. As it was summer the young woman was sleeping outside the house, outside the jacals and the shelters. At midnight the bird swept low along the river course to where the young woman lay asleep. She was already in the bird's claws when she screamed. But it was too late to save her.

"The young woman's father followed the bird which had taken part of his soul. Other good men went with him also, taking weapons. It was far and high to the mountain top, but they reached it by morning. As usual, a new skeleton was found, and among the bones a child. He was alive. The child was taken into the village and was greatly loved by his grandparents.

"Years passed and the boy was old enough to know that he was an orphan. He studied with great interest the art of archery, which he soon brought to command. There was no other Yaqui to bow and arch so sure as this boy. When he had prepared his weapons, he called all the people in the village together. 'I ask permission to go into *Otom kawi* and slay the giant fowl.' But the council answered: 'Many are the good men who have tried to kill the bird. Always they have failed because it is a farsighted animal and vanishes into space when men seek its abiding place. But if you think to go, go. If you require help, it shall be given.' And the boy again spoke, 'I shall go.' Then the young man chose an arch of great power and three arrows of the most exquisite art, and everyone knew his skill as an archer. And so, many offered to accompany him. But he did not consent, saying, 'In three days you may follow me. Whether I fail or prevail will then be known.'

"Early the next morning the boy was ready to go. Thus he instructed his people: 'If I fail, you will see that beautiful carrizo grass in the patio of my house become deathly pale. If I die, so will the grass die. If I am sad, so it will become dry and withered.' Then he said farewell and the drum announced his departure.

"The abiding place of the winged monster was high in *Otom kawi*. Before midnight the boy stood just below, within an arrow's flight of the top of the mountain. On the west side of the mountain all night he remained wakeful and unsteady. When the first rays of morning showed in the east he was greatly surprised to see the enromous bird swinging round and round the top of *Otom kawi* making a noise like a huge wind, until it settled down to its nest on the mountain top. The boy cast one arrow into his bow and moved closer, making his first attempt, which missed. Never before in his life had an arrow of his gone wild. The creature did not even notice it. Another arrow was placed on the bowstring and sprung with force at the bird. This one also failed, though the bird made a movement as if preparing to fly. The boy was disappointed when his aim again failed, and he recalled the warning voices of the older people. He had only one arrow left. If this failed, the bird would escape.

"In the village the carrizo grass began to wither. Quickly the people sent out a score of men to climb the mountain. The grass had only become dry, it had not withered away, and the men went forth against the boy's will. Traveling fast, they made themselves ready for any disaster that might come their way.

"With his last arrow the boy aimed at the bird with care. This time he did not miss. The arrow struck the great bird through its neck. With hoarse cries it tried to fly away. It rose into the air but could not sustain its flight. Down it dropped, striking the cliff, rolling over the slope of the mountain, scattering the trees of the forest, rolling down and down, the boy running wildly after it, a club in his hand. When the bird caught at last in a stump of a tree, the boy came upon it and killed it with the club. When he had done this he shouted and jumped about and sang. At this moment the men arrived. They were afraid to come near the vast animal until the boy assured them that it was dead.

"Meanwhile, in the village there was great rejoicing, for they had seen the carrizo grass become green and bright with life again. Everyone ran all the way up to the slopes of *Otom kawi* to see the bird which had taken so many innocent lives from the villages. Now they were no longer afraid. The boy was taken back into his village and was considered thereafter a great hero."

In this manner did the grandfather tell the story of that mountain which is called *Otom kawi*, Skeleton Mountain. The sun was low and the heat was not overwhelming. The boy who had listened intently went out into the field with a sharp hoe to work in the young corn.

The Singing Tree

Refugio Savala

A big dry tree with all its limbs almost crumbling to the ground appeared in the wilderness every day from sunrise to sunset. This tree was vibrating like the chords of a harp, the sound of which was audible a great distance around. Every day people gathered to hear it.

Wise men from all parts of the country came but no one knew the significance of the sound of this tree. When everyone in the country failed to find an answer about this living tree, an old man stepped out of the crowd and stood before the wise men and spoke: "There is only a slight hope for us to reveal this great mystery which has bound us in confusion for a long time. When I was young, traveling with my father, we found an old woman in the forest. This old woman will interpret the meaning of the sound of this tree, for she is very intelligent, and wisdom crowns her with unmeasured understanding. This woman, if living, is our only hope." Thus he spoke and the wise men after conferring gave the old man an answer. "To lead us out of the obscurity of doubt, it is our will to unmask this mystery, so if you think this woman is wise enough, go forth and bring her. We will make arrangements so that you may depart by sunrise." The next morning the old man and a score of young men moved toward sunrise into the wilderness.

After many days of hardship in the forest they observed from a distance the abiding place of the old woman. It was late in the afternoon when they arrived at her hermitage. The old woman did not show surprise. It was as if she had been expecting these visitors. The messenger upon his arrival saluted, standing far away, fearful that she might turn loose her pet tiger to devour them. She offered them welcome under the shady ramada to rest. This woman had dwelt in the wilderness since the death of her husband, with her only daughter, a young maiden whom she called Seahamut.

When the messenger had settled down, he told the object of his mission. Having explained about the tree, he said: "All the inhabitants of the country are in a profound confusion over this tree. You are the only one not questioned. We ask you to come and interpret the tree yourself, for you are in the grace of cultured wisdom." Though the woman knew these things very well, she pretended ignorance and declared solemnly: "I am advanced in days and the journey through the forest is perilous." This she was saying when at the rear of the hut footsteps sounded. Her daughter arrived with a young stag she had slain. Her mother called her tenderly, and a sturdy young woman appeared before the men. She sat down timidly beside her mother as if she sought her protection.

Raised in this remote wilderness the girl could get along better with the beasts than she could with a human being. She loved and respected her mother who had brought her up in all good things. The mother explained how she had prepared Seahamut in all manners intellectually, and how many years ago she had been told that these things would come to pass. Then she spoke to her daughter: "For this occasion I have prepared you. These are the men you knew were coming since their departure from the living tree." Then the mother told the messenger: "As I must fail to comply myself with your request, I will send forth my daughter. She will interpret the meaning of this message the Almighty sends to the people of the earth." And the old man rejoiced upon hearing this answer for the star of hope shone vividly in his mind.

He mentioned that this would be pleasant news to the people waiting anxiously for an answer, and he asked the girl if she would consent to go. To this she replied timidly: "My mother desires it. In obedience to her I shall go." After she had accepted the petition she prepared the game brought from the forest. By sunset they were eating, and Seahamut became more familiar with the men with whom she was to travel. Evening occupied her mother in instructing her, and the next day at dusk the girl was ready to go. Her mother placed a pretty white tunic in her bag which she would wear upon being presented to the people.

The old messenger told the young men of their great responsibility in taking the girl away from her home. Farewell was said and they departed into the wilderness. They had not gone far when the tame tiger roared a very sad grunt. Seahamut almost turned sharply back, but she realized that her mother was safe with the tiger to guard her. She herself knew every art of self-defense in the forest even better than the men who were traveling with her. During the long weary journey she defended herself and the men in a very skillful manner no man would risk to do. She led them wind-away from the beasts so they did not scent them even at a near distance. She knew when a beast was near and how to avoid it.

The girl was enjoying the journey. She was not even tired when the men began to light up their countenances, seeing their destination at hand. Presently two men were sent on to announce their approach. When the message was received in the village everyone went to the place where they expected to meet an old woman, tired after the long journey. Instead, they were surprised to find a rough, sturdy, wild-looking young woman who did not show the slightest sign of weariness. She was dressed in the neat white tunic her mother had made for her. The most enthusiastic people from the crowd came close to her with the object of kissing her. But this she thought was a challenge and recoiled back in position to charge upon them.

The old messenger had a hard time correcting the enraged girl. When she was again quiet in her mood, the people were afraid to come near her. In presenting her to the wise men the messenger said: "The old woman failed to come herself, but her daughter she has sent to take her place. In presenting Seahamut to you, I do not fail to fulfill what I promised in taking up the journey into the wilderness, for she will interpret the sound of the strange old tree." The wise men were happy, for this would unmask a great secret and their wisdom would improve. So they received Seahamut with honor and did not delay in asking the great question about the living tree.

When the girl prepared to speak, silence reigned all through the multitude of people. Everyone was staring at her.

She listened to the sound of the tree. Then her voice rang clearly in full tone. "This message the Creator of all things sends to the people, a testament that he will establish with the earth: that it must produce all sorts of subsistence for every creature upon it; trees in the forest shall bear edible fruit in abundance; the vegetation of the earth will sustain the beast and the fowl and even the tiniest insect that has life in itself; another thing called seed will also come upon the earth; every bush, shrub or tree which does not bear fruit shall be cut down and the ground cleared for the good seed, then tilled with an instrument called the plow. Thus the groundwill be prepared.

"After the ground is prepared and seed is placed beneath the soil it shall come to pass that, from the seas, water will be lifted in clouds and carried by the winds to the plains in the form of rain. The seed under the soil will burst forth into life and if cultivated properly it shall bear fruit in such quantity doubled, that one seed will produce one hundred, and this shall be for the maintenance of the people.

"But there is another thing to come in exchange for the benefit the earth will provide. It is called death. Together with the sustenance, all creatures upon the earth will receive also death, for death will not spare even the tiniest insect that has life in itself. And it shall come to pass after death that all substance will be swallowed by the earth in payment for the nourishment given during life."

These things did Seahamut tell the people, while the strange old tree vibrated like the chords of a harp when touched by a passing wind. Then it came to silence and remained so forever. The wise men tried to conceal this wisdom from the people, but there was a great change among them. All those who accepted the word remained in their homes and those who did not receive it gathered and danced the farewell dance and disappeared into the morning air, going underground to establish their own kingdom.

Yaqui Literature: Other Sources

Mini Valenzuela Kaczkurkin's collection of Yaqui traditions Yoeme: Lore of the Arizona Yaqui People *(Tucson: Sun Tracks, 1977) is probably the best source on contemporary Yaqui oral traditions. Ruth Gidding's* Yaqui Myths and Legends *(Tucson: Univ. of Arizona, 1959) is a good gathering of Yaqui stories from the Rio Yaqui area in Sonora. Carleton Wilder's* The Deer Dance, *Bureau of American Ethnology Bulletin 186, is a short study of the deer dance as it was performed in the early 1940's at Old Pascua village. It contains translations of twenty deer songs, but it is very technical. Muriel Painter gives a very clear overview of Yaqui ceremonies in her short account of the Yaqui lenten observances* A Yaqui Easter *(Tucson: Univ. of Arizona Press, 1971).*

Two sound recordings of Yaqui song are Yaqui Music of the Pascola and Deer Dance *(Canyon C-6099), recorded in Potam, Sonora, during the Tiniran Fiesta, and* Yaqui Ritual and Festive Music *(Canyon C-6140), pascola, deer dance, matachini and folk songs recorded in Arizona. "Seyewailo: The Flower World: Yaqui Deer Songs" is a one hour color videotape of a Yaqui fiesta recorded near New Pascua Pueblo. In Yaqui with English subtitles, it is narrated by Felipe Molina and available through the Division of Media and Instructional Services at the University of Arizona, Tucson.*

The Tall Candle: The Personal Chronical of a Yaqui Indian *(Lincoln: University of Nebraska Press, 1971) is the life story of Yaqui Rosalio Moises. It was edited by Jane Holden Kelley and William Curry Holden. Moises was grandfather to Mini Kaczkurkin, author of* Yoeme. *Refugio Savala's* The Autobiography of a Yaqui Poet *(Tucson: Univ. of Arizona Press, 1980) is in almost all ways a more representative picture of an Arizona Yaqui life.*

The foremost non-Yaqui authority on Yaqui life is Professor Edward Spicer. His Cycles of Conquest *(Tucson: Univ. of Arizona Press, 1962) gives a complete account of Yaqui documentary history in the context of the histories of the Mexican northwest and the American southwest. Two novels based on Yaqui life which have been very favorably received among Yaqui readers are Curry Holden's* Hill of the Rooster *(New York: Henry Holt and Company, 1956) and Virginia Sorensen's* The Proper Gods *(New York: Harcourt, Brace, and Co., 1951). The writings of Carlos Casteneda are not regarded as accurate portraits of Yaqui life by most* Yoeme. *As Spicer wrote in an early review of* The Teachings of Don Juan, *"it seems wholly gratuitous to emphasize, as the subtitle does, any connection between the subject matter of the book and the cultural traditions of the Yaqui."*

The Yaqui Bulletin *is an occasional publication of the Pascua Yaqui Tribe printed at New Pascua Village, 4730 W. Calle Tetakusin, Tucson, AZ 85710.*

Native American Literature: Other Sources

A mind boggling number of books, articles, records and tapes await the student who wishes to extend his readings in American Indian oral and written literature beyond the four tribal groups included in this collection. For those who wish to continue their readings with a tribal focus, George P. Murdock's Ethnographic Bibliography of North America, *published by the Yale University Press and regularly updated, offers comprehensive bibliographies for each of the North American tribes. A more useful bibliography for the student of literature is Anna Lee Stensland's* Literature by and about the American Indian: An Annotated Bibliography, *first published by the National Council of Teachers of English in 1973 and revised in 1979. Organized by categories, it contains an author index.*

The list we have put together here is organized by genre: oral narrative, song, speeches, fiction, autobiography, and poetry. A few general works are mentioned at the end of the list along with a selection of magazines and journals.

Oral narrative

Tribal. *The best collections of native American stories from oral tradition tend to focus on a single tribe or even a single narrator. Edmund Nequatewa's* Truth of a Hopi *(1936; rpt. Flagstaff: Northland Press, 1967), Ethelou Yazzie's* Navajo History *(Tsaile: Navajo Community College Press, 1974), Paul Radin's* The Trickster *(1956; rpt. New York: Schocken Books, 1972), Dennis Tedlock's* Finding the Center: Narrative Poetry of the Zuni Indians *(1972; rpt. Lincoln: University of Nebraska Press, 1978), and Ekkehart Malotki's* Hopitutuwutsi: Hopi Tales *(Flagstaff: Museum of Northern Arizona Press, 1978) are all available and exemplary. N. Scott Momaday's* The Way To Rainy Mountain *(Albuquerque: University of New Mexico, 1969) is centered on a collection of stories Momaday gathered from his Kiowa kinsmen.*

Jarold Ramsey's Coyote Was Going There *(Seattle: University of Washington Press, 1977) succeeds with a regional focus. It is limited to "Indian literature of the Oregon Country." Among collections with a national scope the best is John Bierhorst's* The Red Swan: Myths and Tales of the American Indians *(New York: Farrar, Straus and Giroux, 1976). It is organized by topics. Stith Thompson's* Tales of the North American Indians *(1929; rpt. Bloomington: Indiana University Press, 1968) is valuable for its voluminous notes.*

For writing about *native American oral narratives, N. Scott Momaday's "The Man Made of Words," in* Indian Voices *(San Francisco: Indian Historian Press, 1970), pp. 44-84, is a good place to begin. In the essay Momaday weaves his personal insights into the oral tradition around more general questions and generous selections from his own work. Melville Jacobs'* The Content and Style of an Oral Literature *(Chicago: University of Chicago Press, 1959) is an exhaustive study of some Clackamas Chinook narratives told by Mrs. Victoria Howard. Barre Toelken gives a very sensitive reading of a very funny Navajo Coyote story in "The Pretty Language of Yellowman,"* Genre, *2 (1969), pp. 211-235. Linguist Dell Hymes has for the last decade sought to "rescue" native north Pacific coast narratives from the archive and to "restore" them to native Americans by re-translating them. His efforts have thus far appeared only in relatively inaccessible academic journals. "Louis Simpson's 'the Deserted Boy',"* Poetics, *5 (1976), pp. 119-155, is one example. Fred McTaggart's discussion of Mesquakie stories* Wolf That I Am *(Boston: Houghton Mifflin, 1976) is attractive for the personal quality of the understandings it reaches. Among all, I find Dennis Tedlock's "Pueblo Literature: Style and Verisimilitude," in* New Perspectives on the Pueblos *(Albuquerque: University of New Mexico Press, 1972), pp. 219-242, to be the most enlightening and satisfying discussion of native American oral narrative.*

Personal narratives. *The personal narratives of native American people have commonly come to us in an "as told to" format. Perhaps the best known of these is* Black Elk Speaks: Being the Life Story of a Holy Man of the Oglala Sioux *as told through John Neihardt. First published in 1932, "discovered" by Carl Jung in the 1950's, and re-issued by the University of Nebraska Press in 1961, it continues to enjoy a wide audience. A good complement is* Lame Deer: Seeker of Visions *(New York: Simon and Schuster, 1972). Written by John Fire/Lame Deer and Richard Erodes, it presents "the life of a Sioux Medicine Man." Another readable pair of personal narratives tell the life story of a Winnebago brother and sister.* The Autobiography of a Winnebago Indian *(1920; rpt. New York: Dover, 1963) was told to Paul Radin and* Mountain Wolf Woman *(Ann Arbor: University of Michigan Press, 1966) to Nancy Oestreich Lurie. Among southwestern peoples Ruth Underhill's* Papago Woman *(1936; rpt. New York: Holt, Rinehart, and Winston, 1979) is clear and powerful. Hopi-Tewa Albert Yava's* Big Falling Snow *(New York: Crown Publishers, 1978), edited and annotated by Harold Courlander, is very readable, as is Hopi Helen Sekaquaptewa's* Me and Mine *(Tucson: University of Arizona Press, 1969).* Stories of Traditional Navajo Life and Culture *(Tsaile: Navajo Community College Press, 1978), edited by Broderick Johnson, contains brief, but full, personal narratives from thirteen Navajo men and women.*

Robert Sayre's "Vision and Experience in Black Elk Speaks," College English, *32 (1971), pp. 509-535, is an unusually helpful discussion of Black Elk's autobiography. William F. Smith's "American Indian Autobiography,"* American Indian Quarterly, *2 (1975), pp. 237-245, offers perspectives on a number of native American personal narratives.*

Speeches

I Have Spoken: American History Through the Voices of the Indian *(Chicago: Swallow Press, 1971), compiled by Virginia Irving Armstrong, is a balanced collection of speeches given by American Indians between 1609 and 1971 for both Indian and non-Indian audiences. Peter Nabokov includes many eloquent native American statements in his "anthology of Indian and white relations,"* Native American Testimony: First Encounter to Dispossession *(New York: Harper and Row, 1979).*

Songs

Appreciating songs as songs *when they come to us as printed words on a page is a perilous undertaking. Before getting too much involved with any of the print collections listed here, it would be a good idea to seek out some of the fine sound recordings of American Indian song widely available.* Indian House Records, *P. O. Box 462, Taos, New Mexico 87571;* Folkways Records, *43 West 61st Street, New York, New York 10023; and* Canyon Records, *4143 North Sixteenth Street, Phoenix, Arizona 85016 all publish catalogues with rich native American listings. The Archive of Folk Song, Library of Congress, Washington, D.C. 20540 specializes in early historic recordings. They are in the midst of a project designed to prepare materials from their archives so that they may be used by Indian people. Color videotapes of native American songs being performed and discussed by performers in their home communities are available from the Division of Media and Instructional Services, University of Arizona, Tucson. Among the programs available are "By This Song I Walk: Navajo Songs,"* "Seyewailo: *The Flower World: Yaqui Deer Songs," and "Songs of My Hunter Heart: Laguna Songs and Poems."*

Most collections of "American Indian poetry," that is, the words of American Indian songs, derive from the work of ethnologists and folklorists published in inaccessible journals and series. Serious students should look at some of these collections. The work of Frances Densmore is a good place to begin. Papago Music, *Bureau of American Ethnology Bulletin 90 (Washington, D. C.: Government Printing Office, 1929) is one of nearly two dozen such collections Ms. Densmore gathered from various tribes. Washington Matthews'* The Night Chant *(New York: The American Museum of Natural History, 1902) gives an authoritative account of the complex song cycles of the Navajo Night Chant. Matthews' translations have been used in countless literary works in recent years, most notably in N. Scott Momaday's* House Made of Dawn *(1968). A new edition of the Night Chant songs with helpful annotation is given in John Bierhorst's* Four Masterworks of American Indian Literature *(New York: Farrar, Straus, and Giroux, 1974). Herbert J. Spinden's* Songs of the Tewa *(New York: Exposition of Indian Tribal Arts, 1933) is a moving collection of song texts with a helpful interpretive essay. Ruth Underhill's* Singing for Power: the Song Magic of the Papago Indians of Southern Arizona *(Berkeley: University of California Press, 1938) contains poetic translations along with enough commentary to give readers a real appreciation of the place of songs and song making in Papago life.*

Out of the many anthologies of American Indian song/poems two stand out. Natalie Burlin Curtis' The Indians' Book *(1907; rpt. New York: Dover, 1968) contains songs Curtis recorded herself from tribes throughout the country. It is unique among other anthologies for the inclusion of musical notation for each song. A. Grove Day's* The Sky Clears: Poetry of the American Indians *(1951; rpt. Lincoln: University of Nebraska Press, 1964) includes both song texts and commentary on them organized by area: Woodlands, Plains, Southwest, and so on. The highly imaginative "workings" of New York poet Jerome Rothenberg found in his* Shaking the Pumpkin *and elsewhere are billed as "traditional poetry of the Indian North Americas." They are emphatically not; and, if it is American Indian expression readers seek, they should avoid Rothenberg and his many imitators. See William Bevis' evaluation of Rothenberg and other poet/"translators" in "American Indian Verse Translations,"* College English, *35 (1974), pp. 693-703. Another good evaluation of translations of song/poems is Dell Hymes' "Some North Pacific Coast Poems: a Problem in Anthropological Philology,"* American Anthropologist, *67 (1965), pp. 316-341, an essay of wider interest than its title suggests. Paula Gunn Allen's essay "The Sacred Hoop" in A. Chapman's* Literature of the American Indians *(New York: New American Library, 1975), pp. 111-135, provides very useful perspectives for readers new to native American literature.*

Fiction

Contemporary native American writing finds many of its deepest roots in the varied writing systems used by native peoples prior to European contact. A good collection and discussion of these early native texts is Gordon Brotherston's Image of the New World *(London: Thames and Hudson, 1979). Garrick Mallery's* Picture-Writing of the American Indians *(1893; rpt. New York: Dover, 1972) is a classic study.*

Simon Pokagon's Queen of the Woods *(Hartford, Michigan: C. H. Engle Publisher, 1899) is said to be the first novel published by a native American. Pokagon's narrative was called by his publisher "a romance of real life by the last hereditary chief of the Pottawattomies." The novels of John Joseph Mathews,* Sundown *(New York: Longmans, 1934); John Okison,* Brothers Three *(New York: Macmillam Co., 1935); and D'Arcy McNickle,* Runner in the Sun *(New York: Holt, Rinehart and Winston, 1954) and* The Surrounded *(1936; rpt. Albuquerque: University of New Mexico, 1978) are well worth reading.*

N. Scott Momaday's House Made of Dawn *(New York: Harper and Row, 1968) won a Pulitzer Prize in 1969 and is probably the best known American Indian novel. It has been followed by a number of superb novels by American Indian authors. James Welch has published two novels set on the northern Plains:* Winter in the Blood *(New York: Harper and Row, 1974) and* The Death of Jim Loney *(New York: Harper and Row, 1979). Leslie Marmon Silko's* Ceremony *(New York: Viking, 1977) is set in Navajo and Pueblo communities in New Mexico. Silko's* Storyteller, *which will be published in 1980, collects her shorter work into a unified statement. Gerald Vizenor's* Darkness in Saint Louis Bearheart *(Saint Paul, Minn.: Truck Press, 1978) is an exciting novel, as is Hyemeyohsts Storm's* Seven Arrows *(New York: Harper and Row, 1972), if only for the controversy it has stirred.*

The Man To Send Rain Clouds *(New York: Viking, 1974), edited by Kenneth Rosen, is a collection of short stories by contemporary American Indian writers. Simon J. Ortiz's* Howbah Indians, *a collection of short stories, was printed by Blue Moon Press, c/o Dept. of English, Univ. of Arizona, Tucson 85721.*

Charles Larson's American Indian Fiction *(Albuquerque: University of New Mexico, 1978) is the only book-length study of American Indian novels by American Indians. It is a useful bibliographic guide.*

Autobiography

Indian people have written a number of superb autobiographies without an anthropologist as intermediary. In 1900 Omaha Indian Francis LaFlesche published an account of his days as a schoolboy at the Presbyterian mission school on the Omaha reservation. The Middle Five: Indian Schoolboys of the Omaha Tribe *(1900; rpt. Madison: University of*

Wisconsin Press, 1963) is as moving a portrait of boarding school life as has ever appeared. Sioux writer Charles Eastman wrote effectively of his life in several books. Indian Boyhood *(1902; rpt. Greenwich, Conn.: Fawcett, 1972) is a good place to begin. Kiowa poet N. Scott Momaday's memoir* The Names *(New York: Harper and Row, 1976) is among the best recent native American autobiographies.*

Poetry

Duane Niatum's Carriers of the Dream Wheel *(New York: Harper and Row, 1975) contains substantial selections of the work of the best contemporary American Indian writers. Kenneth Rosen's* Voices of the Rainbow: Contemporary Poetry by American Indians *(New York: Viking Press, 1975) is well edited and representative. A third general anthology of contemporary native American poetry is* The First Skin Around Me: Contemporary American Tribal Poetry *edited by James L. White in 1976 for The Territorial Press, P. O. Box 775, Moorhead, Minnesota 56560.*

Few works by early Indian poets are in print and available. Creek poet Alexander Lawrence Posey wrote under the pen name Chinnubbie Harjo in the late nineteenth century. The Poems of Alexander Lawrence Posey *(Topeka, Kansas: Crane Publishing Co., 1910) is difficult to find but worth the effort.*

Simon J. Ortiz has published two books of poems which speak eloquently of his Acoma heritage: Going for the Rain *(New York: Harper and Row, 1976) and* The Good Journey *(Berkeley: Turtle Island, 1977). Leslie Silko's* Laguna Woman *was first published by the Greenfield Press in 1972; it will be incorporated in her new collection* Storyteller *(forthcoming 1980). N. Scott Momaday's* The Gourd Dancer *(New York: Harper and Row, 1976) is a collection of Momaday's best work. James Welch's* Riding the Earthboy 40 *(1971; rpt. New York: Harper and Row, 1977) contains powerful poems.*

A number of other writers have printed work with one or another of the small presses around the country. The Blue Cloud Quarterly, *Blue Cloud Abbey, Marvin, South Dakota 57251 regularly prints chapbooks by native American poets. Maurice Kenny's Strawberry Press, P. O. Box 451, Bowling Green Station, New York, New York 10004 also prints many native American poets in a continuing broadside series.*

Kenneth M. Roemer's "Bear and Elk: the Nature(s) of Contemporary Indian Poetry," Journal of Ethnic Studies, *5 (1977), pp. 69-79, defines understandings of the diversity of contemporary American Indian poetic expression. Simon J. Ortiz's essay "Song/Poetry and Language,"* Sun Tracks, *3 (1977), pp. 9-12, is also very helpful.*

Journals

Akwesasne Notes, *Mohawk Nation, Rooseveltown, New York is a monthly news oriented publication. The back page of each issue is regularly devoted to native American poetry. The American Indian Historical Society, 1451 Masonic Avenue, San Francisco, California 94117 prints several publications of interest:* The Indian Historian *is a quarterly journal usually given over to essays but poetry and short stories are occasionally printed as well. "Dreams and Drumbeats," a special poetry issue appeared in the Spring of 1976 as volume 9, number 2.* Wassaja, *a newspaper published by the Society, also prints poems occasionally, as does the* Weewish Tree, *a children's magazine.* Contact II, *edited by Maurice Kenny and J. G. Gosciak, is a literary magazine that regularly devotes space to native American materials.* Alcheringa *(Boston Univ.), a journal of "ethnopoetics," prints native American oral materials. Simon Ortiz is a contributing editor. The UCLA Indian Studies Program has a vigorous publishing program and prints the* American Indian Culture and Research Journal, *which contains occasional essays on literary topics.*

The American Indian Quarterly, *a journal of anthropoloy, history, and literature regularly prints essays on native American literature. A special issue on Leslie Silko's* Ceremony *will appear this year.* Studies in American Indian Literatures *is the newsletter of the Association for Study of American Indian Literatures. Edited by Karl Kroeber at Columbia University, it specializes in reviews and bibliographic data on native American literature.*

Many other small literary magazines have devoted special issues to native American literature over the years. Two from John Milton's South Dakota Review — The American Indian Speaks *(1971) and* American Indian II *(1974) — were among the earliest, though as early as 1918* Poetry *published a special American Indian issue. Other noteworthy special issues are* Nimrod, *vol. 16, no. 2 (1972);* Dacotah Territory 6 *(1973-74);* Scree 4 *(1975); and recently* Shantiah, *vol. 4, no. 2 (1979). Geary Hobson edited an especially good native American issue for* New America *in 1976.*

General works on American Indian Literature

There are dozens of anthologies of American Indian literature on the market and in the library. Most are hastily prepared "cut and paste" efforts and not very useful to the thoughtful reader. I find Frederick Turner's The Portable North American Indian Reader *(New York: Viking, 1974) a useful general anthology. Published by a small press, Geary Hobson's* The Remembered Earth: an Anthology of Contemporary Native American Literature *(Albuquerque: Red Earth Press, P. O. Box 26641, Albuquerque, New Mexico 87125, 1979) is as complete and thorough an anthology available. It is also reasonably priced.*

The only good collection of writing about *American Indian Literature presently available is Abraham Chapman's* Literature of the American Indians *(New York: New American Library, 1975), though several other collections will be published in the next few years. Dexter Fisher's selections for the native American section of her book* The Third Woman: Minority Women Writers of the United States *(Boston: Houghton Mifflin Company, 1980) are especially solid and sensitive, as is her commentary throughout the book.* Studies in American Indian Literatures *(c/o Department of English, Columbia University, New York, New York 10027) is good for current publishing information about American Indian literature.*

Larry Evers